Unholy Alliance

Unholy
Alliance

Religion and Atrocity in Our Time

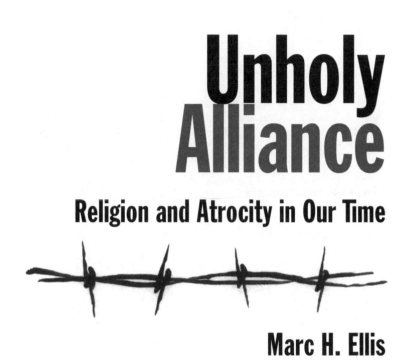

Marc H. Ellis

Fortress Press
Minneapolis

UNHOLY ALLIANCE
Religion and Atrocity in Our Time

Cover graphic: "The Nightmare of Suffering" by Mirella Patruno (stained glass, courtesy of Irvin J. Borowsky)
Book design: Joseph Bonyata
Cover design: Marti Naughton

Library of Congress Cataloging-in-Publication Data

Ellis, Marc H.
    Unholy alliance : religion and atrocity in our time / Marc H. Ellis
  Ellis
        p. cm.
    Includes bibliographical references.
    ISBN 0-8006-3080-7 (alk. paper)
    1. Violence—Religious aspects. 2. Atrocities—History—20th century. I. Title
BL65.V55E55 1997
291.5'697—dc20   96-42502
                                                            CIP

The paper used in this publication meets the minimum requirements of American National Standard for Information Sciences—Permanence of Paper for Printed Library Materials, ANSI Z329.48.1984

Manufactured in the U.S.A.   AF 1-3080

01   00   99   98   97   1   2   3   4   5   6   7   8   9   10

Contents

for Ann

At the source of the longest river
The voice of the hidden waterfall
And the children in the apple-tree
Not known, because not looked for
But heard, half-heard, in the stillness
Between two waves of the sea.
—T. S. Eliot

for Aaron

The Lord said to Aaron, "Go into the wilderness to meet Moses." So he went; and he met him at the mountain of God and kissed him. Moses told Aaron all the words of the Lord which he had sent him, and all the signs with which he had charged him. Then Moses and Aaron went and assembled all the elders of the Israelites. Aaron spoke all the words that the Lord had spoken to Moses, and performed the signs in the sight of the people. The people believed; and when they heard that the Lord had given heed to the Israelites and that he had seen their misery, they bowed down and worshiped.
—Exodus

for Isaiah

Then shall your light blaze forth like the dawn, and your wounds shall quickly heal. Your righteousness shall walk before you, the glory of the Lord shall follow you.
—Isaiah

You are the storm
The storm is within

Acknowledgments

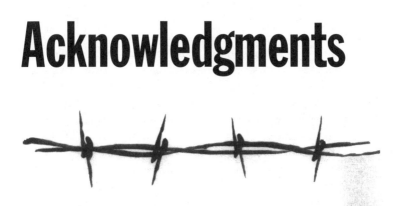

I thank the Center for the Study of World Religions at Harvard University, where I wrote parts of this book as a Senior Fellow in residence during the 1994–1995 academic year. I completed my revisions as a visiting scholar at the Center for Middle Eastern Studies at Harvard University and as a Visiting Professor of Religion at Florida State University during the 1995–1996 academic year. I am particularly grateful to Michael Berenbaum and Joan Ringleheim for inviting me to lecture at the United States Holocaust Memorial Museum during the commemoration of the fiftieth anniversary of the liberation of the death camps. The opportunity to lecture at the museum led me to clarify thoughts important to this work. Support from scholars and staffs at these institutions have been important to the completion of this work, and I am grateful to all involved. I also wish to express my appreciation to Michael West and the staff at Fortress Press for their encouragement and help in editing and publishing this book. In a book publishing world that has become increasingly commercialized and homogenized, it is a pleasure to deal with an editor and staff who understand and engage an author on a substantive level.

Supportive people are important to any work of this nature and I thank in particular David and Cathy Levenson, Leo Sandon, Bill Swain, Walter Moore, Sara Roy, Hilda Silverman, Darshan Ambalavanar, Harvey Cox, Lawrence Carter, Tony Paris, Rosemary Radford Ruether, William Graham, Elaine Hagopian, and Paul Piccard.

Maureen Jackson and Kathleen Woods have been outstanding in their support of my writing, especially with regard to the vagaries of cyberspace. I am also grateful to my students at Florida State University: Andy Taylor, Jaye Huston, John Barich, Harry Coverston, Gary Haile, Diane Whiddon, Bridget Hillyer, Stephanie Crosskey, and Richard Meacham.

During the preparation of this book three important people in my life passed away. The first, Mev Puleo, was close to me through my student, her husband, Mark Chmiel. Mev was an energetic activist on behalf of the poor and, in her short life on earth, she touched many lives. But her importance for me lay in her love for Mark, a brilliant and sensitive man, who has lost a friend and a lover. The second, Gillian Rose, was a philosopher whom I first met on a delegation at Auschwitz. Among other good deeds, she cared for her teacher as he died of AIDS. Gillian was a brilliant philosopher and, more importantly, a beautiful human being. Finally, my teacher William Miller, through his intellect and commitment to a way of life, helped me to find my own way. It was Miller who taught me about eternity; and since I often feel his presence, his teaching has taken on a new level of significance. I miss him tremendously.

Any writer carries a few people of significance with him. I think here of those, named and unnamed, who have been with me through the storm which I have lived in these last years. For their patience and caring, I bow before them. My children, Aaron and Isaiah, are with me always. They strengthen my determination to struggle toward a world without atrocity. Finally, I would like to thank Ann, who brought Aaron and Isaiah into the world and nurtured them with tenderness. Through the years my gratitude and the bond between us endure.

Prologue

Religion and the Cycle of Atrocity

In what conceivable language can a Jew speak to God after Auschwitz, and in what conceivable language can a Jew speak about God?
—George Steiner

In Peru—but the question is perhaps symbolic of all Latin America— we must ask: How are we to do theology while Ayacucho lasts? How are we to speak of God when cruel murder on a massive scale goes on in "the corners of the dead?"
—Gustavo Gutiérrez

A few weeks ago, at a garden cafe in Kigali, the capital of Rwanda, a businessman stopped by my table to greet Gérard Gahima, the Deputy Justice Minister. "How's business?" Mr. Gahima asked him. "Not bad," the man said. "How's justice?" Mr. Gahima shook his head. "Not so good," he said. When we were alone, he put it more bluntly: "After genocide, justice is impossible."

—Philip Gourevitch

For most of my adult life, I have wrestled with the question of atrocity and the language of God. This predicament is due in large part to my Jewish background and my birth as part of the first generation after the Holocaust. This question has propelled me beyond my own community, however, to years of working with and traveling among the poor, most often in the company of committed Christians in different areas of the world. Thus I have experienced the world of Judaism and the world of Christianity as I, and they, continue to ask the perplexing question of how the worship of a good and all-powerful God can allow or even seemingly legitimate horror and death.

The massacre in the Cave of the Patriarchs Shrine in Hebron in February 1994, carried out by Baruch Goldstein, a religious Jew, forced me to a deep reckoning and inspired an attempt to explore the world of Judaism and Christianity and the language of God carried by both religions. To be sure, the massacre at Hebron was simply another episode in the long history of atrocity, a history that has too often been legitimated by religious language. It would, like massacres suffered by Jews and Christians, and in turn perpetrated by them both, soon be forgotten. Mainstream theologians seek to isolate this violence as an aberration and then retreat to the pretense of an innocent world. Such a move allowed the Jewish establishment, in the words of then-Prime Minister Yitzhak Rabin, to in effect "excommunicate" the perpetrator of the massacre. Yet less than a year later, Rabin himself was murdered by another religious Jew, Yigal Amir, who often prayed at Goldstein's shrine and who, like his counterpart, is venerated by many today in Israel. Similarly, just three years earlier, on the occasion of the five-hundredth anniversary of the discovery of the Americas, the Roman Catholic establishment, through the words of Pope John Paul II, asserted that the sufferings of the Americas were secondary to the "immense wealth of Christian life" that arrived with Christopher Columbus. Such pronouncements by Rabin and the pope relegate inherent institutional violence to aberrational or excusable behavior.

My own perspective on Israel and Palestine is that, despite the advances signified by the signing of the Declaration of Principles in 1993 and the subsequent years of dramatic accords and confrontations, the historical facts of occupation, expropriation, murder, and torture must never be forgotten. These actions and their theological legitimation are now a permanent aspect of Jewish memory and a permanent warning about the possibility of Jewish theological complicity in what George Steiner terms the "eruption of barbarism." Israeli foreign policy around the world—including support of Central American authoritarian governments in the 1980s and the South African apartheid regime for decades—must be remembered as well. To seek to cover over this history with a celebrated ending is to do what Christians have been doing for centuries: pretending to an innocence that ultimately results in a new wave of atrocity.

It is the eruption of barbarism in Christendom, in the Holocaust, and in Palestine that forms the central core of my exploration of suffering, religious language, and God. This work emphasizes the responses to barbarism in Jewish and Christian theology and asks whether these responses are substantive and efficacious. A corollary question is whether responses to the suffering, though genuine and searching, function instead to continue a cycle that might allow a renewed assault of barbarism in the future. In this context, my central concern is the analysis of progressive Jewish and Christian theology, that is, the work of, among others, Richard Rubenstein, George Steiner, Elie Wiesel, Johann Baptist Metz, Jürgen Moltmann, James H. Cone, Gustavo Gutiérrez, Joan Casañas, and Elsa Tamez.

Can we speak about God after Christendom and the Holocaust? Do the images of Christmas being celebrated at Auschwitz, of the conquistador Francisco Pizarro drawing a cross with his own blood so that he could die gazing upon it, of Baruch Goldstein executing twenty-nine Palestinian Muslims at prayer during the Ramadan season on the Jewish holy day of Purim, alter our ability to follow the Jewish and Christian path, to speak about justice in the language of these religions, or even to speak about the God whom Jews and Christians traditionally affirm? Does this Jewish and Christian God legitimate the eruption of barbarism or oppose it? Is it possible to frame the question, as is common today among liberation theologians, by counterpoising the God of life to the God of death? Do such religious thinkers as Elizabeth Schüssler Fiorenza, Deborah Lipstadt, Judith Plaskow, Rita Gross, Rosemary Radford Ruether, Emily Culpepper, and Carter Heyward decisively shift the question of God's presence in conquest and suffering from a patriarchal worldview to a more inclusive, creation-centered one? Or do the political and religious sensibilities of such secular thinkers as James Baldwin, Noam Chomsky, Hannah Arendt, and Israel Shahak advance the emergence of a new theology that ends the cycle of conquest and atrocity?

We are now seeing the fruits of a generation of courageous, defiant, and constructive theologians that emerged in the 1960s and have made a revolutionary contribution to the world of religious thought and practice. The tasks these theologians assume—to articulate and speak for a Jewish people emerging from the death camps; for a wounded people of the Americas suffering under economic, political, and religious colonialism; for a majority population under the boot of patriarchy—are very nearly impossible in their dimensions and surely beyond resolution in the brief span of a generation. In exploring the limitations of this generation of theologians, I am, of course, paying homage to them by asking their own questions in the following generation. Will the continuation and expansion of their work address the grim reality of atrocity parading under the guise of innocence and redemption? Is it possible that the religious enterprise which these theologians so ably address is in need of not renewal but abandonment?

These are some of the issues I address in these pages and submit to the reader as an exploration and a dialogue with the reality of atrocity and the possibility of God. This dialogue remains unfinished and flawed, a small contribution from one of the next generation, and perhaps the last generation to raise these questions from within the framework of the Jewish and Christian tradition. For one of the themes that emerges in these pages is that the fight to minimize or abolish atrocity is really the fight to end Judaism and Christianity; it is to recognize that Judaism and Christianity have come to an end, at least in the ways we have known and inherited them. Can this ending be at the same time a birth of a God who never sanctions atrocity?

Chapter 1 opens this dialogue with a look at the massacre at Hebron and the assassination of Yitzhak Rabin; it travels the world of Holocaust thought and theology. In this century, Jews have undergone the horrors of the Holocaust and an unexpected rebirth exemplified by Jewish empowerment in Israel and the United States. Discussion of the meaning of the Holocaust took shape in the 1960s, and during that time the trajectory of post-Holocaust Jewish thought and activity was established. Yet even at the beginning of this discussion, nuance and division were present. Did the Jewish experience of atrocity demand a focus on Jewish survival and empowerment, or did this experience speak to Jews of the need to build a world where atrocity would never happen again to any people? George Steiner poses the question in this way: if, in the Holocaust, Jews experienced the eschatological end of history and of humanity, what remains of the Jewish vocation now, and in what direction should it proceed? If we who come after the Holocaust have a choice, it is one shadowed by an atrocity that challenges our political, cultural, and religious language. For what words can we use, what prayers can we utter, what hopes can we retain, after the Holocaust? As this question haunts those who come after the Holocaust, the contemporary world moves on. Can the language and politics so desperately shaken by the Holocaust respond to the new crisis points in the world, including new and terrible sufferings in Bosnia and Rwanda? What happens when, while continuing to sort out the debris left by the Holocaust, the Jewish community itself commits atrocities in the name of its own survival? Though the question is usu-

ally posed as how Jews speak of God after the Holocaust, the formation of the state of Israel, and the violence attendant in that formation,
have forced the question to a more complex level. For now the struggle is whether it is possible to speak of God in light of suffering that
Jews have endured *and* suffering that Jews have caused.

Chapter 2 explores the evolving world of Christianity after the
Holocaust as a possible response to suffering in the contemporary
world. The Christian world carries a burden into the present as a
prime carrier and perpetrator of atrocity. Though Christians often
proclaim their gospel as if the Christian message and faith were innocent, Jews have experienced the hypocrisy of this claim on their bodies. Yet the Christian claim is even more suspect when its colonial and
missionary history is traced. Paradoxically, the majority of Christians
in the world today— Christians of Africa, Asia, and Latin America—
were evangelized at gunpoint. The difficulty of Jews addressing a God
who permitted atrocity on a mass scale against them is compounded
in Christian communities that have sponsored atrocity for centuries.
For what Christian language can be spoken after conquests that stretch
centuries and continents beyond the Holocaust in Europe? Liberation
theologies, which have grown up among those who were conquered by
Christianity and who now seek to liberate themselves from their
poverty and oppressed state, seem to be an avenue of repair for the
brokenness of the Christian message. Indeed the 1960s, which
spawned the development of Holocaust theology, also gave birth to
liberation theologies, which radically challenge the evils of European
Christian hegemony in language similar to Jewish theology.

Here, too, the question is complex, for can the religion of the conqueror provide the context for the liberation of the oppressed? Is there
something in Christianity that leads to atrocity and that can be rooted
out, for example, in the Black and Latin American liberation theologies
of James H. Cone and Gustavo Gutiérrez? Can these theologies speak to
questions of the Jewish community as well? Because of a shared experience of suffering at the hands of dominant Christians, perhaps the
responses of liberation theology may be instructive to Jews. Yet when
the trajectory of the Jewish community is traced after the Holocaust, its
bonding with the dominant Christians of the West is evident. Unfortunately, this bonding is often solidified in a joint struggle against emerging liberation theologies of the Third World. At the same time, the once-
defiant voices of liberation theologians have been disciplined by
continuing injustice and atrocity and by church hierarchies that hope to
consolidate their own power. Is this the fate of all Christian theolo-

gies—and Jewish ones as well—that no matter what their intentions or perspective, they ultimately become footnotes to a Christianity that may sponsor new episodes of dislocation and death?

Chapters 3 and 4 augment the search in Holocaust theology and liberation theology by looking to Jewish and Christian theologies in the Americas that seek to *renew* the core of Judaism and Christianity or to *alter* that core through feminist and indigenous insights. The difficulty is this: can a history of atrocity force Jews and Christians back to the core of their traditions, making it possible to recover the original and compelling message of each faith and to confront the errant ways of the modern world? If the history of Christianity is infected with atrocity, is the New Testament itself safe from that history? Or if the holy texts themselves are part and parcel of this history, can they be read today without including these events of death as part of the tradition's canon? The history of Christianity may evolve from the texts themselves and surely they cannot be read as if this history had not occurred. Thus, if renewal is to be substantive, the events of atrocity will have to take their place as part of the community's canon. For Christians, the gospel of Matthew is now to be read alongside the gospel of Treblinka; for Jews the book of Exodus will be complimented by the book of Palestine.

With the reading of the history of the community alongside the holy texts—as an expanded and evolving new canon—the core of the tradition is refocused from a pretended innocence to a tradition in struggle with its own culpability. Perhaps a shift from the attempt at religious renewal to an emphasis on struggle, culpability, and solidarity of those who have dominated the tradition with those who have been dominated by it, may bring a new inclusion of the victors and the defeated—including the Gods of both—and thus a way forward. Seen in this light, perhaps the divisions promulgated by the traditions—between Jew and pagan, Christian and Jew, Christian and indigenous people—may prove false. From the perspective of history, the more appropriate division might be seen as between life and death, between Gods of life and death, and between parts of the traditions that promote dignity or atrocity. For inside each tradition are layers that involve commitment to life and to death.

The Jewish, Christian, and indigenous traditions are hardly monolithic, and after this shared history aspects of each are found within the others. Some indigenous aspects of Judaism and Christianity have been covered over and transformed, just as Jewish and Christian understandings and images intermingle. It should not surprise us then that, even though conquered by Judaism and Christianity, indigenous religiosity retains aspects of its own life that may ultimately reorder both religions. Here, too, the humanist critique of religious legitimation of injustice and atrocity takes center stage. For if religious affiliation encourages exploration of a language of hope and well-being, it often counsels silence in the face of religious collaboration with power and destruction. Can the humanist critics of religion break the obligation of silence often imposed by theologians and religious leaders?

Chapter 5 seeks to find a path beyond atrocity and beyond a religiosity that sponsors and is silent before violence. Religious language has been challenged to such a degree that it seems impossible to retrieve without burying the questions that have been raised by history. At the close of the twentieth century, and after thousands of years of Judaism and Christianity, is it part of our fidelity to abandon these religions, at least as we have known them? In their daily lives many people have already done so, and one wonders if many theologians—sometimes articulated in writing but more often spoken of in private—have also reached this place of no return. If this is true, where do Jews and Christians go from here? Those who long ago abandoned the traditions seem as unable to combat the reality and the language of atrocity as those who have remained within religious practice and discourse. Do those without religious affiliation have a deeper connection with others and the earth, with the questions of meaning, love, and suffering, than those who find Judaism and Christianity inadequate? The most powerful religion in the contemporary world is neither Judaism or Christianity but rather the religion of modernity. One wonders if those who worship at the altar of modernity have a language of confrontation with atrocity that seems endemic to this new religion.

Perhaps the task of Jews and Christians may be found in the repositioning of their own discourse, not for the purposes of retrieval or renewal but to empower those dissatisfied with both the Jewish-Christian religion *and* the religion of modernity. In doing this, we explore the truths found in opposition to ancient and modern religious understandings that lead to atrocity, and the hope that might energize us to build a world without barbarism. This is our task and our hope. Though the direction is clear, the path awaits definition. As those who come after, it is incumbent upon us to prevent another generation from shouldering the burden we inherit. In the end, perhaps our work will bear fruit, and a God will come into existence, a God who remembers the forgotten and urges us to create a world beyond barbarism.

1

We Who Come After

The Eruption of Barbarism and the Jewish Search for God

The massacre at the Cave of the Patriarchs Shrine in Hebron on February 25, 1994, perpetrated by a religious Jew, Baruch Goldstein, shocked many around the world. Palestinian outrage was accompanied, at least among some Jews, by a sense of sadness and shame. In a speech before the Israeli Knesset, then-Prime Minister Yitzhak Rabin spoke these words just days after the tragedy:

> Today I stand before you, members of Knesset, and before the citizens of the State of Israel—and in front of the entire world—as a Jew, as an Israeli, as a man and as a human being. I am shamed over the disgrace imposed upon us by a degenerate murderer. The murderer came out of a small and marginal political context. He grew in a swamp whose murderous sources are found here, and across the sea; they are foreign to Judaism. To him and to those like him we say: You are not part of the community of Israel. You are not part of the national democratic camp which we all belong to in this house, and many of the people despise you. You are not partners in the Zionist enterprise. You are a foreign implant. You are an errant weed. Sensible Judaism spits you out.[1]

As Prime Minister Rabin spoke these words, Mohammed Abdullah, a Muslim living in America, was asked for his opinion. "The people who made the World Trade Center bomb, they are not really Muslim. Muslims don't blow up innocent people. The same with the doctor. He was either crazy or he was not a real Jew because real Jews also do not kill innocent people." Leonard Fein, a Jewish journalist, seemed to agree with Rabin and Abdullah when he refused to use the name of the murderer in his monthly column, and instead invoked the Hebrew curse, *Yimach sh'mo v'zichro*—May his name and his memory be erased. Though many observers might quickly agree with Rabin, Abdullah and Fein—that the massacre was an aberration, an embarrassment, a foreign implant, and that the murderer's memory should be erased—the opposite is in fact the truth. Michael Lerner, a Jewish writer and activist, was more perceptive when he wrote that Jews "need to feel shame not only over this massacre but also over the systematic misuse of Judaism and Jewish suffering to justify racist and oppressive treatment of another people."[2]

Rather than an aberration or outcast, Baruch Goldstein should be seen as a logical outgrowth of state policies in Israel, policies which have been legitimated by the Jewish establishment in Europe and America. Richard Goldstein, a columnist for the *Village Voice*, made this observation: "In fact, Goldstein was a militant nationalist. . . But that didn't stop the Israeli army from granting him the rank of major. Four months before the massacre, Palestinian authorities warned the Israelis that Goldstein was bent on perpetrating 'something dreadful' at the mosque. Yet, he was able to enter the shrine, where only four soldiers were on duty despite recent tensions there. Though heavily armed and carrying sound-muffling earphones, he slipped by this detail. And he was able to reload three times before he ran out of ammo and worshipers beat him to death."

Todd Gitlin, a Jewish historian and media critic, confirms Richard Goldstein's interpretation: "The West Bank fascists have as their goal an ethnically cleansed Jewish state, and for a quarter of a century Likud and Labor governments alike have let them strut wherever they pleased, submachine guns at the ready, their fear of Palestinian attacks ready to flick over into vengefulness at the drop of the ammo clip. They have been the state's preferred terrorists."[3]

The act of massacre has much to do with the state of Israel and the recent history of the Jewish people. Baruch Goldstein based his politics on a transposition of Palestinians as Nazis, a transposition not uncommon in Jewish thought and writing. As Richard Goldstein points out, he favored an even richer metaphor: "The Palestinians are like 'an epidemic. . .They are the pathogens that infect us.' Here the process of dehumanization that is central to fascism comes home to roost, in an image not so different from the Nazi representation of Jews as rats infesting Europe." Should it surprise us, then, that the Jewish worshipers adjacent to the Islamic worshipers in the Cave of the Patriarchs resumed their Purim services for more than an hour after the carnage? A Jewish settler who lost track of his teenage boy as hundreds of Muslims rushed out carrying victims of the attack, was grateful that he found his son safe and that no Jews had been hurt in the incident: "Thank God it all ended well," he said.[4]

Surely something has happened to Jews in this century—in the Holocaust, in the birth of Israel, in the occupation and destruction of historic Palestine—that has changed Jews as a people. The militarization of Jewish culture, psyches, and religiosity over the last fifty years cannot be understood or reversed instantaneously. The Israeli-Palestinian accords—accords which, because of their limited nature, guarantee a Jewish victory and a Palestinian defeat—will, unless expanded considerably, do little to help Jews understand what they have done, what they are capable of, and who they have become as a people. Only the reversal of occupation and settlement, only a renewed and transformed Israel/Palestine with Jerusalem as a common capital can initiate this process of self-awareness and critical appraisal. For in the end, Yitzhak Rabin and his generation of 1948 are, from the Palestinian perspective, much closer to Baruch Goldstein than either Rabin or Goldstein would be prepared to admit. This is true as well for the conservative and liberal Jewish establishment in Europe and America, which in legitimating Israeli policies over the decades is complicit in the Hebron massacre and the massacres that preceded it. Even the liberal critics of Rabin, Goldstein, and the Jewish establishment—people such as Leonard Fein, Michael Lerner, and Todd Gitlin—have often critiqued specific policies of injustice in Israel while providing legitimation for the overall process of displacing the Palestinian people. All are tied together in an enterprise which, though understandable within the context of Jewish suffering in Europe, has been an unmitigated disaster for Palestine and the Palestinian people. Do Jews as a people understand the implications of this history, that Jews are no longer innocent, that Jewish redemption has resulted in conquest and exile for the Palestinian people?

In 1948, just months before the war between Jews and Arabs in Palestine was over and Israeli statehood was officially declared, a small

Arab village, Lod, located between Tel Aviv and Jerusalem, was occupied by Jewish forces. As the occupation intensified, Arab forces continued the battle within the walls of the local mosque. The Jewish commander, Shlomo Wolfe, ordered grenades thrown into the mosque
until the sniper fire ceased. Storming the mosque, the Jewish soldiers
found twenty-five Arabs inside, dead. Yet a problem remained, for the
walls were covered with the blood of the combatants and their families.
Since Jewish leaders were sensitive to international opinion, especially
regarding the sanctity of places of worship, the commander ordered
eight Arabs who had surrendered to enter the mosque to remove the
bodies and cleanse the blood from the walls. With the task finished,
Wolfe encountered another problem: these Arabs were now witnesses
to their comrades' deaths and could, if they reached the appropriate
people, communicate this story to the world. For Wolfe, the decision
was obvious, though several of the Jewish soldiers refused his request:
execute those with knowledge of this deed.[5]

Rather than Hebron, then, it was here in this tiny village of Lod that
the cycle of violence began. One wonders what the distance is between
Shlomo Wolfe and Baruch Goldstein, the one at the start of the war
who through execution sought to erase the blood of his deeds; the
other who sought to continue the war by eliminating the "pathogens"
who were ready for—indeed in desperate need of—peace. From the
Palestinian perspective, both are settlers, destined to displace, expro-
priate, and murder. The decades of the existence and expansion of the
state of Israel are to Palestinians one long war, a war in which Palestine
ceased to exist while a warrior state, Israel, was created and continues,
albeit in changed circumstances, to expand.

Yet in a very real sense, the war of Israel and Palestine began almost
1500 years ago with the rise of Christendom and ended in the destruction of European Jewry in the Holocaust. This is why Shlomo Wolfe,
and Rabin himself, could cleanse villages of Palestinian Arabs and yet
be truly horrified by the massacre at Hebron. Rabin meant it when he
spoke of Baruch Goldstein as bringing "shame on Zionism" and being
an "embarrassment to Judaism," for he, like Wolfe and countless other
Jewish military and political leaders, maintain a code of honor understandable within the framework of building a Jewish state. This code
issues from the furnaces of Auschwitz and seeks to close off the possibility of renewed Jewish suffering. To be sure, within this code Jews are
of first and last concern; Palestinians are seen as peripheral, hindering
Jewish security, or, in times of war, seeking to refire the furnaces. Mas-

sacring those at prayer violates this code and, at the same time, sheds a disturbing light on the code itself. Goldstein's act was an indiscriminate one, threatening an anarchy of vengeance. Jews in Israel and the West might not support such acts, and non-Jews in the West would be horrified by them. The blood in the Hebron mosque could throw into question the very code itself, and the Hebron massacre of 1994 might be seen in continuity with the Lod massacre of 1948. The narrative of Jewish suffering and empowerment might be undermined, thus jeopardizing the moral purpose in the building of the Jewish state.

What code of honor could realistically be expected to emerge from Auschwitz? The development and consolidation of codes of honor emerge from history, as does the critique of these codes. In this way, codes of honor are much like theology—often claiming an innocent and redemptive character that tends toward triumphalism, especially when it collaborates with political power. That is why Walter Benjamin, the German Jewish philosopher who committed suicide during the Holocaust, charged the historian with the unenviable and messianic task of rescuing religious and political traditions from consolidation and expansion that often legitimate injustice and oppression they once rebelled against. For Benjamin, the messianic task is a struggle to redeem the dead from an oblivion that has two sources: the rulers of the past *and* the present—who often as not were the powerless of the past—whose orthodoxies triumph with the power of the gun; and the narrative of power disguised in the myths of innocence and redemption.[6]

Palestinians recognize the continuity of Lod and Hebron as crucial to the demythologizing of Jewish innocence and redemption. From their perspective Jews have been anything but innocent, and the Jewish search for redemption after the Holocaust has been a Palestinian calamity. Yet establishing this continuity without distinction is dangerous. It creates a mythological straight line of history that buries the hesitations, the questions, and even the original intentions of Jews regarding what has come to be Israel and Palestine. When affirmed and explored, the complexity of history locates a series of ethical and political contradictions that the narrative in its orthodox variation seeks to silence and ultimately transcend. The possibility of a future beyond atrocity may lie exactly in the recovery and discussion of these contradictions, so long as they do not serve as a justification for an enterprise or seek to become a more sophisticated shield against the most disturbing issues placed before the Jewish people. In the context of Israel and Palestine, this complexity may allow at least two positions which seem at first to be inconsistent: that Shlomo Wolfe and Yitzhak Rabin *did* have a code of honor and that the establishment of the state of Israel *may* have been necessary for the Jewish people while always representing a wrong done to the Palestinian people. This is what Wolfe may have meant when, after ordering the execution of those who cleansed the mosque of blood, he said, "They shuffled off. I heard the shots. Lod was ours. Tel Aviv was saved. I did what was necessary. I'd do it again."

The Broken Covenant

The post-Holocaust Jewish world can be seen within a context of continuity, and indeed the half century that has passed since the end of World War II confirms this view. The moral and ethical critique of Nazi power has remained fairly constant over the years, as have the schools of interpretation regarding the Nazi attempt to annihilate the Jewish people. In general, the interpretative framework of the Holocaust crystallized around the trial of Adolf Eichmann in 1961, as Eichmann was a central figure in the implementation of the Nazi policy to annihilate European Jewry and the highest-level Nazi to be tried in Israel itself. One remembers Hannah Arendt's controversial reports from the trial. Arendt, a German philosopher and emigré to America, wrote of the banality of evil, as she found Eichmann to be a superficial, career-oriented functionary within the bureaucratically organized attempt to destroy the Jewish people, rather than a hate-filled anti-Semite. She also wrote of the capacity of victims to organize for their own demise, especially through the Jewish Councils of Europe which, though subservient to Nazi power, functioned as governments within the Jewish ghettos. Finally, Arendt saw the crimes of Eichmann, and indeed of the Nazi regime, as crimes against humanity committed on the body of the Jewish people. Lesser known are the writings of a young Holocaust survivor, Elie Wiesel, in which the suffering of the Jews is emphasized and the trial becomes a referendum on crimes against the Jewish people during the Nazi period *and* through all of Jewish history. For Wiesel, Eichmann symbolizes less the banality of evil—as an official in a bureaucratic organization with a goal to be accomplished—than he symbolizes every attempt to persecute and annihilate Jews throughout history. If Arendt criticizes the legal arguments of both the defense and prosecution lawyers, Wiesel wonders how a defense could even be presented at all, and if a defense was demanded, how a Jew could agree to conduct that defense. For Wiesel, a Jew defending Eichmann is an outrage.[7]

The universal and particular understanding of Jewish suffering presented by Arendt and Wiesel respectively, were hardly neutral positions. By the time of the Eichmann trial these positions are more accurately described as a battleground where the questions of European, Christian, and Jewish history are fought. That is why the response to Arendt's analysis of the trial was so strong and personalized, exemplified by Gershom Scholem, the great scholar of Jewish mysticism, when he wrote: "In the Jewish tradition there is a concept, hard to define and yet concrete enough, which we know as *Ahabath Israel*, 'Love of the Jewish people. . .' In you, dear Hannah, as in so many intellectuals who came from the German left, I find little trace of this." Scholem's internal discussion was complemented by Wiesel's outrage against those outside the Jewish community who criticized the execution of Eichmann by the Israeli state: "When millions of Jews were listening for one voice of conscience, those now protesting were dumb and blind. Today, when it is a question not of saving the lives of millions of innocent victims but of preserving the tainted life of a mass murderer, they have suddenly found their tongues and their sensitivity. Let those who were silent then remain silent now."[8]

Just five years later, in the wake of Israel's victory in the 1967 war, the intellectual, philosophical, and theological battleground yielded a decisive victory, one which essentially adopted the emphasis on the particularity of Jewish suffering and history over the universal. Sensing her defeat and viewing the continuation of her argument as a losing effort that generated less insight than anger, Arendt refused to write on the subject any longer. Arendt's earlier prediction that the search for unanimity of opinion on the question of the Holocaust and Israel was an ominous endeavor that would destroy diversity and protection from that "God-like certainty which stops all discussion and reduces social relationships to those of an ant heap" was fulfilled after the 1967 war. For Arendt, the attempt to enforce unanimity leads to the elimination of those who differ, and "spreads like an infection into every related issue."[9]

In many ways, the views of Arendt and Wiesel define the trajectory of Jewish interpretation of the Holocaust. Arendt saw the attempted destruction of the Jews as an attack on the safety and dignity of all humanity. When the Jews were at risk, humanity was as well. The lesson was to construct a civilization and a world order where all were protected from the barbarism endemic to the Nazi period. Wiesel saw the Nazi assault in more particular terms, as an assault on the Jews, Jewish history, and the Jewish God. Why else would Hitler have singled out the Jews and why would he have continued the slaughter long after the war was lost, even when the material and manpower were needed for the war effort? If there were universal lessons in this assault, so be it. But the primary crime was against the Jewish people and the essential lesson was for them as well. To universalize the question of Jewish suffering was to lose its significance. In Wiesel's view, this universalization would soon overwhelm and forget the suffering of the Jews. In Arendt's view, the particular suffering of the Jews took on meaning precisely in its application to the universal. Their dispute was less about the significance of the Holocaust than about the arena in which its lessons are to be found.

It is not surprising that contrasting opinions on the lessons of the Holocaust led to divergent understandings of what Jewish empowerment should be sought in the post-Holocaust world. From the 1940s onward, Arendt was binationalist Zionist in the tradition of Judah Magnes and Martin Buber. She was in favor of a Jewish homeland in Palestine that emphasized the revival of Jewish culture and the Hebrew language. A homeland also would allow Jewish intellectual and social experimentation found in the establishment of Hebrew University and the kibbutz movement. Arendt saw a Jewish homeland as important to the internal development of the Jewish people, as well as to the larger project of humanizing a world in crisis. It was difficult, however, for Arendt to see how these contributions could be developed without, at the same time, recognizing the full human and national rights of the Arabs in Palestine. The binationalist aspect of Palestine was worth preserving from an ethical and strategic standpoint. Arendt wrote prophetically in 1948 of the consequences of pursuing a policy of separation and statehood: "The land that would come into being would be something quite other than the dream of world Jewry, Zionist and non-Zionist. The victorious Jews would live surrounded by an entirely hostile Arab population, secluded within threatened borders. Defense would dominate other interests and activities, including the social and intellectual experiments, which would be discarded as impractical luxuries. Politics and economics would center around military strategy and be determined exclusively by the exigencies of war."[10]

After the 1967 war, Arendt's view of binationalism, like her understanding of the universal meaning of Jewish suffering, became marginal to Jewish discourse, even to the point of vanishing. Though Wiesel's early position on binationalism and the Jewish homeland is unclear, his overall celebration of Israel's victory in 1967, with his almost mystical discussion of the reunification of Jerusalem, became the order of the day. For Arendt, the response to the Holocaust and the overall collapse of Western civilization make necessary an attempt to rebuild particular human institutions and value-centers that might coalesce into a larger construct protected by ethical political values. Wiesel's emphasis is elsewhere: the victory of Israel in 1967 is a miracle that bespeaks the faintest whispering of a God who was absent in the death camps.

Arendt was not alone in her understanding that new insights were needed to guide the West after the collapse that the Nazis embodied. Viktor Frankl, an Austrian Jew who survived Auschwitz and Dachau, applied his training as a psychologist to the experience of the death camps and developed logotherapy, a school of psychology that emphasizes the search for meaning as central to human existence. Like Arendt, Frankl sought universal lessons from the Holocaust, as it challenged humanity at the deepest level of depravity. The Holocaust revealed that the drive of the person to endure is present even amid collapse and that hope for a future beyond catastrophe is essential to the ability to live through impossible circumstances. Whereas Wiesel emphasized the brokenness of humanity and God, Frankl saw the Holocaust as revealing the core of the human search for wholeness and meaning. Even the suffering in the death camps revealed a lesson for all persons, regardless of the situation they found themselves in. Frankl writes of inmates who dealt with their suffering by finding meaning and dignity: "Do not think that these considerations are unworldly and too far removed from life. It is true that only a few people are capable of reaching such high moral standards. Of the prisoners only a few kept their inner liberty and obtained those values which their suffering afforded, but even one such example is sufficient proof that man's inner strength may raise him above his outward fate. Such men are not only in concentration camps. Everywhere man is confronted with fate, with the chance of achieving something through his own suffering." In Frankl's work no distinction is drawn between Jews and non-Jews, either in their suffering or in their search for meaning. The role of religion and ideological commitment is written of in a positive way as part of the human search for meaning; general themes override the particular. Frankl's meditation on the importance of love exemplifies the

universal message of the Holocaust: "Then I grasped the meaning of
the greatest secret that human poetry and human thought and belief
have to impart: *The salvation of man is through love and in love.* In a
position of utter desolation, when man cannot express himself in positive action, when his only achievement may consist in enduring his
sufferings in the right way—an honorable way—in such a position
man can, through loving contemplation of the image he carries of his
beloved, achieve fulfillment." Published in Austria in 1946, Frankl's
work was one of the first works after the Holocaust.[11]

There was also writing on Jews and Judaism after the Holocaust that
emphasized the particularity of Jewish life as a contribution to the universal struggle of humanity. Eric Gutkind, a refugee from Nazi Germany, wrote during and after the war of a reinvigorated Judaism and
Jewish life, precisely to do battle with the universal crisis that was
destroying humanity. The challenge of Jewish life was to lead in this
struggle for the humanization of the globe against the forces of darkness. In fact, the complacency of German-Jewish "assimilationists,"
which ended in the "torture chambers," is, for Gutkind, the lesson of
contemporary Jewish history: that the particular mission of the Jews is
to contribute to the global uplift and that mission cannot be dispensed
with. After the Holocaust, destiny beckons with a particular attention
to the lowly and the outcast. As a people who have experienced exile,
the Jews' role is to be present to the poor of the contemporary world.
By delving deeper into one's Jewishness, a unity with the struggles of
all peoples comes into view: "The more intensely the Jew loves the people Israel the nearer he comes to mankind as a whole," writes Gutkind.
"His love is not a discriminatory love, pitting one against the other; it
is not a preferential love, but the most decided form of universalism
one can think of. The closer the Jew is in uniting himself with the people Israel the closer he comes to humanity and the less remote is he
from the Unity of Mankind." Writing in 1952, Gutkind titled his collection of essays *Choose Life* with the subtitle *The Biblical Call to Revolt.*
Just seven years after the Holocaust, Gutkind calls for a Jewish theology of liberation in service to humanity.[12]

The passion and perspective of Holocaust writing change with the
1967 war. Wiesel describes this period as a watershed for himself,
where he became a child again, "astonished and vulnerable, threatened
by nightmare," as well as for the Jewish people, who suddenly became
"children of the Holocaust." The watershed involves a military victory
and a religious manifestation to be interpreted, in Wiesel's words, by

poets and kabbalists. Indeed, the details of the war can hardly describe "the great mystery in which we are encloaked, as if by the command of the Almighty." Religious and secular Jews alike interpreted the experience of victory as a religious one, compelling each Jew to "confront his people, his past, and his God." Jewish theologian Eugene Borowitz describes the 1967 war in similar images: "The three-day news blackout after the war began was a time of hideous imagination, of deep soul-searching, of religious hope and consternation, and produced an overwhelming, voluntary outpouring of help, most notably from Jews who had never previously included themselves in the community. Then news came of the staggering Israeli victory. World Jewry experienced an elation that transcended relief from dread or rejoicing at Israeli prowess; the Bible calls it deliverance. Jews everywhere found themselves uncomprehendingly overwhelmed by the sight of soldiers converging on the Temple Mount's Western Wall; atheists, agnostics, and believers alike found themselves moved to prayer."[13]

The celebration of Wiesel and Borowitz diminished the already receding voices of Arendt, Frankl, and Gutkind. The particularity of the Holocaust as a Jewish experience to be guarded and explained by Jews was on the ascendancy. Coupled with the victory of 1967, the emphasis on the particularity of Jewish life and experience was complete. Yet even that celebration was hardly evident when the troubling questions of the Holocaust were as yet free of Israel's lightning victory. Even as late as the spring of 1967, the Holocaust remained very much on its own. To be sure, Israel was a state and the question of a unified Palestine with equal Jewish and Arab partners had receded; still Israel was not yet linked to the Holocaust as *the* response to suffering. Perhaps it is more accurate to state that Israel had yet to be joined to the Holocaust in the sense that both could still be seen and analyzed separately. After 1967, the Holocaust and Israel become central to Jewish life as a package, and the discussion about one is seen to be at the same time a discussion about the other.

In the twinning of Holocaust and Israel, insights are gained and lost. A continuity is established between experiences of suffering and empowerment. Weak and helpless in the Holocaust, Jews are now strong. In this way, Jewish identity and self-respect are strengthened; a pride emerges where once there was ambivalence and shame. One can see other effects as well, however. With the increasing power of Israel, the Holocaust too becomes empowered, almost militarized. In speech and action the Holocaust becomes an exclusive Jewish property, a property in need of a theology to articulate its uniqueness and justify its owners. The result is the development of Holocaust theology, a theology that seeks to guide the Jewish community through despair, celebration, and over the years through an increasingly ambivalent empowerment. In the end, this theology looks forward to empowerment rather than critically engaging it, and celebrates Jewish survival while neglecting the disaster that befalls the Palestinian people. In Holocaust theology, Jewish empowerment remains essentially innocent.[14]

Here we reflect on the generation of theologians who came to prominence after the 1967 war. Though they are pictured together as a harmonious group, with contributions from each coming together into an overall interpretation, their consensus is retrospective. Harvesting the insights of Holocaust theologians as they are absorbed in Jewish memory testifies to the power of their thought while glossing over the struggle for the heart and soul of the Jewish people. The seeming inevitability and acceptance of their theological insights is similarly a myth. For like the Eichmann trial, Holocaust theology was initially a battleground with dramatic stakes: Jewish survival, continuity, tradition, and even God. After the death camps, could Jews believe in a God of history? After Auschwitz, could one affirm a covenantal relationship as the essence of Jewish life? What did it mean to be Jewish after the Holocaust? Was empowerment of the Jewish people, especially in Israel, a Jewish commandment, after powerlessness led to mass death?

Each theologian had his own personality and insight. Richard Rubenstein, a rabbi, Hillel chaplain, and religious studies professor at Florida State University, emphasized the difficulty of accepting the traditional Jewish God and the covenant at the center of Jewish life; Emil Fackenheim, a concentration camp survivor and philosophy professor at the University of Toronto, emphasized Jewish survival as a victory over Hitler, implying, of course, that those who ceased to be Jews were accomplices of Hitler; Irving Greenberg, who founded his own institute to promote Jewish learning and leadership, emphasized the centrality of Israel as the way of Jewish commitment in an age when God is silent; Elie Wiesel continued to articulate an almost mystical view of the Holocaust, embracing Fackenheim and Greenberg while vehemently rejecting Rubenstein's approach.

For Wiesel and Fackenheim, Rubenstein's break with the Jewish God of history threatened to undermine a fragile consensus about the continuation of Jewish life after Auschwitz. This dispute between Rubenstein and Wiesel came to a head in 1970 at the first Annual

Scholars Conference on the Holocaust in Detroit, Michigan, when Wiesel discarded his prepared lecture to respond to Rubenstein's earlier presentation. It was a dramatic moment in which Wiesel lectured Rubenstein on the truly difficult task after the Holocaust: to continue with God and the Jewish people, to affirm within despair, and to recognize the validity of the survivor's testimony over against Rubenstein's academic declarations. Instead of representing the brokenness of the tradition, the Holocaust for Wiesel brought out its many strengths. To Rubenstein's statement that the death of millions of Jews, for no reason other than that they were Jews, deprived Jews even of martyrdom, Wiesel responded that many Jews, especially the rabbis, could have saved their lives. The overwhelming number of rabbis chose to remain with their endangered community, even unto death. For Wiesel, this commitment was worthy of reflection, even wonder. To Rubenstein's comment that it was difficult to live in a world without God, Wiesel responded that it was even more difficult to choose, after the Holocaust, to live *with* God.[15]

Yet Wiesel betrays a naiveté about his own position, for he also breaks with the rabbinic tradition by placing the experience of death, rather than study and piety, at the center of Jewish theology. His understanding that after the Holocaust the covenant is no longer between God and the Jewish people, but rather between the Jewish people and their memories of pain and death, of God and meaning, is hardly rabbinic in its sensibility. In this covenant, the past of Israel is emphasized, and Israel's overwhelming experience of death, its memory of a world infused with meaning, and even the memory of a God who was present to the people, is all that remains. All begins with destruction; the power of God is a memory to be recalled rather than a presence expected to manifest itself in the future. Israel's victory in the war is an exception that may portend a future of a God who was absent in the Holocaust. Still, the shadow remains and the covenant of old is no longer binding. Over the long run, it is uncertain whether Wiesel's sense of a post-Holocaust covenant or even his mysticism guarantees a substantive future for Jewish life any more than does Rubenstein's vision of the void. Perhaps it is the sources through which each man interprets the break with normative Judaism that provides the anger: for Wiesel, a reinterpreted Torah and Hasidic tales, for Rubenstein, the lectures of the Protestant theologian Paul Tillich, the letters of Paul, and the psychoanalysis of Freud. Is it right to assume with Wiesel that his memories of a world of meaning provides a future for Jewish living in Western, Christian, modern and secular life and that Rubenstein's explorations lead Jews astray?[16]

At least in his early years, the anger of Wiesel is comparable to Rubenstein's. And like Rubenstein, some of that anger is directed at the Jewish community itself. For contrary to what one might assume, much of the Jewish world held survivors at arms' length even as they spoke in their name. Wiesel accuses Rubenstein of this failing, but his criticism goes far beyond him. Though the material needs of the survivors were taken care of, it was often done in a condescending manner, as if the survivors were incompetents, misfits, or even carriers of disease. As Wiesel writes, it was "proper to give them sympathy, but from afar. Let them stay in the background, where they could do no harm or attract attention. Tell me, were you afraid or ashamed of them?" And Wiesel's autobiographical *Night*, which details his experiences in Auschwitz, is laced with an anger toward God comparable to Rubenstein's anger. For what kind of God would allow the innocent to be sent to their deaths? If many characterize *Night* as a dialogue with the God of history, it is also more; a bitter, ironic, and accusatory memoir would be a more accurate description. Perhaps, then, it was the male ego and the desperate fight to define the future of Jewish life that made their relationship so explosive. Perhaps, in listening to Rubenstein's analysis, Wiesel realized the direction that his own thought might lead to. If the logical extension of Wiesel's anger with God and the community led to a flight from Jewish life, this was not his intention. Over the years, the tenor of Wiesel's language changes, as the harshness dissipates and his message becomes more accommodating to his growing audiences.[17]

The struggle of Rubenstein and Wiesel had consequences beyond the Jewish world, for both became major figures in the public sharing of the Holocaust story and, at the same time, resources for the deconstruction and reconstruction of Christian theology in the West. The influence of Rubenstein and Wiesel can be seen in the Jewish liturgy of destruction prominently displayed in the United States Holocaust Memorial Museum in Washington D.C. and the Christian Holocaust theology developed over the years by Franklin Littell, Paul van Buren, and Robert McAfee Brown, among others. The liturgy of destruction emphasizes the difficulty with God that both Rubenstein and Wiesel share, and the narrative of destruction in the museum combines Rubenstein's later emphasis on the systematically organized, bureaucratically administered destruction of the Jews with Wiesel's evocation of the void that the Holocaust leaves behind. Christian Holocaust theology accepts their challenge of Christian complicity in the mass slaughter of the Jewish people.[18]

But this is to get ahead of the story, for it is the break with the normative rather than its enshrinement as part of a new orthodoxy which is of interest. For it was here, when Holocaust theology was being birthed, that it subverted the known and accepted, and it is here that clues are found that might bring us beyond the orthodoxy of the present. Yet it is also here that we are cautioned to step slowly, to linger, as it were, in a despair and a questioning that have largely been lost.

It was in 1965 when Richard Rubenstein first traveled to Auschwitz. Several days after his visit, he became the first Jewish theologian ever to lecture at the Catholic University of Lublin. This was a dubious honor, as before the Holocaust over half of the population of Lublin had been Jewish and the city was the seat of many important rabbinical academies. Rubenstein was both moved and saddened by the occasion and burdened by the knowledge that he was compelled to speak for the dead. He knew that his religious perspectives would not have been shared by most of Lublin's Jews had they lived to express themselves, as they would have "affirmed their confidence in the Lord God of Israel who would in time bind their wounds and send everlasting healing. They would never have deviated from their belief that God is good, that He mysteriously performs all things for the best." Rubenstein could affirm none of this, largely because of their fate. How could he speak of God's goodness after Auschwitz? "I could and did affirm His terrible holiness, but I could never speak of His goodness. I could not praise God's handiwork or His ultimate purposes. I could not even say with Job, 'Though He slay me, yet will I trust in Him.'"[19]

Rubenstein published a collection of essays the following year with the provocative title *After Auschwitz*. The essays were somber in tone, almost despairing. While it is true that Jews survived the Nazi onslaught, Rubenstein questions the world in which that survival occurred. The world of the death camps is past and, at the same time, remains a potential future. Rubenstein is unable to accept a limited God who was powerless to save the Jews or an omnipotent God who could have done so but chose not to intervene to end the slaughter; the burden of the present is to live without the traditional Jewish God. The prospect of human solidarity is also suspect, for the Nazis and the surrounding populations hunted Jews, turned back Jewish partisans, built and maintained the death camps, and even provided the expertise to make death more efficient. "Having lost everything, we have nothing further to lose and no future fear of loss," Rubenstein laments, "Our existence has in truth been a being unto death. We have passed beyond all illusion and hope. We have learned in the crisis that we were totally and nakedly alone, that we could expect neither support nor succor from God or from our fellow creatures." It is in a world devoid of God and human solidarity that the state of Israel becomes a testimony to Jewish dignity and self-defense. Rubenstein writes that through its power Israel has "radically escalated the cost of killing Jews." As importantly, however, Rubenstein asserts that Israel is "no royal road back to the God of History."[20]

In his support of Israel, Rubenstein joins a consensus of Holocaust theologians. Yet he does so with such explicit language—escalating the cost of taking Jewish lives—that the Jewish theological mainstream is loathe to embrace him even on a position of overriding importance. Their argument for Israel is based on the history of Jewish suffering and the prospect that Israel will limit or end that suffering; Israel is to protect Jewish lives and if necessary to inflict damage that the enemy will find unacceptable. But the argument is made along moral lines. Because of atrocity against the Jews in Europe, a Jewish state is necessary. That state is peace loving, progressive, innovative, and a model of democracy. Jews are innocent sufferers who fight only in self-defense, and if the Arab states accept Israel all will be well. The fight with Europe and Christianity is behind the Jews; they along with the Americans support Israel for historical, moral, and even theological reasons. It is also important for Holocaust theologians to argue that even God might be part of this endeavor of returning Jews to their soil after centuries of dispersion. In this way, the dramatic history of the Jews and their return to Israel are elevated to the ultimate level, one which a repentant Christianity can embrace.

The moral drama of the Jews is therefore a crucial aspect of a narrative that will elicit support for the state of Israel. At the same time, the themes of Jewish innocence in suffering *and* empowerment and the possibility that Israel is a redemptive response to the Holocaust are also crucial to attract Jewish support in the West for an economically, politically, and strategically dependent state. For Rubenstein, by contrast, innocence and morality have little if anything to do with the political empowerment of the Jewish people; nor is it a theologically charged issue, as if the demonstrated power of Israel is dependent on God. At the moment of history when God was needed the only response was absence. Jews have no need or expectation of God. Indeed the military prowess of the Israeli state reflects its knowledge that the only protection that Jews have is the one they devise for themselves. To bring morality and God into the narrative of self-defense and the ability to damage the opponent is the same mistake Jews have made in their previous unempowered existence. For Rubenstein, a narrative of morality and God is the royal road back to disaster.

Rubenstein's explosive denunciation of the German-Jewish philosopher and biblical scholar Martin Buber should be understood within this context. Delivered at the Buber Centenary Conference in West Germany, a conference chaired by Walter Scheel, then-President of the Federal Republic of Germany, Rubenstein critiques Buber's theology and political leadership during the Nazi period. Rubenstein sees Buber's mystical understandings of the human-divine relationship as lacking in substance and institutional weight, while at the same time underestimating the reality of evil in the world. For Rubenstein, Buber's venture into politics was almost always utopian and messianic, and because of this Buber misunderstood what was at stake with the Nazis and the ancient theological conflict between Judaism and Christianity. In Rubenstein's view, Buber's tendency to underestimate the power of evil affected his politics and his theology. Because Buber viewed evil as privation of dialogue, he was more concerned with attempting to restore the broken dialogue than to face the necessity of creating and sustaining political power structures able to contain evil. Since a principal concern of politics is to create a system of officially sanctioned coercion, Buber's politics were, to Rubenstein, foolhardy and dangerous.[21]

Because of these views, Buber had little or no place for the Holocaust in his theological thinking. Seeing evil fundamentally as absence of relationship, Buber was unprepared to see in the Holocaust the presence or absence of God. In Rubenstein's understanding this allows Buber to continue on after Auschwitz without engaging the critical theological categories of covenant, election, and God's action in history. Still, Rubenstein is as interested in the political aspects of Buber's categories as in their theological efficacy: at a time when it is imperative to escalate the cost of taking Jewish lives, Buber pleads for increased tolerance and understanding between Jews and Christians in Germany. Rubenstein finds no discussion of the relationship between power and dignity in Buber's understanding of the interpersonal encounter of I and Thou or even in Buber's controversial lectures in

Germany in 1953. In Rubenstein's view, even after the Holocaust, Buber failed to grasp the most important lesson of the entire period: "The Holocaust reminds us that he who lacks the power to defend himself, yet is unprepared to choose death, must be prepared for the possibility that an adversary may inflict upon him and his family any obscenity whatsoever, as indeed was the lot of the Jews during World War II." For Rubenstein, this fact about the human condition was clearly understood by the Zealots at Masada, as they chose death rather than to "endure the predictable consequences of impotent servility."[22]

Buber's theological and political understandings also informed his Zionism, a binational Zionism similar to that of Judah Magnes and Hannah Arendt, and his socialism, a utopian socialism which he continued to affirm after the Holocaust. Rubenstein criticizes Buber's distrust of the state and its institutions as a "messianic attempt to create a *Gemeinschaft*" as unworkable in Palestine because neither the Jews nor the Arabs could trust the other community with control over the state's instruments of coercion. This naiveté was again illustrated in Buber's opposition to the execution of Adolf Eichmann, though Rubenstein agrees with Buber's idea that a far worse punishment for Eichmann than death would be to live out his natural life as a prisoner of the very people he did so much to destroy. Rubenstein disagrees with Buber's understanding that the state has no right to take a person's life, for, in Rubenstein's mind, this is exactly the purpose of the Israel, to offer the hope that the surviving Jewish community would "no longer be the gathering place of future defenseless victims." To Buber's understanding, shared with Arendt, that Eichmann's crimes against humanity were no less monstrous than his crimes against the Jews, Rubenstein responds that the more one studies the Holocaust, the more apparent it becomes that, "far from being a crime against humanity, a very significant proportion of the political and the religious leaders of the Western world regarded it as a convenient operation so long as their police and armed forces were not directly involved." When Buber asserts that Eichmann's crimes against humanity were at least as great as his crimes against the Jewish people, Rubenstein feels that Buber is in effect diminishing the significance of the violence done to the Jewish people by upholding an empty and misleading abstraction. Here again Rubenstein finds a "strange inability" on Buber's part to weigh seriously the reality of evil, suffering, and tragedy.[23]

Though Rubenstein's critique of Buber is strong, there is also a sensitivity to the circumstances in which Buber lived. In a sense, Buber was fated to be a tragic figure in a tragic period in history. With other Jews, Buber was heir to a theological and political tradition that, according to Rubenstein, had already sealed the fate of the European Jews. This fate began with the surrender of Jerusalem in 70 and 135 c.e., as well as in the bargain struck by the rabbis in those surrenders: political submission for the imperial assurance of Jewish religious and cultural autonomy. It is Rubenstein's conviction that no other course was available to the Jews at the time nor later in the European diaspora. Therefore he finds no fault in the Pharisees for having accepted Roman domination. Nevertheless, the indignities visited upon diaspora Jews over the centuries, including the Holocaust, were a predictable consequence of this initial surrender. Rubenstein believes that the Pharisees consented to lead a community whose dignity and security rested upon the "power, the interests, and the whim of strangers," who often regarded Jews as enemies. The "daring risk" that the Pharisees embraced, that Caesar would be a trustworthy master, could not guarantee that *"every* heir to the power and authority of Caesar would also refrain from abusing his unlimited power over the Jews." For Rubenstein, Adolf Hitler was the legitimate head of the German Reich, and therefore heir to the power and authority of the Caesars. When Rubenstein concludes about Buber that a man whose "thought had so little relevance to the concrete experience of his own time and people is hardly likely to be of much relevance to ours," Rubenstein is actually speaking about a two-thousand-year history which, like Buber, is a relic to be studied rather than a tradition worth continuing.[24]

With these thoughts, it is surprising that Rubenstein's final paragraph relating to Buber's worldwide eminence should end in a lament. "Perhaps Buber's eminence reveals more about us than it does about him," Rubenstein writes, "There were other great Jewish teachers in our terrible century. Why did all of us bestow our laurels upon him? When Buber's life and thought is viewed in light of the Holocaust, I must confess that I have no answer to that question. Of one thing, however, I am certain. We needed him. Why, I do not know." This final response, so different in character than Rubenstein's previous analysis, is reminiscent of the final act of the bitter exchange between Elie Wiesel and Rubenstein. After Wiesel finished his response to Rubenstein, Rubenstein stood up and stated that he wished to say something. Expecting a refutation, Wiesel was stunned when Rubenstein simply replied: "I as a rabbi want to give you my blessing."[25]

In these emotional moments at the beginning of the journey

beyond rabbinic Judaism and before Holocaust theology was established as normative, Rubenstein recognizes that the battle with Wiesel and Buber over the struggle to define the future of Jewish life is really an attempt to cope with a tradition that has few answers for the dead or the living. What future is there for such a tradition? Rubenstein longs for a world where Buber and Wiesel make sense, and he feels that the breach of solidarity between God and the human engenders so much divisiveness and rage that the future might not be worth inheriting. Perhaps Rubenstein was close to Wiesel in sentiment when, just months before the 1967 war, in a symposium on Jewish Values in the Post-Holocaust Future, Wiesel said:

> The question is asked: Why did the Jews oppose spiritual resistance to physical threat and physical resistance to spiritual threat? The Midrash explains this paradox in the following way: The Jewish people entered into a covenant with God. We are to protect His Torah, and He, in turn, assumes responsibility for Israel's presence in the world. Thus, when our spirituality—the Torah—was in danger, we used force in protecting it; but when our physical existence was threatened, we simply reminded God of His duties and promises deriving from the covenant. Well, it seems that, for the first time in our history, this very covenant was broken. That is why the Holocaust has terrifying theological implications. Whether we want it or not, because of its sheer dimensions, the event transcends man and involves more than him alone. It can be explained neither with God nor without Him. . . . For the first time in our history, the Jewish people was totally abandoned. God's failure was matched by man's.[26]

Perhaps Rubenstein also longed to assent to what Buber spoke of in Germany in 1953:

> When I think of the German people of the days of Auschwitz and Treblinka, I see, first of all, the great many who knew that the monstrous event was taking place and did not oppose it. But my heart, which tells me of the weakness of men, refuses to condemn my neighbor because he was not able to bring himself to become a martyr. Next there emerges before me the mass of those who remained ignorant of what was withheld from the German public, but also did not undertake to discover what reality lay behind the rumors which were circulating. When I think of these men, I am seized by the thought of the anxiety—likewise well-known to me—of the human creature before a truth which he fears that he cannot stand. But finally there appears before me, from reliable reports, some who have become as familiar to me by sight, action, and

voice as if they were friends—those who refused to carry out or to continue to carry out the orders and suffered death or put themselves to
death, or those who learned what was taking place and opposed it and
were put to death, or those who learned what was taking place and
because they could do nothing to stop it killed themselves. I see these
men very near before me in that special intimacy which binds us at
times to the dead and to them alone; and now reverence and love for
these German men fills my heart.[27]

By the 1970s, these longings were noticeably absent from Rubenstein's writings. The debate had become a war, the division of opinion
a bitterness which seemed unabating. For Rubenstein, there was no
royal road back to the God of history, nor was there a road back to his
own people.

Crimes against the Future

With Elie Wiesel at the symposium was the German-born Canadian,
Emil Fackenheim. In his early years as a philosopher, Fackenheim
wrote extensively and approvingly of Martin Buber and found little
room in his own reflections for the significance of the Holocaust. Yet
in this symposium he moved radically to include the Holocaust,
proposing after Auschwitz a 614th commandment: "The authentic Jew
of today is forbidden to hand Hitler yet another, posthumous victory."
This commandment is relevant to both the agnostic and believing Jew,
as he redefines the center of Jewish life and practice:

> If the 614th commandment is binding upon the authentic Jew, then we
> are, first, commanded to survive as Jews, lest the Jewish people perish.
> We are commanded, second, to remember in our very guts and bones
> the martyrs of the Holocaust, lest their memory perish. We are forbid-
> den, thirdly, to deny or despair of God, however much we may have to
> contend with him or with belief in Him, lest Judaism perish. We are for-
> bidden, finally, to despair of the world as the place which is to become
> the kingdom of God, lest we help make it a meaningless place in which
> God is dead or irrelevant and everything is permitted.

Fackenheim, here, is recalling the particularity of the Jewish vocation
and warning that Jews cannot disguise the uniqueness of Nazi evil
under the comfortable generality of persecution-in-general. After the
Holocaust, that particularity must be affirmed in radically different
circumstances. If the Jewish vocation begins with the commanding
voice of Sinai, it continues today with the commanding voice of

Auschwitz. Fackenheim understands this 614th commandment as issuing from victims of Auschwitz themselves. If the origin of the Jewish community is found in response to the voice of God, contemporary Jews must listen to their own voices, the tears and cries that arise from the dead.[28]

As do Rubenstein and Wiesel, Fackenheim breaks with normative Judaism. The original commandments are given by God at Sinai, and they form the way of life that the covenant demands. The commandments are a sign of and witness to God's presence in history; they provide the structure for the life of God's people. But with the Holocaust, the source of the commandments, the covenant, and chosenness is thrown into question. The whole structure of Jewish life, even the desire to remain Jewish and to create a Jewish future, is threatened. For if there is no God, or if the God who exists could not or did not act at the time of greatest need, why affirm the covenant? Wiesel's understanding of the memories of Jewish history and of God's presence influences Fackenheim to mobilize Jewish life in the present so that the memories are preserved. The present experience of the Holocaust casts all into doubt, even Buber's sensibility, which Fackenheim clung to for years. Though the memories cannot create a future, without them a future is impossible. What is needed is a commandment to continue on so that a community remains to sort out the past, the Holocaust, and a future which is faithful to both. The commandment proceeds from the memory of the covenant *and* the slaughter, demanding a fidelity to the Jewish people itself. The voice comes from history, so that all that has gone before, including those who died with loyalty to the faith, will not be lost; if God has lost the power to render their sacrifice meaningful, then we must assume that role. The commanding voice of Auschwitz compliments Wiesel's evocation of the martyrs of the Holocaust and confronts Rubenstein's sense that the history of the Jewish people might be at its end.

In the discussion that followed the prepared presentations, the question of the Jewish vocation and the uniqueness of the Holocaust predominated. Wiesel agreed with Fackenheim, noting that as a Jew he considered the Holocaust experience mainly as a Jewish experience, and the event as both irrational and unique: "In the beginning there was the Holocaust. We must therefore start all over again. . . . Today no poet can write poems without justifying himself against that background. This applies to all of us. Today we know that all roads and all words lead to the Holocaust." Another participant, George Steiner, a literary critic who was then Director of English Studies at Churchill College, Cambridge University, agreed with the "absoluteness, the ontological horror of the catastrophe," but disagreed with the direction of Fackenheim's and Wiesel's analysis. Steiner speaks forcefully of hundreds of thousands of Indonesians who are being massacred because of their alleged Marxist affiliations, and with no intervention by Western powers to stop the bloodshed. "This evening we'll go to our friends, to our dinners, to our good sleep, while torture is going on and many human beings are being burned alive," Steiner comments. "And the great difference is this: it is at least conceivable that when the first news got through about Auschwitz—and there is some evidence on this—there was not actually in the minds of those who heard it the possibility of believing it; it seemed outside the categories of understanding. *We who come after* know that whatever the news is, it may be so."[29]

Steiner first broached this haunting phrase "we who come after" in 1966, the same year as the publication of Rubenstein's *After Auschwitz*. For Steiner, the implications of the Holocaust for speech, writing, and action are profound, as a new knowledge has come into being: "We know now that a man can read Goethe or Rilke in the evening, that he can play Bach and Schubert, and go to his day's work at Auschwitz in the morning." There is a specificity as well for what Steiner labels the "eruption of barbarism" in modern Europe: "The blackness of it did not spring up in the Gobi Desert or the rain forests of the Amazon. It rose from within, and from the core of European civilization. The cry of the murdered sounded in earshot of the universities; the sadism went on a street away from the theaters and museums." Steiner refers to the Enlightenment philosopher, Voltaire, who looked confidently to the end of torture and ideological massacre. That confidence was betrayed in our own century when the "high places of literacy, of philosophy, of artistic expression, became the setting for Belsen." In Steiner's view, we have become post-Auschwitz humans because the evidence at Auschwitz—"the photographs of the sea of bones and gold fillings, of children's shoes and hands leaving a black claw-mark on oven walls"—alters our sense of the possible: "Hearing whisperings out of hell again we would know how to interpret the code; the skin of our hopes has grown thinner."[30]

For Steiner, Hitler's crime was particular, that is, against the Jews, *and* universal, that is, against humanity, because the death of a specific culture affects all cultures. To illustrate this, Steiner describes the death of Chaim Aron Kaplan, a teacher of Hebrew, an essayist, and historian in the Warsaw Ghetto, as a unique tragedy. To be sure, this is so of every death, as an absolute uniqueness passes from humanity. For Steiner, though, despite its outward democracy death is not entirely equal: "The integrity, the fineness of intelligence, the human rationalism exhibited on every page of [Kaplan's] indispensable book—representing a specific tradition of feeling, of linguistic practice—are irretrievably lost. The particular type of human possibility realized in central and east European Judaism is extinct." In murdering Chaim Kaplan and those like him, the Germans deprived human history of one of the versions of its future. Genocide is the ultimate crime because it preempts the future, tearing up one of the roots from which history emerges. Because there can be no repair of the crime, forgiveness is impossible. It is the crime against the human future that constitutes "both the persistence of the Nazi action and the slow, sad vengeance of the unremembered dead."[31]

At the same time that the Nazis denied humanity a part of its future, they also made more difficult the discussion of God. Steiner describes the human act of speech as a way of approaching God; it is the frontier of language which gives proof of a transcendent presence in the fabric of the world. The poems of St. John of the Cross and of the mystic tradition point to this transcendence: "It is just because we can go no further, because speech so marvelously fails us, that we experience the certitude of a divine meaning surpassing and enfolding ours. What lies beyond man's word is eloquent of God." Clearly we are in a different world from Holocaust theology's. Steiner is, at least in the beginning of his exploration, lamenting the nuances of transcendence now lost in the mystery of language. Language is in many ways tied to the unfolding of the religious traditions, but the literature that Steiner is dealing with is already distant from the covenantal language that Rubenstein, Wiesel, and Fackenheim are working through. The echoes of transcendence are real for Steiner and they, too, like the covenant at Sinai, are in danger of being lost.[32]

When language itself becomes an instrument of barbarism, the assault on transcendence increases. In legitimating atrocity, language further restricts the human approach to transcendence and God. As a legitimator of atrocity, and as an explorer of meaning after atrocity, language faces an almost impossible task. Still, Steiner recognizes the possibility that language might serve as a way of healing, of reapproaching the transcendent in a time of barbarism. By raising this possibility, Steiner seeks a way within and beyond the Holocaust theology debates and in so doing moves the language of theology to another place of encounter. In a sense, though, Steiner simply extends the point he made at the symposium in 1967, when in response to Elie Wiesel he commented, "No, the Holocaust doesn't teach abstractly, but it may teach us something extremely simple. If you forbid one to compare the agony of someone now being tortured and burned to those who were then— and that's what you're doing, I think, Elie—this is a fiat I think untrue to the deepest genius of the Jews and the Jewish sense of implication in man's fate." By doing this, Steiner continues, "we are accepting an eschatological end to history, namely, an end to our humanity."[33]

Here is the question that Steiner poses: at the eschatological end to history and of humanity, what is the vocation of a people who in its very history has experienced both at an accelerated level? What does it mean to be Jewish for those who have come after? Again this vision is partially present in the haunting image—one might say messianic image—which Steiner presents, that of the Jewish French historian of the medieval period, Marc Bloch, who returned to France, joined the underground, was captured, tortured, and executed in Grenoble. As he was being taken out for execution, Bloch saw a boy of fourteen or fifteen who was also to be shot. Seeing that the boy was terribly afraid, Bloch asked the Germans for permission that they be shot together. Bloch comforted the boy to the very end. Steiner comments: "The values of that moment, the historian's training, the gift of humanity— these belong to all men, not alone to the Jews. But the Jew, I think, may have an uncomfortable obligation and privilege of practicing them right now pretty constantly and at whatever price of discomfort."[34]

The courage of Bloch's return to France, and the comfort he was able to lend the boy, comes from a tradition which houses a homeland in a text, or rather a series of texts, beginning with the Torah and expanding over time to include the likes of Karl Marx, Sigmund Freud, Ludwig Wittgenstein, and Franz Kafka. In this unfolding discussion, and within the context of immense suffering, a messianic horizon is established. From the beginning of the Jewish tradition the concepts of contract and covenant are less metaphoric than they are moral, legalistic, and above all textual. Hence for Steiner, Judaism is a "literal instrument, a spoken-written deed of trust, subject not only to constant personal and communal ratification, but to close probing." If God 'keeps book' on the Jewish people, Jews also 'keep book' on God. The covenant is a two-way operation, open to verification, argument, and even dismissal.[35]

In the heart of the covenant is terror and the possibility of rehabilitation. The covenant is a script of wandering, dispersal, and return, which Jews were promised in the beginning and have lived out in history. Jews have carried this script "on their back" through the millennia, and it is this textual fabric—the interpretative practices in Judaism—which is ontologically and historically at the heart of Jewish identity. Steiner defines the Jewish world as immersed in a "concentric tradition of reading," involving the holy books and commentary on them, as well as a developed and ongoing tradition of satellite texts. Within this context, then, Kafka can be seen as an heir to the prophets in his work as a modern commentator. After all, Kafka felt coerced into writing, as if he was not worthy; in this attitude he resembles the prophets and their attempt to evade the burden of their insight and the commandment to speak. For Steiner, Jeremiah's "I do not know how to speak," and Jonah's flight from foretelling, have their parallel in Kafka's "impossibility of writing, impossibility of not writing." To those who say that this textual tradition is simply a substitute for an anchored political and social identity, as Rubenstein might, Steiner argues the opposite: "The point is that sometimes hallucinatory techniques and disciplines of attention to the text, the mystique of fidelity to the written word, the reverence bestowed on its expositors and transmitters, concentrated within Judaic sensibility unique strengths and purities of disinterested purpose."[36]

Yet it is here that the shadow lies. For Steiner, the Jewish calling is a "pure hunt for truth," regardless of the consequences. Prophetic act and critical thought are the nationhood of Judaism. The patriotism of the truth-seeker is antithetical to the civic option posited by philosophers like Jean-Jacques Rousseau. The citizenship of the Jew is one of critical humanism; the Jew at home in the text is a conscientious objector to flag and anthem. In Steiner's understanding, the locus of truth is always extraterritorial; its "diffusion is made clandestine by the barbed wire and watch-towers of national dogma." This truth was announced in Jeremiah and remains valid today: "The royal city, the nation are laid waste; the text and its transmitter endure, *there* and *now*. The Temple may be destroyed; the texts which it housed sing in the winds that scatter them."[37]

After Auschwitz, Steiner's statements are provocative, even to some dangerous. They invite speculation that he seeks a return to a pre-Holocaust, unempowered Jewish existence. Some Jews might feel this a prelude to another disaster, an end to the Jewish people, including the Jewish text. Can the text be carried and the concentric tradition of reading be continued, without an empowered Jewish state? Here Steiner addresses the question of Israel, the most difficult arena of discussion, especially in the post-1967 war era. Here, too, he is provocative. It is clear to Steiner that a majority of Jews are not prophets or idealists; especially after persecution, displacement, and death, Jews seek a normal existence. They would, like other peoples and nations, "vanquish their enemies rather than be oppressed and scattered by them; if harsh reality dictates, they would rather occupy, censor, even torture than be occupied and censored and tortured as they have been for so long." And so it is with Israel, a nation-state that lives as an armed garrison. The sad irony is that Israel has made others homeless and disinherited in order to survive, whereas for two millennia the dignity of the Jew was bound to the inability to make any other human being as disinherited as Jews themselves. Today the virtues of Israel are similar to those of Sparta, with its propaganda and self-deception. Steiner sees no singular vice in the practices of the state of Israel, as these follow logically the demands of the modern nation-state. Still the consequences are profound, for when Judaism trades its homeland in the text for territory, Judaism becomes homeless to itself.[38]

For Steiner, it is implausible that the difficult road of Jewish history should have as its end, or its justification, a small state in the Middle East, especially one "crushed by military burdens, petty and even corrupt in its politics, shrill in its parochialism." Though the state of Israel is wholly understandable, perhaps historically inescapable, and in many respects admirable, Steiner sees it as an attempt to make the condition and meaning of Judaism like that of other people's. In this way, the state threatens to eradicate the deeper truth of "inhousedness" which is the legacy of the prophets and the keepers of the text. Steiner recalls a visit to Jerusalem when he was taken to the Shrine of the Scrolls, where some of the Dead Sea scrolls and biblical papyri are kept. The guide explained the hidden hydraulic mechanism whereby the entire display can be made to sink safely below the ground in case of shelling or bombardment. Though such precautions are indispensable because nation-states, including Israel, live by the sword, in Steiner's mind such precautions are also metaphysical and ethical barbarism: "Words cannot be broken by artillery, nor thought live in bomb-shelters." Hence his conclusion: "Locked materially in a material homeland, the text may, in fact, lose its life-force, and its truth values may be betrayed. But when the text *is* the homeland, even when it is rooted only in the exact remembrance and seeking of a handful of wanderers, nomads of the word, it cannot be extinguished. Time is truth's passport and its native ground. What better lodging for the Jew?"[39]

For Holocaust theologians, Steiner's view of Israel is unique and completely unacceptable. In many ways, Steiner is more traditional than the others, in that he embraces a diaspora existence as the essence of Judaism and Jewish life. The diaspora is a place of longing and commitment, even freedom, for without a state Jews can engage the vocation of thought and discernment. With a state they are burdened with responsibilities that are time-consuming and morally ambiguous. Why build and maintain a state when that can be done by others whose vocation is different or undefined? Steiner's understanding is similar to the pre-Holocaust rabbinic understanding of the diaspora, only without the law or prayer, an understanding that Holocaust theologians discredit as irresponsible after the European catastrophe. He is also in line with the European Jewish intellectual tradition, which existed before the Holocaust and was decimated in it. Steiner therefore stands in an interesting and provocative tradition, one which was overwhelmed by the physical violence of the Holocaust and by the Holocaust narrative that became normative in the Jewish world after the 1967 war, but one that still haunts contemporary Jewish life. For, after all, the majority of Jews live by choice in the diaspora, even after the Holocaust. After the theological statements and the mobilization of emotions, do most Jews think that their tradition of thought and ethics has been enhanced by having a state? If Steiner is correct to say that Jews want to live normal lives, does that mean that they no longer see a distinctive quality in Jewish life apart from the pride of possessing a powerful state? Many Jews might answer that after the Holocaust the alternative to empowerment is unacceptable, despite the diminution of thought and ethics that has arguably accompanied it. Abandonment of the state today would simply place millions of Jews in jeopardy. The more important argument is about the new constellation of Jewish life and how ethics and empowerment, the text and government, are to be balanced in a way that is responsible and just. But Steiner would argue that to start at that place of balancing reality and the ideal is already breaking the prophetic ideal, or at least collapsing the dynamic of Jewish life over the millennia. At the very least, Steiner is the last major European Jewish intellectual figure to be explicitly and publicly anti-Zionist.

In an essay on metaphor and the Holocaust, Steiner returns to the themes of textuality, vocation, and statehood with renewed vigor. One is immediately caught up, however, in another dimension only hinted at in earlier essays. Here the discussion is less about the call of the text, the fulfillment of the text, or even its interpretation or betrayal, but whether the text has lost its authenticity because of the Holocaust experience. The text carried weight throughout Jewish history because the major actors in the text, God and humans, could carry on a discourse without entering the realm of speculation and theology. For Steiner, the most authentic and lasting strength in Jewish sensibility lay outside of reflection and metaphysical discourse on the nature and attributes of God. Rather, from Abraham onward there was a covenant of dialogue between the Jew and God, an understanding of "living in His presence." This allowed for a language world of Judaism in relation to God as one of "idiomatic affinity."[40]

One of the consequences of the Holocaust is that this language world has been violently and irreparably shattered. The hermeneutical dilemma of how to speak about God, or rather how to construct a systematic theology about God—a foreign concept to Judaism—now moves to the center. Living in God's presence, one is faced with the question of whether there is a human form of language adequate to conceptualize and understand Auschwitz. In Steiner's words one hears echoes of Rubenstein and Wiesel: "In what conceivable language can a Jew speak *to* God after Auschwitz, and in what conceivable language can he speak *about* God?" The language of prayer is also suspect; can it be anything but cynical, accusatory, or despairing? Speech about God is problematic, for what forms can it take, what plausibility can it establish after Auschwitz? The choices are stark in this situation; to be silent is one option, though for a Jew to be silent about formative historical events is self-mutilation. The other option is to speak and possibly trivialize the experience of death and the end of meaningful linguistic expression. Steiner understands that after the Holocaust, metaphors that once made it possible for language to speak about God are no longer available to us. It may be that after the "gassing, starvation, live burial, slow torture, burning of millions of men, women, and children in the heartland of so-called civilization, we no longer have cause or need to speak to or about a God whose overwhelming attribute became that of absence, of nothingness." One finds here a reciprocal failure: words fail us as we fail them. It is this reciprocal failing that comes nearest to justifying the concept of the death of God or, as Steiner prefers to think of it, the exit of God from language, that is, from the bounds of human experience.[41]

The problem of language and the ability of the Jew to continue a discourse with God revolves to some extent around the question of the uniqueness of the Holocaust. Steiner cites previous and post-Holocaust atrocities, concluding that the uniqueness debate is more than a discussion about historical fact and comparison. Regardless of the objective reality, it is clear that the presumed uniqueness of the Holocaust has become vital to Judaism, in essence the cement of Jewish identity. Steiner regards this development as perhaps inevitable and ambiguous, masking profound differences within the Jewish world and serving historically as a justification for Israel's more extreme policies at home and abroad. It provides a self-flattering and self-dramatizing "aura of tragic belonging," and a disturbing commercialized pathos of horror with a "compensating fascination" with violence. "We are, in certain respects, a traumatized, a crazed people," Steiner remarks, "How could we not be?"[42]

Still the question remains, why the Jews? Here Steiner explores uniqueness at a symbolic and metaphysical-theological level, concluding that the Jews were singled out in Europe precisely because Jewish contributions to Western history are also confrontations with that history. These contributions/confrontations are accepted in their depth or rejected out of hand. Since the Jews carry these contributions/confrontations in their communal life and texts, and since their physical bodies remind others of the presence of these challenges, rejection and annihilation are predictable, if not inevitable. For Steiner, the contributions/confrontations revolve around a religious and secular summons prompted by the ancient and modern Jewish people—to worship an infinite, invisible, and ethically imperative God who is involved in the meaning of history and who demands a life of abnegation and the abolition of the ego, private property, and privilege. The religious option is presented in the Judaic understanding of monotheism and then exemplified in Jesus the Jew, who sharpens the Mosaic law even as he continues the vision of the prophets. The secular option is exemplified by Karl Marx, who was utterly Judaic in his secular, justice-oriented messianism. In Marx, the religious and secular are closely tied together. When Marx asks that we "exchange love for love, and justice for justice," Steiner believes he is speaking the language of Isaiah, Amos, and Jesus.[43]

Jews have confronted Western culture with these claims and ideals, and for this they have been rejected. It is not the charge of deicide that created and sustained Jew-hatred in the Christian civilization of the West, although this charge plays its part. Rather, it is as inventor and carrier of a God who is powerful and demanding that Jews have suffered. As Hitler reportedly said in his tabletalk: "The Jews invented conscience," and, for Steiner, this is simply another way of saying: "The Jews invented God." Therefore, to eliminate the Jews is to make everything permissible. In Steiner's view, no other approach illuminates the drivenness of the Nazis to eradicate the Jew and Judaism from Europe; no other approach explains the Christian and post-Christian obsession with Jews, a mix of dream and fantasy turned demonic.[44]

The Loss of Jewish Innocence

After Auschwitz, the life-giving mystery of meaningful metaphor and therefore the organization of that metaphor in poetry, philosophy, and theology may be fated. That fate is logical in view of the death camps. Still, the compulsion to articulate truth within Judaism, even the "commandment of dialogue" with or against a God who no longer speaks, may continue. Certainly the question of Auschwitz looms larger than ever before, and analysis of the pathology of politics or social-ethnic conflicts, though important, is insufficient. For Steiner, it is a question of the existence or nonexistence of God, of the one who made us, who did not speak out of the "death wind," and who is now on trial: "In that court, which is the court of man in history, how can the language spoken in indictment or defense, in witness or denial, be one from which He is absent, one in which no psalm can be spoken against Him?"[45]

Steiner's understanding of the connection between language and humanity, language and God, as being bound to a people's activity and witness in history, comes full circle, or so it seems. A possible outcome is the end of German as a language because of the deeds that the language justified. German becomes Nazified; Nazism pollutes German. "Everything forgets," Steiner writes, "but not a language. When it has been injected with falsehood, only the most drastic truth can cleanse it." In an interesting transposition, Steiner wonders whether this history of complicity demands that this very language carry on the discussion of the Holocaust. It is precisely because the language carried the ideas of death that it may be able to carry the seeds of healing. That is one possibility; the other, horrible to contemplate, is that the language that carried death is incapable of making this transition. Hence, in the discussion of the Nazi period, German language and culture do so in a terminal way. Because of this terminal character, the oppressors' confession might then cease. Steiner cites Martin Luther's pamphlets of the early 1540s in their incitement to eliminate the Jews from Europe and cites Johann Fichte's "Address to the German Nation" as a call to German nationhood where hatred of Jews is given the sanction of a major philosophy. Steiner writes: "The literally unspeakable words that are used to plan, to prescribe, to record, to justify the Shoah; the words that entail and set down the burning alive of children in front of their parent's eyes; the slow drowning of old men and women in excrement; the eradication of millions in a verbose bureaucracy of murder—these are German words." At the same time, however, it is German that carried the warnings of Heinrich Heine, Friedrich Nietzsche, and Franz Kafka and, after the Holocaust, the poetry of Paul Celan. This raises the possibility that a rehumanization and a restoration to language of its capacities to speak to and about God may come within the "death-idiom" itself.[46]

There have been some who suggest that Hebrew as the language of the surviving Jewish nation is the logical extension of this transposition, that the breach implemented by the Nazis and carried by the German language can only be healed in the language of the victims and their survivors. Steiner probes the force of this position yet issues a caveat, as the relations between modern Hebrew and the realities of Auschwitz are complex: "How could the rebirth of Israel, how could the modulation of Hebrew into the future tense—one, precisely, lacking in the temporal present tense of Biblical Hebrew—incorporate the Shoah without risking self-destruction, without relinquishing the life-giving grammar of hope?" It is difficult to imagine the victims and survivors of Nazism carrying the burden of transition and transposition without sinking under its weight.[47]

Still, there is another difficulty which Steiner does not mention: the use of Hebrew in Israel to carry out its policies of occupation, expropriation, torture, and death. If, as Steiner notes, Israel as a nation-state has made the decision to "occupy, censor, even torture" and if, as Steiner records, the Holocaust has been used as a justification for some of the most extreme gestures of its domestic and foreign policies, then Hebrew as a language is burdened by the Nazi era *and* the Israeli state, by its status as victim *and* by its status as victor. If German has been infected by the deeds that it legitimated, is this not true for Hebrew as well? Of course, the problem is hardly limited to the Hebrew language in which occupation policies were ordered and carried out. It would seem to apply also to Jewish speech in America and Europe through which the Holocaust narrative was created and in which these Israeli policies were legitimated, or at least protected from criticism. In spoken words that encouraged these policies and in the silence encouraged by speech which averted its eyes—and helped avert the eyes of others—it would seem that Holocaust theologians are implicated as well.

It may be that the Jewish people have already lost their opportunity to heal the break with the human and God because of their life and policies after Auschwitz. Is it possible that the survivors of the barbarism in Europe appear, at least to the Palestinians, as purveyors of barbarism in Palestine? If it is true that barbarism prevailed in the very heart of Christian humanism, Renaissance culture, and classic rationalism—a barbarism that continues to haunt these traditions more than fifty years after the Holocaust—then it must be said that barbarism prevails at the very ground of Jewish humanism and religion. Steiner is right when he posits the seemingly implausible, that some who devised and administered Auschwitz read Shakespeare and Goethe (and, it must be added, the New Testament as well). Yet it also is true that later among those who occupied, displaced, and tortured— as well as those who covered over and denied these realities—are Jews learned in Jewish history and Jewish texts, that is, Jews within the concentric tradition of reading that defines the essence of Judaism. It could be, at another level, that this tradition not only fails to prevent the misuse of Jewish power after the Holocaust, but in its misuse shields Jews from this very realization, thereby impeding the ability to stop before it is too late.

If the force of the Jewish world acted as a shield against recognizing whom Jews had become as a people in the present—that is, not simply victims, but also perpetrators—then the Jewish contributions to, and confrontations with, the world need to be seen in a new constellation. If it is true that Jews in history presented to the world ideals that were rejected—monotheism, Jesus and Marx—then it is also true that Jews rejected these ideals as well. In this sense, Steiner is replicating, albeit unintentionally, the speech of those Jews who legitimate and carry out acts he finds reprehensible. That is, Jewish speech which emphasizes innocence, contribution, suffering—in essence a Jewish chosenness that is self-referential and self-validating—makes it difficult, if not impossible, to allow others to interact critically with Jewish self-perception and internal language. Could it be that along with the rightness and desirability of monotheism, Jesus, and Marx, the Jewish world also carries with it a tendency toward authoritarianism and militarism, a tendency sometimes recorded in Jewish sacred books and the books which have come after? This pretense of innocence might be the reason that Steiner, even in his critique of language and God, Nazism and state power—and with specific reference to Israel—is unable to make the very connections implicit in his own analysis. In short, for Steiner, the vehicle of Jewish life, haunted by the Nazi period and endangered by the Israeli state, retains an innocence and a redemptive quality. It is almost as if the inner life of Jews and Judaism is divorced historically, and can be divorced today, from the actuality of its life in the world. This is a divorce that is correctly denied to Germany and the German language.

There remains an opening, however, for Steiner's rescue of the German language and German history. This opening is possible because of the witnesses who warned of the Nazi peril. Though Steiner is silent on this aspect of the Jewish world, warnings have been present. Clearly he presents such a warning, and there have been others, before and after the Holocaust. In their own way, Hannah Arendt and Martin Buber presented warnings in this area, as does an entire literature of dissent that has been largely ignored or even repressed in the post-Holocaust period.

The examples are many, relating largely to the Jewish experience in Palestine and Israel. As early as November 1929, for example, Hans Kohn, a disciple of Buber's binationalism and utopian socialism, left the Zionist movement because of its treatment of Palestinian Arabs. In a letter to Berthold Feiwel, a mutual friend of his and Buber's and one of the directors of the Palestine Foundation Fund, Kohn wrote of his increasing awareness that the official policy of the Zionist Organization and the opinion of the vast majority of Zionists were becoming incompatible with his own convictions. In fact, Kohn's Zionism was less political than it was moral and spiritual, as he viewed Palestine as a place where Jewish pacifism and humanism might be realized. Widespread unrest, exemplified by the Arab-Jewish riots of 1929, prompted Kohn to rethink the disparity between his ideals and the enterprise he was part of: "We pretend to be innocent victims. . . . But we are obliged to look into the deeper cause of this revolt. We have been in Palestine for twelve years without having even once made a serious attempt at seeking through negotiations the consent of the indigenous people. . . . We have set ourselves goals which by their very nature had to lead to conflict with the Arabs. We ought to have recognized that these goals would be the cause, the just cause, of a national uprising against us."[48]

By the time of the Israeli invasion of Lebanon in 1982, Israeli poets were recalling the victims of the Holocaust and the Palestinians suffering in Lebanon in almost interchangeable ways. Efraim Sidon, an Israeli poet, uses the remembrance of the Holocaust explicitly to discard it as justification for the war in Lebanon. To do so he pronounces the guilt of Arab children in a mocking way:

> I accuse the children in Sidon and Tyre
> whose numbers are still uncounted
> Three-year-olds, seven-year-olds, and
> others of all ages, of the crime of living
> next door to terrorists.
> If you hadn't lived near them, children,
> You could have been students today.
> Now you will be punished.

Sidon concludes the poem in calculated irony by blaming everyone in Lebanon for the Holocaust and thus in need of punishment:

> I accuse the residents of Lebanon—all of them
> For the Nazis' mistreatment of us in the World War.
> Because from generation to generation,
> everyone must see himself
> As if he were destroying Hitler
> Always, always
> And that's what Begin is doing.
>
> I accuse you all!
> Naturally.
> Because I am always, always the victim.[49]

The poetry of Dahlia Ravikovitch similarly connects Jewish ideals and Jewish behavior. In her poem "One Cannot Kill a Baby Twice," Ravikovitch uses Holocaust imagery drawn from the Jewish poet Chaim Bialik to illumine the massacres at Sabra and Shatilla in 1982; once again it is the children who focus the loss of Jewish innocence:

> Upon sewage puddles in Sabra and Shatilla
> There you transferred masses of people
> Great masses
> From the world of the living to the world of the dead.
>
> Night after night.
> First they shot
> After that they hung
> Finally they slaughtered with knives.

> Terrified women appeared in haste
> Above a dusk hillock:
> "There they slaughter us,
> In Shatilla."
>
> A delicate tail of a new moon was hung
> Above the camps.
> Our soldiers illuminated the place with flares
> Like daylight.
> "Return to the camps, march!" the soldier commanded
> The screaming women from Sabra and Shatilla.
> He had orders to follow.
> And the children were already laid in filthy puddles
> Their mouths wide open
> Calm.
> Nobody will hurt them anymore.
> One cannot kill a baby twice. . .[50]

In the creation of victims, in carrying out, legitimating, and opposing policies that created victims, Jewish symbolism, metaphor, language, and history changed. The poets, and before them the pacifist and binationalist Zionists, all pointed in one direction: contemporary Jews come after the Holocaust *and* after Israel.

This loss of innocence is even more vividly illustrated in the Jewish response to the Palestinian uprising. It was in December 1987, that the uprising began and with it the policy of might and beatings promulgated by then-defense minister Yitzhak Rabin. At that time, Israel Shahak, an Israeli and a survivor of the Nazi concentration camps, began to publish translations of Hebrew press accounts of the Israeli response to the uprising. In his first collection, Shahak penned this foreword:

> It must be remembered that the reports of the atrocities committed by the Israeli Army which are translated in this collection are only a small part of those reported in the Hebrew press, which in turn are a negligible part of *the horrors which are daily perpetrated against the whole Palestinian population of the territories.* Item No. 2 illustrates that those horrors, in all their present details, had their beginning, *as a well developed method,* during the invasion of Lebanon in 1982. . . . It should be clear to everybody who reads this collection of testimonies, that the systematic use of the atrocities, which in their intensity and the special intention to humiliate are Nazi-like and *should* be compared to the analogous German Nazi methods, *is intentional and in fact constitutes the*

Israeli method for ruling the Palestinians. There cannot be any doubt in my opinion that those Nazi-like methods, in whose effectiveness the stupid Israeli Army top command reposes a blind faith, have been devised by 'experts'. . . and probably will *become worse,* if not stopped from outside and their use can lead to an actual genocide, whether by a "Transfer" or by an extermination. Indeed, this is one of my reasons for assembling this collection: To show that THE ACTUAL GENOCIDE OF THE PALESTINIANS IN THE TERRITORIES IS NOW POSSIBLE, SINCE THOSE ISRAELI SOLDIERS AND OFFICERS WHO HAVE COMMITTED THE OUTRAGES RECORDED HERE ARE CAPABLE OF ANYTHING AND EVERYTHING, AND LIKE THE COMMANDER IN ITEM NO. 1 WILL CONSIDER THAT THEY ARE ONLY CARRYING OUT THEIR ORDERS. [51]

Shahak's words are harsh, especially his reference to the possibility of genocide against the Palestinians. Yet his panic derives from his own experience. Did the world believe that the Germans were capable of pursuing a policy of genocide against the Jews? To be sure, the Nazi rhetoric was extreme and the riots against the Jews were awful, but did anyone think that this would lead to Auschwitz? The policy of transferring Palestinians had already been practiced in the 1948 and 1967 wars, one of the architects of both policies being Yitzhak Rabin. Important here is that the imagery of genocide is available and intimate to Shahak because he has suffered the reality himself. What seems like an exaggeration becomes a warning that Shahak has to shout as a way of being faithful to the Jewish experience of Holocaust.

As provocative is a poem of Jason Moore, which carries the title "Burning Children." Moore, a Jew living in America, takes as an epigraph to his poem the words of the Holocaust theologian, Irving Greenberg, that after the Holocaust "no statement, theological or otherwise, can be made which is not credible in the presence of the burning children." In Greenberg's understanding the burning children are Jewish victims of the Holocaust, but at the beginning of the poem Moore applies this to Palestinian children he visited in the hospitals after the uprising began:

> In Jerusalem, in Nazareth, in Jericho and in Hebron
> The soldiers guard the return against the enemy.
> Hospitals full of children
> Beaten, shot, paralyzed, brain dead
> Martyrs framed by tears and kefiyahs.
> On the pillows and on the blankets
> On the chairs and on the walls
> Palestinian flags everywhere.

The burning children are now Palestinian children wounded by the advancing Israeli army. A further confusion results as Moore is no longer certain whom to side with, the soldiers or the children. The Israeli soldiers in Jeeps remind him of the Nazi patrols outside the Warsaw ghetto; in the imagery the Palestinian towns become the Jewish ghettoes. Moore concludes:

> I see these images of children burning
> This time they are not our own
> Or are they
> Burning everywhere.[52]

Moore's poem completes the odyssey from the Holocaust to the present by asking if the history of the Jews and Palestinians is now a shared one, bonded by atrocity. Are the Palestinian children now to be seen in the same light as the Jewish children, that is, intimate to the future of Jewish history? At the same time, Moore confronts Rubenstein's analysis of escalating the cost of killing Jews and Wiesel's and Fackenheim's moral narrative about Israel. Moore accepts Greenberg's radical assertion of credibility and reverses it: statements about Israel are only credible in the face of those Palestinian children he has seen in the hospitals.

As Moore was writing his poem, Elie Wiesel and seventy-five other Nobel Prize winners gathered for a conference in France. Louis Marton, whose mother was killed at Bergen-Belsen, wrote bitterly of Wiesel and his refusal to speak directly and openly about Israeli brutality against the Palestinians. Marton, with others, was standing in the rain, a few yards from the Israeli embassy in Paris, shouting slogans against the oppression and in favor of a two-state solution. Across the street from them, other Jews were singing about the strength of Israel and the need to repress the Palestinians. Just one hundred yards down the street, the Nobel laureates were having tea with the President of the French Republic. Marton surmises that they were probably talking about weighty world issues but neglecting, so as not to embarrass Wiesel, the "bloodletting" in Gaza and Nablus. As far as Marton could see, the silence was significant: "From 9 December to the present, one Palestinian youth has on the average been killed *per day*. When the tally will reach 10 or 50 or 100 per day, perhaps even Wiesel will find himself compelled to speak up rather than beat around the bush. But then it will already be too late, honor will be lost. His honor and the honor of his father, killed at Auschwitz; my honor and the honor of my mother, killed at Bergen Belsen. All of it."[53]

The Inverted Shema

For contemporary Jews, who experience the dual sense of coming after, the situation is at the same time demanding and hopeful. The difficulty in articulating language about God, and the near impossibility of addressing God without accusation and bitterness, are intensified by Jewish behavior in Israel. Hebrew as a language has carried the burden of suffering; now it carries the burden of oppression. Jews addressing God carry the bitterness of the victim but are also chastened by a new community of accusers, Palestinians, who are also part of the discourse. The haunting images of Palestinian refugees shadow Jewish speech and activity. At the same time, recognition of this duality of victim and victor may make possible a more honest and humble discourse in the future.

The prospect of healing nonetheless recedes for now, as the burden is more complicated, heavier, more intimate. When Steiner writes that Jews are a traumatized, crazed people, his reference is to the Nazi period. Jewish oppression of the Palestinians, however, adds a further layer to the trauma and craziness, even to a foundational confusion. When Prime Minister Menachem Begin responded to a reporter's question about Israel's bombing of Beirut with his own question, "And if Hitler himself was hiding in a building with twenty innocent citizens, you still wouldn't bomb the building?"—thus equating Yassir Arafat with Adolph Hitler and Palestinians with Nazis—a level of Jewish discourse was degraded. The response by the Israeli novelist Amos Oz and Holocaust historian Yehuda Bauer was, "No, Mr. Prime Minister, your example is not an equivalent. . . . Beirut is not Berlin." Their response sought to address this confusion, though in a sense it was already too late. For the world that Steiner analyzed years earlier had already changed in fundamental ways; his analysis of the Jewish contribution/confrontation with the West and with humanity has lost its force. The policies of might and beatings in response to the Palestinian uprising only worsened the situation, as did Elie Wiesel's silence. Could the beautiful sentiments of Yitzhak Rabin, expressed at the signing of the Israeli-Palestinian accords, that Jews and Palestinians should get over the scars of the past and begin to build "a future without fear, without the eyes of frightened children, without pain," be trusted by a people who had experienced his policy of might and beatings and his promise just six years earlier to continue the "confrontations, the hitting, the arresting, the introduction of the plastic bullet and the curfews on a large scale"? The limited quality of these agreements also betrayed the beautiful rhetoric. For could Palestinians be healed of their trauma while they were denied full equality in the land they once called their own? Could the Hebrew language and Jewish speech in general convey a solidarity contradicted in history and the present by its policies and deeds?[54]

When Baruch Goldstein entered the Hebron mosque in 1994, the outcry was strong, but the language could no longer carry the burden. Even the Nazi references—in the poetry, in the article titles—seemed tired. The only possibility left was to invert Jewish speech about the Holocaust as Rami Heilbronn, a Jewish-Israeli, did to Primo Levi's famous poem "Shema," which was written after Levi's experience in Auschwitz. In a memorial service for the victims of the massacre at a West London synagogue, Heilbronn recited the inverted Shema as a confession:

> You who live secure
> In your warm houses,
> Who return at evening to find
> Hot food and friendly faces:
>
> Consider whether this is a man,
>
> Consider whether this is a woman,
>
> Now consider the dead
> In the Cave of the Patriarchs
> Consider that this has been:
> I commend these words to you.
> Engrave them on your hearts
> When you are in your house,
> When you walk on your way,
> When you go to bed
> When you rise
> Repeat them to your children.
>
> Or may your house crumble,
> Disease render you powerless
> Your offspring avert their faces from you.

For Heilbronn, the coming peace could never erase the Hebron slaughter, nor the other massacres that he recalled: Sabra and Shatilla in 1982, Kafr Kassem in 1956, or Deir Yassin in 1948. Just before reciting the poem, Heilbronn spoke these words: "Now we must all do much more than follow the impulse to flinch and look away from the horror and outrage, rush to explain or try to put together fragments of reason or meaning to it, or frantically attempt to exclude, expel, vomit that man and his machine gun. We must start by facing it, as painful and deep as it may lie, and for as long as it takes."[55]

There was no word from George Steiner, or perhaps in fact his word had already been fulfilled. "*We who come after* know that whatever the news is, it may be so," Steiner writes, "Whatever the massacre, the torture, the children being burned now in our name—it may be so." Then came the news of the assassination of Rabin, the man who spoke of peace, who shook the hand of the once demonized Yassir Arafat, who during the 1948 Israeli War of Independence had expelled thousands of Palestinians from Lydda and Ramle and who, forty years later, ordered the policies of might and beatings which shocked the world. Was Rabin, at the end of his life, trying to break the cycle he helped initiate? And did he die at the hands of a man who sought, above all else, to make sure that the cycle continued until the Palestinians were permanently expelled from the land? Perhaps we can say that Rabin was a victim of a process that he helped set in motion and that had taken on a life of its own.

The assassination was carried out by a devout Jew, Yigal Amir, who kept in his bedroom a book praising Baruch Goldstein. As with the massacre in Hebron, most commentators sought to distance themselves, the Jewish people, and Jewish religiosity from this act of murder. Amir, however, stood firm in his convictions. Through compromise, Rabin endangered the Jewish nation whose survival depended on the cleansing of Palestinians from the greater land of Israel. The Torah itself had provisions for such a traitor. The sentence was death.

A few days after the assassination, a banner flew atop the orthodox religious settlement, Maale Amos, as a sign of solidarity with the assassin. It read, "We are all Yigal Amir." In the midst of Palestinian land and just ten miles south of Jerusalem, the settlement is located at, and named for, the birthplace of the prophet Amos.[56]

2
Subverting the Religion of the Conqueror

Evangelization, Resistance, and the Judgment of God

From the image of Marc Bloch, an agnostic, going to his death comforting a child, to the image of Baruch Goldstein, a religious Jew with a rapid-fire assault weapon murdering men prostrate at worship, is a great leap and difficult to articulate in language. Yet, unlike Bloch, Baruch Goldstein was sure of God's presence and the mission that God had laid before him. Thousands of Jews attended his funeral with the same certainty. Rabin's assassin honored Goldstein.

Two weeks after the massacre, Daniel Bar-On, an Israeli psychologist who has worked over the last decade for a healing of Jewish and Palestinian pain, was unable to attend a Holocaust conference in Berlin that he had helped plan. Living in Beer-Sheva, only twenty-five miles from Hebron, Bar-On was afraid of leaving his family at this time of crisis. But there was another reason as well. Since the massacre his heart was broken and he felt no desire to be with others. "A person who claimed to be a religious Jew, went and killed, in cold blood, twenty-nine Moslems and injured scores of others during their holy Ramadan prayer—can that be true?" Bar-On wrote incredulously, "He committed that mass-murder in the holy place, in which according to our tradition, Abraham had buried Sarah. Abraham, who is the father of the Arabs and the Jews." For Bar-On, it was a small minority of religious Jews expressing hate and the desire to expel the Palestinians from their land. "They believe they serve God," Baron continued, "but in their heart there is only Satan."[1]

Jewish Power, Christian Power

For Goldstein, the "cleansing" of Palestinians from Abraham's burial site and the cleansing of Palestinians from Hebron, Jerusalem, and the entire West Bank, was part of God's plan, a *mitzvah*, a commandment. Did Goldstein see the cleansing of Palestinians from the greater Land of Israel as the 615th commandment, the logical continuation of the 614th commandment, that of Jewish survival after the Holocaust, posited by Emil Fackenheim on Purim in 1967? Was this a logical extension, at least in Goldstein's mind, of Richard Rubenstein's idea that the significance of Israel lies in the fact that the state has radically escalated the cost of killing Jews? Goldstein saw his action as a preemptive strike against those who might after worship, or somewhere in the future, or their children's future, threaten Jewish lives. The massacre of Muslim worshipers recalls the image of the "Shrine of the Scrolls" in Jerusalem being protected by advanced technology in the case of warfare, and the thought that "words cannot be broken by artillery, nor thought live in bomb shelters." Perhaps Goldstein knew in a perverse and intimate way that words can be broken and reshaped in artillery and thought, that religious thought and practice can live in bomb shelters and thrive in the cleansing and conquering of others.

At the same conference that Bar-On could not attend, and in the city where just decades earlier the orders were issued to cleanse Europe of Jews, this is the conclusion Richard Rubenstein reached in his keynote address. Analyzing the relationship between the Holocaust, holy war, and ethnic cleansing in Europe during the Nazi period and in the Balkans during the post-cold war period, Rubenstein reflected on the massacre: "What Goldstein attempted to bring about, and what we are witnessing in the Balkans today, are modern versions of a holy war whose objective is the elimination of all those who do not share the dominant majority's symbolic universe." By analyzing the Nazi aggression and the war in the Balkans as examples of Christian holy war, that is, the desire to cleanse the Jews from Europe then, and through ethnic cleansing to make sure that no Islamic state would arise in Europe now, Rubenstein articulated a sensibility vis-à-vis European Christianity that lay in the background of Jewish thought and theology after Auschwitz. For after all, the need to escalate the cost of taking Jewish lives after the Holocaust is related to Europe and European Christianity. The reason for a Jewish state is unrelated to the Palestinians; Israel represents the need to escape from Europe and the symbolic universe of Christianity. One wonders if Goldstein was clearing in Palestine space for Jewish life and its symbolic universe, historically denied Jews in Europe. Perhaps Goldstein was acting out a power that could have ensured Jewish survival during the Nazi period yet was impossible even to imagine then. It is sadly ironic, even tragic, that the power necessary to make the Nazis think twice about persecuting Jews is now in place, too late, at the expense of another people and in the wrong geographical location. Still for many Jews the poison of anti-Jewishness was simply empowered to another level by the Nazis, a continuation, as it were, or perhaps even an unfolding of Christian doctrine and belief.[2]

This was Rubenstein's position when he announced that his thought had come full circle over three decades: from emphasizing the strongly anti-Christian elements in National Socialist ideology, to seeing the Holocaust—especially after his visit to Serbia and Croatia in 1993—as a modern version of the holy war whose objective was to eliminate the Jews as a political, cultural, and demographic presence within Christendom. For Rubenstein, this sensibility is in character with the Christian character of Europe, as Europe was organized and blessed by Latin Christianity. Full fellowship in European society has traditionally been accorded to those who share the common faith or, more importantly, the symbolic universe and discourse of Christendom. As the heartland of Christianity, European Christian traditions form the basis for naming its seasons and celebrating or commemorating its important events. Divorced from its Christian roots, European civilization—its art, literature, music, philosophy, religion, and politics—is hardly understandable. For Rubenstein, European secularism is simply the unintended consequence of Europe's Christian culture. To be European means to be Christian. Within this context Jews, no matter their talent or wealth, whether Einstein or the Rothschilds, are at best regarded as outsiders, at worst as enemies. Even Jewish contributions to European culture have often been seen as threats to Christian identity. To meet that threat, Europeans have resorted to whatever methods were necessary, including holy wars, expulsions, inquisitions, and even mass extermination.[3]

Rubenstein notes differences between the Crusades of the eleventh century and the Nazis of the twentieth century, while citing a common European Christian perspective. Both sought an end to the Jew as the disconfirming other, thereby reducing the dissonance that comes from a group which gave birth to the central identity of Christianity and, at the same time, embodies the rejection of that identity. To reinforce the identity of Christianity, it was necessary to reduce or even eliminate the presence of that other which, whatever its own behavior, could only be seen as subversive. By the Nazi period, the subversive Jew was racialized and assimilated, thus adding the dynamic of visibility and invisibility. The desire for their elimination accelerated. That the Holocaust was a modern version of a Christian holy war carried out by a National-Socialist state responds to the question of which groups and institutions regarded the elimination of the Jews as a long-term benefit. Rubenstein answers simply by citing the groups and institutions for whom the integrity of the Christian symbolic universe was essential. These entities could perpetrate or acquiesce in the destruction of the Jews. Rubenstein points out that in 1939 the overwhelming majority of European Christian leaders were convinced that the greatest threats to the integrity of Christendom came from Bolshevism and from unconverted Jews—Jews who were religious, socialist, Zionist, secular, or assimilationist. At the same time, Bolshevism was largely thought of as Jewish in origin and spirit. Because Pope Pius XII regarded Germany as the bulwark against the communization of Europe, his interest in the Jewish question and Jews was bound up with the fight against communism. According to Rubenstein, the pope's great fear of Bolshevism accounts for his disappointment that the United States and Great Britain were unwilling to join with Nazi Germany in defense of Christian Europe. This disappointment was registered long after the Vatican knew of the plans for the final solution.[4]

Yet it is important to note that Rubenstein is not singling out Roman Catholicism for blame, for the Protestant Reformation was a religious and sociopolitical vanguard for the annihilation of Jews in Europe as well. The waging of holy war against Jews was always a temptation within Christianity, though it was limited historically for theological reasons. On the one hand, the impoverishment and ghettoization of Jews was seen as a sign of God's punishment for the Jewish rejection of Christ. On the other hand, Jewish conversion to Christianity could be seen as a sign of the imminent messianic return of Christ. Jews were both despised and valued, the disconfirming other who was also a confirmation. The Protestant Reformation unleashed a series of millenarian movements that, in destabilizing the dominant Catholic symbolic universe, also sought a restabilization of that universe, often to the detriment of the Jews.

The process of rationalization and utilitarian valuation that the Reformation fomented is also pertinent. For Rubenstein, it is no coincidence that the land of the Reformation bore the seeds of the death camps, as it was there that bureaucracy achieved its most completely objective form. The logical outcome of this development in its most thoroughly secularized, rationalized, and dehumanized creation is the death camp. Before human beings could acquire the dehumanized attitude of bureaucracy—in which the personal elements of life, including the irrational and emotional, are eliminated—a disenchantment had to become culturally and religiously predominant. Only when God and the world has become radically disjoined, does it become possible to treat both the political and the natural order with an uncompromisingly dispassionate objectivity. This separation of God and the world was a central feature of Martin Luther's two-kingdom approach and thus to the Protestant ethos. Rubenstein's view of the annihilation of the European Jews comes into focus with the understanding that the death camps were a culmination of foundational religious and political values in the West. Even the anti-Christian aspect of the Nazis was part of a European and Christian cycle. When the Nazi rebels against Christianity denounced the Jews, the church could only stand by, allowing a deed buried deep in the Christian psyche. The Jewish community in Europe was doomed.[5]

The victory of Christianity that Rubenstein depicts so chillingly also carries a cost that Rubenstein fails to note. In disciplining, defeating, expelling, and massacring Jews to protect its own universe from subversion, Christianity disconfirmed its own underlying plausibility. What Steiner writes of language, can easily be said of Christianity: "Languages have great reserves of life. They can absorb masses of hysteria, illiteracy and cheapness. But there comes a breaking point. Use a language to conceive, organize and justify Belsen; use it to make out specifications for gas ovens; use it to dehumanize man during twelve years of calculated bestiality. Something will happen to it." As a consequence of such barbarism, language—indeed Christianity—will languish; a cancer sets in and the two principal contributions of language and religion, conveying a humane order (law) and the human spirit (grace), atrophy. Such is Steiner's meaning when he writes that Auschwitz is central to the "terminal belief" of Christianity. Yet one is shocked by the longevity of this terminal belief when in April 1993, Metropolitan Nikolaj, the highest ranking church official in Bosnia, stood between General Ratko Mladic and Bosnian Serb President Radovan Karadzic—architects of ethnic cleansing—and spoke of the Bosnian Serbs' struggle as following the "hard road of Christ."[6]

Rescuing Christianity

At the outset, then, Rubenstein and Steiner posit two seemingly contradictory post-Holocaust Jewish views of Christianity: that Christianity is relentless in its calculation and in its defense of European hegemony; and that Christianity effectively died in Auschwitz. Seen from the institutional perspective, Christianity continues as if the Holocaust did not occur. The imperative of the church's self-perception as the carrier of the message of redemption, and the logical unfolding of its corporate and bureaucratic structure propel it forward, regardless of the lapses in its ethical witness. From the ethical perspective the view is quite different, for the possibility of the church proclaiming its message as the good news of salvation is compromised, if not eviscerated. Do burned and scattered bodies speak of a deserved punishment or proclaim a messianic age to come? Rubenstein analyzes the church's silence in the matter of the elimination of the Jews from Europe in a calm and detached manner, as predictable, understandable, and inevitable. In fact, he shifts the question by asking why Jewish leadership did not recognize and act to escape this logical unfolding. For Rubenstein, the state of Israel is the Jewish counterpart to the European church; its possession of nuclear weapons and its willingness to use them in protection of its sovereignty are also predictable, understandable and, in certain circumstances, inevitable. Steiner's understanding of the Jewish state is somewhat like his understanding of European Christianity: as an institutional framework that, in its foundations, lies and abuses and makes more difficult, if not impossible, discourse about humanity and God.

Yet beneath and around this analysis of Christian relentlessness and defeat is another series of relationships between Jews and Christians. Rubenstein illustrates this in his fondness for his teacher, Paul Tillich, the great Protestant theologian, who helped Rubenstein sort out his difficult path as a Jewish theologian after the Holocaust, and for the apostle Paul, whose break with normative Judaism in the first century served as a model for Rubenstein's own break with normative Judaism in the twentieth century. To be sure, Rubenstein admires Paul's courage rather than his ultimate vision of the risen Christ, and it is psychoanalysis rather than Christian faith that is Rubenstein's initiation into new life. Still, in Rubenstein's discussion of Paul Tillich and Paul of Tsaurus, there is an undeniable attraction to the certainties of Christian faith,which both Pauls had achieved. Perhaps at a subconscious level, Rubenstein's attraction to elements of Christian theology and faith after Auschwitz may be strategic. After all, Rubenstein and most other Jewish theologians live in Europe and in America, which is properly seen as an extension of Christian Europe. Perhaps this represents an attempt to ally oneself with a relentless enemy which might in a new era become a relentless protector and friend. [7]

Rubenstein is more direct about his contact with Christianity than is Steiner, though the Christian elements in Steiner's thought are pronounced. It seems paradoxical, for example, that even after the Holocaust, Steiner proposes that the greatest contribution of the Jewish faith and sensibility to the world is Jesus the Jew. What Steiner claims is incredible; that Judaic sensibility is the highest form of morality and ethics and that the messenger of that sensibility, Jesus the Jew, has been stolen and perverted by Christianity, used against his own people, and in that violation and violence has brought to an end Christianity's flawed enterprise. Does this perhaps represent, again subconsciously, an attempt to convince Christians that they can become authentic human beings and perhaps Christianity can be revived, if only they and their religion become Jewish? The proposal is double-edged: Christians must remain who they are with the new understanding that the carriers of the message of Jesus are the Jews themselves. To harm the Jews is to deny Jesus and thus distance Christians from the one they claim to be savior. Access to Jesus is through the Jews. In this view, Christians cannot claim a self-sufficiency in terms of salvation; they cannot become Jews but must be Jewish oriented. Without the Jews they are lost.

The ambivalence is clear and one wonders how, after this history, it could be otherwise. To begin with, the narrative of the Holocaust is listened to in the Christian West which produced the death camps. Jewish theologians and commentators on the Holocaust often receive a more generous hearing among Christians than among Jews, a hearing that produced an identifiable revolution in Christian language and theology in the 1950s and early 1960s. During that time, Jewish theologians like Abraham Joshua Heschel and Will Herberg proposed an alliance between Judaism and Christianity, intimating that Judaism and Christianity are indispensable to one another because they hold two messages in a dynamic tension, the need to redeem an unredeemed world and the possibility that redemption has already occurred. The need was mutual. From the Christian side, Reinhold Niebuhr announced a similar dependency of Christianity on Judaism, as the Hebraic foundation of Christianity—the material and the prophetic—was necessary to keep Christianity from pretending to an otherworldliness which allowed ethical improprieties, perhaps even the Holocaust.[8]

An ecumenical dialogue is born through mutual need. From the Jewish side the relentless aspect of Christianity and its terminal belief are held at the same time that a new and fruitful dialogue is initiated and pursued. From the Christian side, the disconfirming other, the Jew, is in need of embrace, thereby becoming fuel for Christian renewal. In Buber's terminology a "genuine conversation" is at hand, but it is also a strategic deal, as Jews are to be comforted and protected by a Christianity in search of renewal. In fact, Jews and Christians do comfort and protect each other in a post-Holocaust and increasingly secular world. Jewish identity is respected, a major aspect of that identity articulated as the survival and flourishing of the state of Israel. In this exchange, Christianity becomes more Judaic, and Jews are admitted, totally and with honor, into the Christian West.

In a sad and ironic way, the Holocaust becomes the honored entry point of Jews into Western Christian civilization. A reversal takes place in Christian history which is profound and problematic. The German Catholic theologian Johann Baptist Metz articulates this reversal in his writing on the relationship of Christians and Jews after Auschwitz. Metz begins with a question to his fellow Christians: "Will we actually allow Auschwitz to be the end point, the disruption which it really was, the catastrophe of our history, out of which we can find a way only through a radical change of direction achieved via new standards of action? Or will we see it only as a monstrous accident within this history but not affecting history's course?" Metz answers his own question by asserting that the future of Christianity is dependent on an affirmative answer to the need for a radical change of direction. This cannot be accomplished, however, through abstract reflection on dogma or even on the complicity of the church; it cannot be accomplished by personal Christian reflection or even institutional action alone. The change can occur only by embracing the suffering and the heirs to that suffering.[9]

According to Metz, Christians are from now on assigned to the victims of Auschwitz in an alliance belonging to the "very heart of saving history." Metz considers insulting and incomplete any attempts at Christian theology and language about meaning when they are initiated outside the Holocaust or try in some way to transcend it. Meaning, especially divine meaning, can be invoked only to the extent that such meaning was not abandoned in Auschwitz itself. This is why Metz responds to the question whether it is possible for a Christian to pray after Auschwitz in the affirmative: "We can pray after Auschwitz because people prayed *in* Auschwitz."[10]

Metz's work has depth because he stands accused and humbled by the experience of the Holocaust and the acknowledged Christian complicity in the Holocaust. He remains in the experience of Holocaust and refrains from moving beyond the suggestion of a mutual future. Jürgen Moltmann also sees the Holocaust as a question central to Christian theology and practice. Like Metz, Moltmann's theological reflections arise out of the recent history of the German people and from a generation that came of age during the Holocaust. For young Germans like himself who began the study of theology after the war, Auschwitz becomes a turning point: "We became painfully aware that we must live, inescapably, in the shadow of the Holocaust, which had been committed against the Jewish people in the name of our people. 'After Auschwitz' became our concrete context for theology. With the name of the place of the crime we not only marked a political or moral crisis of our people, but also a theological and church crisis." What was incomprehensible about Auschwitz for Moltmann and his generation went far beyond the technique of mass death or even the experience of the hiddenness of God. For them, it was the silence of the men and women who had looked on or looked away, or closed their eyes to the abandoned, to the victims, and ultimately to mass murder. Rather than the question of suffering and God, Auschwitz presents German Christians the challenge of living with a tremendous burden of guilt, shame, and sorrow. Regarding the Jews and Judaism, Moltmann is near to Metz when he writes that Jews and Christians are moving on the same path, but with different tasks. Their union will be brought about in messianic time, as Christianity can gain salvation only together with Israel: "For the sake of the Jew Jesus there is no ultimate separation between the Church and Israel. For the sake of the gospel there is provisionally, before the eschatological future, also no fusion. But there is the communal way of hoping ones."[11]

Here Metz and Moltmann encounter *the* Christian predicament after the Holocaust. If it is impossible to chart a Christian future that leaves behind the death camps, it is difficult, if not impossible, to envision a positive expression of Christianity with the death camps it helped to construct at its center. Instead, what occurs is an attempt by Christian theologians, including Metz and Moltmann, to use the Holocaust as a way of bypassing the "terminal" condition of Christian belief. If the Holocaust symbolizes the demonization of the Jews and in this way represents the alienation of Christianity from its source, by recovering the beauty of the Judaic faith and by realizing that Israel is chosen and that the gentiles are grafted onto that chosenness, the history of Christianity can be confessed *and* jettisoned. By looking to the Jews as the authentic people and themselves as a secondary, grafted upon people, the history of triumphalism comes to be seen as alien, a detour which is now realized as such. The task of the Jews remains, especially because Christians now understand their task. In light of the Holocaust, it is almost incongruous that it is by relationship with the Jews, past and present, that salvation for the non-Jew is approached. Though it is an understanding reached through critical appraisal and soul-searching, it also functions to relieve Christians of a history that is difficult to identify with in a positive manner.

This is a major theme of Paul van Buren's work on Christian theology and its relation to the Jewish people. For van Buren, the church's Bible begins with Israel's Torah. The failure to understand that connection has had disastrous consequences for the Jewish people, as it resulted in centuries of persecution, and for the church, because it blinded Christianity to the witness of God's people. This in turn led to a further misunderstanding of Torah, exemplified in the false theological division between law and gospel. It is by listening to Israel's Torah that the church assumes its proper vocation and witness to the gentiles, as confirming Israel's chosenness and Israel's God. In van Buren's view, the church cannot replace the Jewish witness with its own; rather it adds its witness to that of Israel's as a way confirming Israel's witness. There is only one covenant or promise, which is with the Jewish people. Those who draw near to the Jews find in that promise a confirmation of their own possibility of drawing near to God.[12]

Other Christian theologians voice similar views. Clark Williamson understands the God of Jesus Christ to be the God of Abraham, Sarah, Jacob, Moses, and David. Because the God of Christians and Jews is the same God, the people Israel are connected with the Christian faith in God. This connection with the people Israel becomes part of the church's proclamation of its faith in God. That the salvation of Christianity comes through the Jews is a proposition made most vividly by A. Roy Eckardt. For Eckardt, the question to the Christian community is whether God will deliver the Christian church from its estrangement from God—a condition intimately related to its treatment of Jews over the centuries—and deliver it from its continuing propensity to devalue Jewish culture and survival: "Is there somewhere a special historical event that judges and redeems the victimizing Resurrection? Is there somewhere an event of God that in the very moment Christians are assailed by the moral trauma of necessarily rejecting the Resurrection in its victimizing aspects, will nevertheless bring assurance, an event that will say 'I accept you'?" In Eckardt's view that event may be the state of Israel seen as a sign from the God of Israel.[13]

The people Israel and the state of Israel as rescue for the Christian community, emphasized and nurtured in different ways by these theologians, is a decidedly mixed blessing for Jews. The disconfirming other becomes *the* confirming other upon which all the anxieties and hopes of Christians are placed. God's continuing covenant with the Jews, a covenant that now includes the state of Israel, is proof of the continuing life of the church—that is, the wanderings of the Jews, even their sins, did not sever God's covenant with the people. Hence Christians are guaranteed this same fidelity, in a sense saving them from the anxiety their own history of destruction and death elicits. Salvation is of Christ and of the Jews. That the Jews may fall short again has extreme consequences for Christian belief, consequences one can hear in tone, at least, in the writings of Paul van Buren. For van Buren, the danger is found in the peculiar secularization process among Jews which finds a centering of loyalty on peoplehood rather than on attachment to the Torah. Since a Christian theology of the Jewish people can only understand the peoplehood of the Jews as a divine calling, an ethnic identification cannot be decisive; a Jewish ethnicity as such is of no more interest than any other: "Presumed racial characteristics are hardly the stuff on which a theology of the God of Abraham and Sinai can build solidly. A Gentile church that is absolutely dependent, ontologically and teleologically, on the continuing existence of God's Israel, can hardly demand but must certainly trust that the Jewish people will continue to produce out of themselves that remnant by which it has maintained itself in its covenant with God."[14]

With these theologians the instability of Christian life, historically related to the Jews as the disconfirming other, is reintroduced in the present as confirming other. Christianity's symbolic universe is devastated by the Holocaust *and* is renewed by the victims of the Holocaust. Unfortunately, this view of the Jews is to romanticize the once demonized; the victims of the Holocaust are innocent and empowered Jews are also innocent. The possibility that Jews are normal, with the flaws and strengths of the human, is rarely mentioned or, if mentioned, is subsumed within the transcendental category of chosenness. What happens when the flawed quality of the Jews is too obvious to bury in theological categories? Should this other side reappear, or be thought to reappear, the consequences to Jews and Christians are almost too grave to contemplate. Have not the Jews always and everywhere disappointed Christians? The romanticization of the once-demonized reflects a continued ambivalence of Christians about Jews that is, at heart, an ambivalence about who Christians are as believers and as a community. For what if the flaw of Christians is not simply the drama of their sins, but the fact that even with their beliefs they are simply normal in their failings and successes? Does this mean that even the Jews might not save them from themselves? Does this suggest that even Jesus Christ has failed to deliver Christians from themselves? Can Jews succeed where Christ has failed?

George Steiner worries about post-Holocaust Christian theologies that emphasize patience and self-questioning. If Christianity itself is fragmentary and culpable, then the Jew is emphasized because the "potentiality of the truly ecumenical contains within itself the only access to genuine realization of God's promise in and through Christ." For Steiner, this metaphoric construct and symbol dramatization is enormous in its implication or, if you will, charged with enormity. This very enormity and the instability of this construct and dramatization—the ultimate inability of the victim to rescue the victimizer and the victimizer's universe—might paradoxically reconfirm Richard Rubenstein's vision of the state of Israel as a place of safety from the relentless nature of Christianity militant in its empowerment *and* in its renewal. Surely post-Holocaust Christians have retained what Rubenstein thought crucial to their faith and their crusade against the Jews: the mythical, magical, and theological categories which for Christians define the Jews and from which Jews may suffer in the future.[15]

It is interesting that the renewal of mainstream Christianity after the Holocaust links with a once-victimized and now increasingly affluent Jewish community. In fact it is within the context of Jewish ascendancy—in the universities, business, politics, and the media—that the discussion of Jewish suffering becomes public and Holocaust theology becomes normative for the Jewish community and, to some extent, for the Christian West as well. The awarding of the Nobel Prize for Peace to Elie Wiesel is just one example of the public recognition afforded the story of Jewish suffering; the United States Holocaust Memorial Museum, located on the mall in the nation's capital, is another. In sum, a chastened, dominant Christianity joins a once-suffering and now ascendant Jewish community to discuss the future of Judeo-Christian civilization.

Confronting the Ecumenical Deal

From the Palestinian perspective, Christian celebration of Jewish renewal is part of the Palestinian catastrophe, as it became a cornerstone of European and American support for the Israeli occupation of East Jerusalem, the West Bank, and Gaza. Edward Said, a foremost Palestinian intellectual, cites the contradiction of Israeli Prime Minister Menachem Begin receiving an honorary doctorate of law at Northwestern University in May 1978, just a month after the invading Israeli army created 300,000 new refugees in southern Lebanon and despite continuing Israeli occupation of Palestinian land in violation of international law. On the theological level, Palestinian Christians were thrown into an almost irresolvable crisis by the development of Christian Holocaust theology in the West. At a Jerusalem conference on Palestinian liberation theology, held at the height of the Palestinian uprising, Naim Ateek, a Palestinian Anglican priest, spoke of the Bible being used by Jews and Western Christians to "silence us, to make us invisible, to turn us into the negated antithesis of God's 'chosen people.'" For Ateek, as for many Palestinian Christians, the use of the Bible and theology against them forces a dilemma: "Israel was using power in a terrible way to oppress us, and these Jewish and Christian people were celebrating this kind of Israeli power as something redemptive and from God."[16]

Ateek points out that in contemporary Christian theology Palestinians hardly exist. Like the Jewish experience in the Holocaust, Palestinian suffering raises the question of God: "Where is God in all of this?

Why does God allow the confiscation of our land? Why does God allow the occupation and oppression of our people?" This leads Munir Fasheh, a Palestinian educator at Bir Zeit University, to declare that Palestinian Christians are not a part of the Christianity that helped "plunder five continents, enslave people in many regions, and wipe out people and civilizations in North America and Australia, and is now threatening the Palestinians with a similar fate. As Palestinian Christians we have to declare with a loud voice that it has been Christianity, which accompanied capitalism, more than Zionism, that is at the root of many problems in the world today." Historically the Christianity Fasheh condemns was also anti-Jewish, and it is ironic to him that as the sin of anti-Jewishness is identified and fought against, the invisibility of and the force against the Palestinians increases. In a Palestinian setting, Fasheh's singling out Christianity over Zionism for critical focus is bold indeed. For Fasheh the problem is Western Christianity, a fatally flawed enterprise from which he seeks to disassociate himself.[17]

Years earlier, the African American novelist and essayist James Baldwin wrote of another transposition in Jewish history that comes with the embrace of dominant Christians in the West. If the embrace has theological ramifications, it carries political and economic consequences as well, especially in the Middle East and America. It begins with a common classification as white, a classification denied Jews in pre-Holocaust Europe. Many Jews accept this "white" classification to advance in American society but object to its use on moral grounds. Nonetheless, the difficulties some African Americans have with Jews is less related to their Jewishness than to their whiteness and the privileges they enjoy as whites in America. For Baldwin, Jews not only enjoy the theological and moral support of white Christians; in effect Jews have become Christians in the West, assimilating to a power that makes invisible those on the other side of that power. It is important to follow Baldwin's analysis as it points out another dilemma of Jewish and Christian existence after the Holocaust as seen by Christians who are now oppressed by the Jewish-Christian renewal of the empowered and the affluent. The Palestinian situation outside the West is now complemented in Baldwin's analysis by African American people within the West. Both are victims of dominant Western Christianity now joined by the heirs of the Holocaust.

Baldwin's major essay on this theme was published just two weeks after the symposium on Jewish values in the post-Holocaust future. His analysis carried an incredible irony in that, just as Emil Fackenheim posited the 614th commandment as essential to the survival of the Jewish people, a Black American thinker was asserting that, in the eyes of African Americans, Jews and white Christians had become indistinguishable. In the 1960s, African Americans encountered Jews in the ghettos, as slum landlords, grocers, merchants, in effect empowered brokers of the American and Christian society that oppressed Blacks. The anti-Semitism of people in the ghetto therefore has to do with the whiteness of Jews who benefit from an exploitative system. For African Americans, the discussion of Jewish suffering serves to mask this complicity. Baldwin notes the irony of Jewish success in America; the condemnation of Jews by some Blacks is for the Jew "having become an American white man—for having become, in effect, a Christian." Jews profit from an elevated status in America and for this reason must expect a level of distrust among Blacks. "The Jew does not realize that the credential he offers, the fact that he has been despised and slaughtered, does not increase the Negro's understanding," Baldwin writes. "It increases the Negro's rage. For it is not here, and not now, that the Jew is being slaughtered, and he is never despised, here, as the Negro is, because he is an American. The Jewish travail occurred across the sea and America rescued him from the house of bondage. But America is the house of bondage for the Negro, and no country can rescue him. What happens to the Negro here happens to him because he is an American." Jews are singled out by African Americans not because they are different from other whites, but because they act essentially the same. The history of Christendom victimized both Blacks and Jews; in Harlem, Jews continue in the historic role assigned them by Christian civilization, that is, to do their dirty work.[18]

The agony is compounded by the fact that one victim, the Jews, has survived and ascended while the other, African Americans, remains in virtual slavery. Baldwin writes that Jewish suffering is recognized as part of the moral history of the world, and Jews are recognized as contributors to world history. If Jewish history is known and honored, Black history has been "blasted, maligned, and despised." The Jew is seen as white, and when whites rise up against oppression, they are celebrated as heroes. When Blacks rise up, they are seen as reverting to their "native savagery." Baldwin uses irony to justify his assertion that the Warsaw Ghetto uprising was not described as a riot, and its participants are celebrated rather than being maligned as hoodlums. The uprisings in Watts and Harlem are for Baldwin an almost analogous situation to the Jewish situation during the early Nazi period. The negative characterization of Black uprisings reminds young African Americans of their situation; it also reminds them of the fact of Jewish empowerment even as Jews claim to be victims. In any case, Baldwin finds this does not help in building a positive view toward Jews in the Black community. At the same time, it helps little when Jews maintain that because of their suffering in Europe it is impossible for Jews to be exploitive or bigoted in America. For Baldwin, it is "galling to be told by a Jew whom you know to be exploiting you that he cannot possibly be doing what you know he is doing because he is a Jew."[19]

Still, Baldwin's anger is directed mainly at the Christian world. Baldwin again states his case quite boldly: "We won our Christianity, our faith, at the point of a gun, not because of the example afforded by white Christians, but in spite of it. It was very difficult to become a Christian if you were a Black man on a slave ship, and the slave ship was called 'The Good Ship Jesus.' These crimes, for one must call them crimes, against the human being have brought the Church and the entire Western world to the dangerous place we find ourselves in today." Because of this witness, it is necessary for Baldwin and other African Americans to be attentive to what Christianity does rather than what it says about itself. What it did historically and what it does today may make desirable, even necessary, the "destruction of the Christian Church as it is presently constituted." Baldwin agrees with Malcolm X, the Black Muslim leader, when he stated in Harlem: "If you want to know what the white Christian man is, examine his deeds. Forget his words. He's got a whole lot of pretty sounding words. Watch his deeds. His deeds are like the deeds of a snake, the deeds of a beast." Malcolm X wrote that Christianity is the white man's religion and that the Bible has been the ideological weapon for enslaving millions of nonwhites around the world. "Every country the white man has conquered with his guns, he has always paved the way, and salved his conscience, by carrying the Bible and interpreting it to call people 'heathens' and 'pagans,'" Malcolm wrote. "Then he sends his guns, then his missionaries behind the guns to mop up."[20]

This analysis brings the critique of Christianity full circle. While German theologians take on the victims of the Holocaust as intimate to the future of Christian life, and while American Protestant theologians place Christianity as grafted on to the Jewish people and the state of Israel, Palestinian and African American theologians and intellectuals critique the rapprochement of Judaism and Christianity. This latter group understands this ecumenism as a regrouping of a dominant

Western Christianity that oppresses Palestinians and African Americans, as well as other peoples around the world. As Palestinians and African Americans lay the responsibility for the death camps at the feet of European Christianity, they exponentially increase the accusation against it: that the history of Christianity is one of violence and expansion and the attempt to annihilate the Jews is only one example of this history. In this perspective, Jews are placed in continuity with other suffering peoples who have been and are today victims of Christianity. We might say that these victims are products of 1492, when Europe and European Christianity rose from chaos and poverty to conquer and enslave large areas of the Americas and Africa by the sword and the cross. When Malcolm X addressed the African American crowds in Harlem, he was addressing victims of 1492, a process that continues in the present. Metz's challenge of the victors carrying the victims with them into the future assumes an unimaginable burden, adding the victims of 1492 to the victims of the Holocaust.

For Jews their grouping with dominant Christians represents a dilemma. On the one hand, Jews, like any people, desire survival, and, as much as any people, Jews know what it is like to exist on the other side of Christian power. On the other hand, it is strange for Jews to be grouped with dominant Christians over against struggling minorities. The fate of struggling minorities *is* the fate of the Jews, at least in Jewish consciousness. The angry response to Palestinians and African Americans can be seen in this light; they point to a reversal of position of such magnitude in such a short time that it is almost impossible for Jews to absorb, much less articulate. Jews are no longer an unempowered minority but rather an empowered one, which in America means identification with whiteness. What Baldwin states boldly is that Jews want it both ways; to be empowered and to be identified as a particular oppressed minority, at least when narratives of suffering are aired publicly. This allows Jews affluence and an ethical status, in short, access to power and recourse to innocence. Perhaps one of the tasks of Holocaust theology is to articulate innocence and empowerment in a framework that overpowers those who experience Jews differently. For Holocaust theologians, Jews are not white and Israel is not a colonial power, from any viewpoint, Jewish or otherwise. To their mind it is simply impossible. This insistence betrays an anxiety toward Palestinians and African Americans, not unlike Christian anxiety when faced with the critical appraisal of Jews.

The Christianity of the Conquered

The victims of 1492, of course, are not simply victims. Victimized historically by imperialism and colonialism and today in a more sophisticated international monetary and trade system, they remain, at the same time, subjects of their own history. Perhaps it is more accurate to say that they are struggling to master their own history by recreating and renewing their own narrative. Yet for most of the peoples of 1492, in Africa, Asia, Latin America, and North America, European and American power continues its assault. To be sure, the continuation of this assault has been called by different names and assumed different forms over time: imperialism, neocolonialism, the North-South conflict, core versus periphery. The important fact is that the Euro-American conquest of the world continues today, long after the voyage of Columbus.[21]

There is little need to catalogue the 500 years of conquest, or even the continuation of the conquest in the present. Perhaps it is a coincidence that the quincentenary of Columbus' voyage was also the fiftieth anniversary of the Nazis' conversion of Auschwitz from a concentration camp into a death camp designed to annihilate Europe's Jews and others whom the Nazis had characterized as "useless lives." David Stannard, an American historian, thinks the connection is significant, because one of the preconditions for Spanish and Anglo-American genocides against the Native Americans was a definition of the natives as inherently inferior beings, a definition later applied to Jews. The conquering Spanish legitimated their definition by appealing to ancient Christian and European truths, for example, the philosophy of Thomas Aquinas and Aristotle. Since the colonizing British and subsequently the Americans were more interested in Native American land than Native American servitude, they appealed to other Christian and European sources of wisdom to justify their genocide. This wisdom saw Native Americans as Satan's helpers, lascivious and murderous wild men, as vermin. Because of these views, many were deemed unfit for conversion to Christianity or for civil life. Because the British and Americans preferred Africans as slaves, the mass killing of the Indians could proceed.[22]

The movement of conquest is always accompanied by language and religion. A narrative that seeks to legitimate conquest is developed; its role is to subvert the narrative of the conquered and reinforce the conquest. In relation to colonialism and conquest, the Christian narrative seeks to expand the Christian faith over against other religious sensibilities and, in doing so, subvert and eliminate disconfirming others. While the Jews are the most intimate other to Christianity, the expansion of Europe in 1492 introduced Christianity to peoples around the world who, even if dwelling in "ignorance" before Christian contact, had the potential for rejecting the proffered salvation. If conversion was rejected, the people moved from an ignorant to a disconfirming other. Therefore the expansion of Christianity held promise and anxiety. Would the peoples that Christians encountered recognize the truth of Christianity or reject it as unimportant or even false? Ultimately, and unexpectedly, a new anxiety surfaces as the conquered adopts the Christian religion as a form of survival, and later of liberation, and this with the same symbols and name of the conqueror.

In this process of expansion, Christianity also encountered Islam. Like Judaism, Islam contains a real provocation to Christianity. In a geographic and cultural way, Islam is close to Christianity, drawing on Judeo-Hellenic traditions. It has also experienced military and political successes that, at certain times in history, threatened Christianity and its European hegemony. Indeed, from the seventh century until the battle of Lepanto in 1571, Islam in either its Arab, Ottoman, North African, or Spanish form dominated or effectively threatened European Christianity. As important, Arabic and Hebrew are Semitic languages; in Edward Said's understanding they "dispose and redispose of material that is urgently important to Christianity." To overcome this dual threat from the power and narrative of Islam, the Middle East was subdued, invaded, and redefined in the eyes of the foreign invader. If the area was seen as strange and disconfirming, it could be recreated in the language and faith of European Christian civilization. This recreation tames and ultimately makes entire peoples subservient or even invisible. Said labels this "Orientalism," defined as a movement of military and intellectual power that seeks European and Christian hegemony over an established, though by the eighteenth century weakened, Islamic foe. This power is exercised through a concerted strategic apparatus that combines state, military, and narrative hegemony. To define and redefine the other is a power that seeks subjugation and authority over the people and cultures. At the end of this process, the tragic irony is that people from the "Orient" travel to Europe and America, the place of their dispossession, to learn who they are.[23]

Orientalism is a relatively late extension of European hegemony, first practiced and perfected in the Americas. George Tinker, an Osage, Cherokee Native American, identifies Europe's colonial conquest of the Americas as proceeding on two separate but connected fronts: the first involving the political and military strategy, which cleansed Native Americans from their land, deprived native peoples of self-governance and self-determination and made room for the conqueror. The second front involved Christian missionaries, who cleansed Native Americans of the religious connection to their tribe and their geography and substituted Christian religion. Vine Deloria, a Sioux Native American, argues that the substitution of Christianity for native religiosity represented a radical change of worldviews from a native, local, and geographic religiosity to a Christian linear view of revelation history. The ultimate effect of this transformation was to uproot his people from their land and from their geographic and symbolic universe.[24]

This happened in the Philippines as well. Here again conquest and conversion proceed hand in hand. For Vincent Rafael, Filipino priest and author, conversion, like conquest, is a process of crossing over into someone else's world and claiming it as one's own. This crossing over involves annexation and restructuring of the world one has invaded. It forges a new hierarchy of interests and values and seeks a conversion to this hierarchy, as if by giving up what is yours and deferring to what is theirs the culture, religion, and language have been elevated. The Spanish colonization of the Tagalogs, the largest and most prominent ethnolinguistic group in the Philippines, is an example of the ties between colonialism and evangelization, mediated by Christianity and Castilian Spanish. For Rafael, the Spanish colonizers introduced into the culture of the Tagalogs a new kind of power relation between ruler and ruled, one premised on the adherence of both to a transcendental order. But they also did more, for they sought to establish a different way of perceiving the world, thereby dramatically changing the religious and political way of conceiving the relation between self and society in Tagalog culture.[25]

This effort could only be legitimated and regulated within the context of the Spaniards' Christianizing mission. Catholicism provided Spain's colonial enterprise with its ideological framework as it legitimated the structure of colonial rule with the practice of religious conversion. For Rafael, the religious invasion of the Tagalog language provided the most intimate and longlasting aspect of the Spanish invasion. Long after the end of colonial rule, the Castilian language, the language of imperial Christianity, remained. Even when the Taga-log language was employed to transmit Christianity, the local language still underwent change. Because the Spaniards saw Tagalog as an infe-rior language unable to carry the ultimate meaning of the Christian faith, they found no adequate equivalent in Tagalog language for the significant language of Christianity such as *Dios*, *Espiritu Santo*, and *Jesucristo*. To reach salvation, the worldview of the Tagalog people had to be left behind.[26]

A curious development in this process ensues. The Christian ethos that accompanies European civilization helps to conquer a people, invade their language and culture, reorganize their patterns of life and authority and, at the same time, converts the conquered people so they become co-religionists. In the European mind, the debased pre-Chris-tian reality is elevated through military and religious conquest; the people experience this elevation as an eruption of barbarism. Those who survive this eruption struggle to survive and over time to achieve equality within a shared religious framework. The struggle, however, takes place within a linguistic, religious, and political framework pro-mulgated by the conqueror. The struggle takes place, in essence, on imperial turf. Through conquest and conversion the conquerors deprive humanity of one of the versions of its future; the oppressed struggle to create a future in the language and religious symbolism of the oppressors. This can hardly be understood as the distinctive and original future before the conquest. Rather, it is a struggle to survive within a future bequeathed by empire. It is important to note that both George Tinker and Vincent Rafael, a Native American and a Tagalog respectively, are members of the Christian clergy, their books are pub-lished by Christian publishers, and their reading audience is predomi-nantly Christian.

The fate of a majority of Christians in the world is to seek liberation within the religion that participated in their conquest. Liberation the-ologies, originating in the 1960s among Christians of the Third World, attempt to move those conquered by Christianity to a level of political and cultural empowerment within the religion that legitimated their conquest. Ironically, European and American Christians, who are heirs of the victory of 1492, often renew their own Christian faith through the development of these liberation theologies. If Steiner's sense of the terminal belief of Christianity built into the Nazi annihi-lation of the Jews is true, the victory of those who prevailed in 1492 may seem hollow. Yet struggles for liberation and the theologies of liberation that develop within those struggles may seem, like Christian Holocaust theology, a place of rescue. Could significant segments of the European and American Christian world be aligning itself with Jews and Third-World Christians as a way to invest its triumph with meaning and purpose, thus tempering its barbarism with a "whole lot of pretty sounding words," as Malcolm X claimed years ago? Perhaps this is the true commonality between the Jews of Auschwitz and those Christians conquered in the experience of 1492, to argue after their survival for a place in the political and symbolic universe of the Christian conqueror, who in turn might be renewed in the process.

Christian liberation theologians argue on two levels: the first level invokes a common Christianity that obligates the dominant Christian to repent and allow the conquered a full and equal place in the material and spiritual world. The second level articulates a Christianity of the oppressed as being quite different from the Christianity of the powerful. Often liberation theology operates on both grounds alternately and simultaneously. The first level continues to be elusive; no people of 1492 conquered by Christianity has reached political, economic, or religious parity with European and American Christians. The second level seems even more distant, since it is difficult, if not impossible, to subvert the oppressive religion from within its own parameters and language. The attempt at subversion is often dismissed or quickly usurped and, in that usurpation, transformed into the normative, which can be used against the oppressed. Are these lessons learned in the three decades of contemporary liberation theology?

The complexity of this process is often dismissed, if considered at all. Christianity claims a universality and submerges the particular histories of the people it conquers. Emphasizing the universal over the particular can lead to an embrace that transcends racial and cultural barriers. But it can also legitimate a conquest and erase that people's history; in so doing it seeks to erase the history of the conquest as well. This leaves those who are conquered in a quandary, for as their native culture and language recede they are left with a religion that speaks of their equality with other Christians, even as their material reality contradicts that equality. The notion of equality is typically raised after Christianity has lost its imperial power. It may even become the new strategy to retain the importance of Christianity in the lives of people who begin to recognize their history of subjection. The theoretical and theological understanding of the universality of Christianity that is now asserted has been experienced by the conquered people as an ordeal of destruction and atrocity. Third-World people arrive at the table of Christianity, late, out of breath, and dependent on the charity of their hosts. These are the same hosts who, in disguising the people's loss of their world in the glory of Christian faith, also disguise their victory with the language of liberation.

Theology and the Struggle of African Americans

The work of African American theologian James H. Cone is instructive here. In his first books on the relationship of Black power and Christianity, published in the late 1960s and the early 1970s, Cone begins with a fundamental challenge: If Christianity was given to African slaves as the oppressor religion in hopes that it would convince them to remain slaves, and if white Christian religion continues to be racist and oppressive, then how can Blacks hold to such a religion in the present? The answer is simple and profound. For Cone, Christianity and whiteness are opposites. No true revelation of God comes without a condition of oppression that develops into a struggle for liberation. Hence revelation is only for the "oppressed of the land." Accordingly, white Christian theology is that of the anti-Christ while Black theology, arising from an identification with the oppressed Black community, is true Christian theology. To the proposition that God is for all people, Cone is adamant that "either God is for Blacks in their fight for liberation from white oppressors, or God is not. God cannot be both for us and for white oppressors at the same time."[27]

The dichotomy that Cone proposes has its own anxiety. In his discussion of God, Cone pointedly reminds the reader that there is no use for a God who loves white oppressors the same as oppressed African Americans. In fact, it is this equal distribution of love, often proposed by the white oppressor to mollify African Americans, that is most dangerous to the Black freedom struggle. What African Americans need is God's love as expressed in Black power, the power to destroy their oppressors by any means at their disposal. Unless God is participating in the activity of liberation, Cone counsels a rejection of God's love. Still, rejection is only one option left to the Black liberationist: "If Jesus Christ is white and not Black, he is an oppressor, and we must kill him. The appearance of Black theology means that the Black community is now ready to do something about the white Jesus, so that he cannot get in the way of our revolution." For Cone, rather than dying to save white Christians, Jesus dies to destroy them, to "dissolve their whiteness in the fire of judgment," for it is in this destruction that the possibility of revolution, and therefore the wholeness of humanity, might be realized.[28]

Still the problem remains, as white Christians claim God and Christ, and the continued oppression of African Americans renders debatable belief in a God of liberation. Cone is aware of these problems and cites with approval Richard Rubenstein's theology. For Cone, Rubenstein rejects a view of God that contributes to oppression of the Jewish people and takes seriously the division of oppressor and oppressed neglected in traditional Christian theology. Rubenstein's understanding is crucial to African Americans who experience white racism as an "insanity comparable to Nazism" and in a country where the genocide of Native Americans serves as a reminder that white oppressors are capable of pursuing a course of "complete annihilation of everything Black." The very history of Christianity makes belief suspect, if not impossible, and Cone, like Rubenstein, stresses the Protestant Reformation as symbolic and culpable. Martin Luther's condemnation of the Peasant Revolt is instructive, as it reminds Cone of the white churches' condemnation of Black ghetto uprisings. Other Protestant reformers, like John Calvin and John Wesley are similarly suspect, as there was, according to Cone, an easy affinity between Calvinism, capitalism, and slave trading. Wesley said little and did less with regard to slaveholding.[29]

The question remains as to whether this human suffering can be in accordance with the divine plan. Here is Cone's wager: to believe that human suffering is part of God's plan would mean that the death of six million Jews, the genocide of Native Americans, and the enslavement and lynching of Blacks happened with the knowledge and approval of God. Only oppressors can make such a claim. The alternative is affirming the Blackness of God and the presence of a Black Christ who has been with African Americans in their struggle. This presence cannot be rejected because of white distortion and abuse. Instead, Black theology must affirm with the people that as creator, redeemer, and holy spirit, God identified with the oppressed of Israel and participated in the birth of their peoplehood, became oppressed himself in order that all may be free from oppression, and continues the work of liberation today. In America, this spirit is found among African Americans gathering in the community for their historic encounter with whites, whom Cone identifies as the anti-Christ.[30]

The underlying theme of Cone's early work is the attempt to distance himself and the African American freedom struggle from false religion and a false God. The biblical witness is crucial, for here the choice of God to be a God of the oppressed is clear and unequivocal. This choice is seen within the context of African American history as well, for that community has felt God's presence in their suffering and struggle. One way of seeing African American history is as a struggle of the people to affirm themselves as authentic persons rather than as slaves. In opposing slavery and seeking freedom, Black theology seeks to accompany and articulate the force of that history. For Cone, Black theology began when the Black clergy realized that killing slave masters was doing the work of God, refused to see the white racist church as part of God's gospel, and organized instead the Black church. The African American experience of Jesus Christ, then, is quite different than the white systematic exposition of the meaning of God and Christ. The difficult question of God's presence in history as the people continue to be oppressed is recognized by Cone as authentic and yet humbled by the experience of African Americans in relation to Christ the liberator.[31]

Cone's work on a Black theology of liberation became a lightning rod for affirmation and critique. Criticized for being antiwhite and decrying the possibility of reconciliation with the oppressors, thus equating European-American Christianity with the anti-Christ, Cone responds that he had little patience with people who expected him to remain calm in the face of racist theology: "I kept thinking about my mother and father (and all the poor Blacks they symbolized in African American history and culture) in order to keep my theological vocation clearly focused and my immediate purpose sharply defined. God did not call me into the ministry for the purpose of making the gospel intelligible to privileged white intellectuals." In light of racist theological discourse, Cone speaks prophetically about the righteousness of God in clear and uncompromising language. There is an irony in the sons of slave traders and slave holders defining the nature of the gospel and characterizing Black theology as antiwhite and racism in reverse. Cone cites Catholic sociologist Andrew Greeley's response to Black theology as a "Nazi mentality . . . a theology filled with hatred for white people and the assumption of a moral superiority of Black over white." Greeley's critique, like white theology in general, is conveniently more interested in the theoretical aspects of Christian theology than the actual deeds of the history Cone was detailing.[32]

At the same time that Cone defended his early work, however, he retreated from aspects of his theological explorations and from the overall methodology he employed in creating a Black theology of liberation. In the intervening years, Cone has come into contact with the world of suffering outside of the United States, and his theological vision has expanded to include struggling peoples around the world. Aspects of African American empowerment also affect Cone's vision; so he laments his earlier, almost exclusive focus on racial injustice and the lack of analysis of the effects of corporate capitalism on the poor of all races and ethnic backgrounds. To be sure, Cone finds very few differences between African American and European-American capitalists. "We are all—Blacks and whites, men and women, young and old—sinners, and thus capable of exploiting the poor in order to promote our economic and political interests," he writes. As important are Cone's revised thoughts on theological method. No longer would he create a theological structure that begins with divine revelation and then proceeds to explain the doctrines of God, Christ, world, and eschatology. By the mid-1980s, Cone is unable to affirm a revelation independent of human experiences to which theologians can appeal to verify their understanding of the gospel.[33]

Cone's work on Martin Luther King Jr. and Malcolm X in the 1990s represents a shift in emphasis from theology to history. In Cone's early work, the liberating message of the Bible and Jesus is seen as abused by white European and American Christianity and discovered by the slaves and their descendants. His exploration elicits a new methodology for discovering a liberating message within the two major streams of African American history, that of integration and nation-building, represented by King and Malcolm X. By detailing the backgrounds and struggles of both leaders within the context of the broader African American struggle, nuances and bold discoveries are recounted. The battle is no longer with white theology, nor does the struggle to create an African American theology take center stage. Rather the insights, tendencies, failures, and hopes of two men destined to lead African Americans and to die for them, are explored. The tradition of African American protest is the center from which theological insights emerge.

For Cone, it is this grounding in Black protest that allows King and Malcolm X to become master critics of American Christianity and its racism. King as a Christian contributed a powerful internal critique, while Malcolm X as a Black Muslim contributed a "devastating" external one. "The best surgeon for cutting out the cancer of racism in Christian churches is Malcolm X," Cone writes. "Malcolm's Black theology is not a replacement for the Christian theology of Black churches or even of white churches. Rather it is an *indispensable corrective*." This corrective can help keep African American churches from simply duplicating white churches; in Cone's view it may also help white churches understand what community might be like without racism. Hence Cone's conclusion that Black and white Christian churches need to "practice and preach the gospel according to Martin and Malcolm." If this is done, America and the world will be a better place to live.[34]

Cone's work on King and Malcolm X is nuanced compared to his earlier work on a Black theology of liberation. He is more cognizant of history and class issues, and less interested in proving the satanic elements of white Christianity or the almost unqualified beauty of African American Christianity. The Christianity that African Americans practice remains indigenous to their community, and Cone analyzes at length the African American roots of King's vision, especially since most white commentators stress the influence of personalist philosophy on King's ministry. Cone's incorporation of Malcolm X in the redefining of Black and white Christianity is subversive, for in the European Christian tradition few outside the community are allowed to speak to the core of Christian faith and practice. The shift in Cone's framework and style over the last decades, however, suggests that his original definition of the separation of Black and white as, on the one hand, heirs to the promise of the kingdom and, on the other hand, the anti-Christ, is no longer operative. This shift could have resulted because Cone's argument was so persuasive that it was absorbed into the broader Christian theological ethos and therefore no longer needed to stand on its own. More likely Cone's understanding of Malcolm X's role in relation to Martin Luther King Jr. that of corrective, is now Cone's own role in relation to white Christian theology.

Absorption of elements of Cone's theology into white Christian theology did not fundamentally reorient the practice of Christians in America in relation to race. It is difficult to argue that the masses of African Americans are empowered in white America, or even, in a substantive way, closer to the goal of liberation than when a Black theology of liberation was articulated. If white Christian theology has over the years whitened the legacy of Martin Luther King Jr. transforming his prophetic speech into a comfortable, almost status quo philosophy, is it not too far off when Malcolm X may undergo the same whitening? On the race question, King has functioned for white Christians as a point of rescue, delaying what Cone felt in his early work to be their terminal condition. Perhaps Malcolm X will ultimately function in the same way. The issue is less what Cone or King or Malcolm X propose or hope; rather it is the continuing power of the terminal patient which resurrects itself over the bodies of dead Jews and African Americans by incorporating the voices of the dead to bring the builders of the death camps and the slave ships new life. In the two levels of Christian liberation theological argument, the assertion of a common Christianity and the articulation of a radically different Christianity carried by the oppressed, the former is victorious.

Evangelization at Gunpoint

At the same time that Cone was writing on the revolutionary potential of Black Christianity in the United States, Gustavo Gutiérrez, a Peruvian priest and theologian, began lecturing and writing on a Latin American theology of liberation. If the backdrop of Cone's analysis is the tradition of Black protest, which includes, among other events, resistance to slavery, organizing for civil rights, and the emerging Black power movement, Gutiérrez's sensibility is informed by the failure of policies of development, as well as the failures of guerrilla movements in Peru in the 1960s. In the larger Latin American reality, the question of liberation also responds to the failure of John F. Kennedy's Alliance for Progress, as well as revolutionary movements and popular resistance in Cuba, Bolivia, Mexico, and Santo Domingo during the twentieth century. The deaths of revolutionary figures, such as Camilo Torres and Ernesto Che Guevara, were also instrumental, as was the rise of a Marxist critique of capitalism and Christian democracy. As in the Unites States, Christianity was part of the problem in Latin America, where the historical role of 1492 was, if anything, even more apparent. In general, then, Latin American liberation theology emerges within two crises: the crisis of the system of domination and the rise of popular movements to challenge that system.[35]

Gutiérrez's lectures and his subsequent book on a theology of liberation are mild in language compared to Cone's early work. Gutiérrez posits the theology of liberation as evolutionary within the Catholic communion and specifically within the guidelines of the recently completed Vatican Council II. The Council tried to balance the universality of the Catholic church with the particular historical and geographical contexts of local Catholic communities. Hence the emphasis on the use of the vernacular in liturgy and the realization that the expression of Catholic commitment would, while maintaining an essential uniformity, vary in its expression according to local demands and exigencies. Gutiérrez's analysis proceeds in this light, moving from a classic view of theology as an intellectual understanding of faith that stresses the effort of intelligence to comprehend revelation and faith, to a more liberationist perspective that stresses an existential commitment to God and to the human community. It is this shift from a theology defining the absolute and transcendent to a theology reflecting on the historical events of humanity that is seen to be revolutionary. Gutiérrez proposes a theology which represents a progressive and continuing reflection that comes after commitment and action. The central element of commitment is charity in its broadest and most dynamic sense; theology arrives later on.[36]

Gutiérrez realized the pastoral consequences of this analysis, for here the people lead with their desire for freedom: the theologian, indeed the church, accompanies the people or is left behind. History is the place of action and the road to salvation. The coming of the messiah is identified with the alleviation of oppression in the world. As Gutiérrez understands it, the messiah arrives when injustice is overcome: "When we struggle for a just world in which there is no servitude, oppression, or slavery, we are signifying the coming of the messiah." To illustrate this understanding, Gutiérrez quotes passages from Karl Marx and Isaiah as dual challenges to Christian commitment. The challenge is whether contemporary Christians will realize the prophecy of Isaiah to participate in the creation of a new Jerusalem or fulfill Marx's analysis of Christianity as having the characteristics of servility and cowardice. For Gutiérrez, this is "precisely what is at stake in our epoch."[37]

In the early 1970s, Gutiérrez's work was translated into English, upon which it received a worldwide readership. His ideas about theology and the Christian community began a controversy on the role and meaning of theology which continues to this day. Quoting Marx as a challenge to Christian theology was often interpreted as replacing Christian theology with Marxism. The Marxian analysis that posited differing economic and social classes within the society *and* within the church—proposing that there were Christians who were part of the dominant (and oppressive) classes and Christians who were poor (and oppressed)—was seen by some as a call for class warfare within society *and* within the church. The option for the poor as it develops in Gutiérrez's work, however, simply calls for a recognition of this division. As Gutiérrez writes, the church is split already and to pretend a unity has dire consequences: "To try piously to cover over this social division with a fictitious and formalistic unity is to avoid a difficult and conflicted reality and definitely to join the dominant class." For Gutiérrez, the option for the dominant class represents a decision against authentic love, which is demonstrated in class solidarity and social struggle. To be sure, serious divisions can occur precisely by recognizing and understanding that social classes and class struggle already exist within the church without being affirmed; analyzing the reality brings to light these classes and this struggle as well as the "*peculiarly religious* myth of the 'community of the faithful' and the (catholic) universality of the Church."[38]

Recognition of the struggle and the myths that seek to deny that struggle is not to exclude the dominant from Christian love; rather it seeks to include justice in the very definition of love. For Gutiérrez, love does not mean that the oppressors cease to be enemies, nor does it eliminate the radicalness of the struggle against them. Love of enemies does not ease tensions; rather it challenges the whole system and becomes a subversive formula. Participation in class struggle is the necessary and inescapable means of making love concrete. It is in this context that Gutiérrez is critical of Johann Baptist Metz and Jürgen Moltmann and the political theology that they and other European theologians were developing in the 1960s. As a critic of European theology and Christianity, Metz, for example, postulates the church and theology as institutional voices of social criticism within the broad movement of history. Metz's theology comes from the crisis of European history and in the midst of contemporary European affluence; within this context his theology is understandable, perhaps even necessary. Yet it is inadequate in light of Europe's exploitation and injustice in relation to the Third World. Because Metz is far from the revolutionary ferment of Third World countries, Gutiérrez believes he cannot understand the injustice and exploitation in which most of humankind dwells. Metz's work may be a confrontation with aspects of internal European history, especially as it relates to the history of the Jews. It does not lead to the confrontation needed in Latin America for the liberation of the masses.[39]

By the end of the 1970s, Gutiérrez sees this insufficiency as central, and shifts his attention from the church and its theology to those who are the victims of history. Gutiérrez further distances himself from European Christianity precisely through the question of the poor in history. European theology responds to the questions of science and secularism and seeks to answer the questions of the nonbeliever. Latin

American liberation theology confronts the challenge of the poor and displaced and seeks to respond to those who are considered by society to be nonpersons. Therefore liberation theology has not only a different point of departure; it is for Gutiérrez in historical contradiction to progressive theology. With roots in the social reality of the poor, liberation theology is an expression of a dialectical opposition to bourgeois ideology and the dominant European culture it reflects. Gutiérrez believes that European theology marginalizes the historical agent, that is, the exploited and despised segments of society who form the underside of history and a repository of a new understanding of faith. For Gutiérrez, these are the people whom the Bible calls "the poor."[40]

As segments of the church opt for the poor and the marginalized, a new martyrdom comes into being. Some, especially those associated with the institutional church, are well known, but for Gutiérrez as important are the *campesinos*, laborers, and students who have been kidnapped, tortured, or murdered. These are history's anonymous witnesses—"protagonists of hope in the midst of repression, faceless as the poor from whom they spring and for whom they die." Above all, these witnesses express the right of the poor to think and to a human life. The poor become the engine of history and the locus of a theology defined as their "expression of the right to think and be." Here, too, the fullness of life brought by Jesus and the power of the poor are discovered. Gutiérrez describes this as Easter gladness—"joy that passes through death and pain, in intensity, in profound hope."[41]

Yet Gutiérrez knows that these affirmations of hope are difficult, especially as the situation of suffering is longstanding and increasing over time. By the 1980s and especially in his writings on the Book of Job, Gutiérrez shows an awareness of this ambiguity and challenge. The failure of developmentalism and revolution to alleviate poverty, and the failure of traditional theology and liberation theology to counter the worsening situation of the masses, provides the framework for an exploration of Job. The questions framing Gutiérrez's reading of Job are clear. How are Latin Americans to talk about a God of love in a situation of poverty and oppression? How are they to proclaim the God of life to those who die prematurely and unjustly? Is it possible to acknowledge a God of love and justice when the suffering of the innocent is ever-present? What language can convey to those who are not even regarded as persons that they are the sons and daughters of God? For Gutiérrez, the answers lie in the interplay of gratuitousness and revelation, silence and speech, for silence, contemplation, and practice are all necessary in thinking about God and doing theology. Theology is speech that has been enriched by silence and practice. Still the challenge remains. Can Christians proclaim that Christ is the center of the world when the innocent suffer on a mass scale? Can Christians proclaim that the "crucified Jesus dwells there and with him all who suffer unjustly, all the poor and despised of the earth?"[42]

For Gutiérrez these are challenges found within histories shaped by European Christianity. The suffering of the innocent is a key difficulty facing a mature discourse about God, and here Gutiérrez refers to the European theological crisis after Auschwitz. Citing the work of Johann Baptist Metz and Richard Rubenstein, Gutiérrez refers to the "terrible holocaust" of millions of Jews as an "inescapable challenge to the Christian conscience and an inexcusable reproach to the silence of many Christians in the face of that dreadful event." To Gutiérrez, Metz and Rubenstein ask the right question, that is, how we can speak about God when God seems absent in the face of immense human suffering? Gutiérrez offers no answer to this question in relation to the Jewish Holocaust. For Latin Americans, however, the problem is not precisely how to do theology after Auschwitz but how to do theology in Latin America, where the people are presently experiencing the violation of human rights, torture, and murder that Gutiérrez finds so horrible in the Jewish Holocaust. The task of the theologian is to find words with which to talk about God in the midst of starvation, systematic social injustice, disappearances, terrorism, and what Gutiérrez refers to as the corpse-filled common graves of Ayacucho: "In Peru, therefore—but the question is perhaps symbolic of all Latin America—we must ask: How are we to do theology *while Ayacucho lasts*? How are we to speak of the God of life when cruel murder on a massive scale goes on in 'the corners of the dead'?"[43]

Here Gutiérrez finds the message of Job compelling, as one who, on the dung heap of history, protests, challenges and embraces; as one who, in his argument with God about the suffering of the innocent, searches for justice and ultimately accepts the gratuitousness of God's plan for history. Job speaks to the contemporary world in a prophetic language that makes it possible to draw near to a God who refuses to be confined to human categories, even the category of justice. This God has a predilection for the poor without demanding proof of their moral or religious superiority; God's love of the poor is based simply on the fact that they are poor and living in situations that are contrary to God's will. The basis for the privileged position of the poor is found within God, in the gratuitousness and universality of God's *agapic* love. At the end of his journey, Gutiérrez's Job learns that belief in God and God's gratuitous love leads to a preferential option for the poor and to solidarity with those who suffer exploitation and contempt: "The God of utter freedom and gratuitousness who has been revealed to Job can alone explain the privileged place of those whom the powerful and the self-righteous of society treat unjustly and make outcasts." In God's revelation, gratuitousness and preferential love for the poor are inseparable, as is the Christian's contemplation of God and concern for the disinherited of this world. Gutiérrez learns that prophecy and contemplation are part of a journey that must be traveled without turning from unjust human suffering, which continues to be "heartrending and insatiable." The journey never ends, nor does the protest that Job exemplifies. If the challenge of talking about God has become more explicit, it continues to be mysterious, as "awesome and as alluring as ever."[44]

The distance traveled from the sketches of a theology of liberation to the biblical figure of Job is significant. Though Gutiérrez was well aware of Job at the time of his first writings on liberation theology, the emphasis on poverty and injustice was addressed in more strident, class-oriented terms. The new emphasis on Job is important and stems from a variety of factors, including the worsening situation of Latin America. From the perspective of the political, social, and religious realms, the failure (at least in the immediate sense of relieving poverty and empowering the poor) is obvious. The poor continue to die before their time and in massive anonymous numbers; martyrdom, too, increases daily. In his early work, Gutiérrez accepts the challenge of Karl Marx and the response of Isaiah as the challenge of the age, that is, the redefinition of Christianity as the task of working with God to usher in the messianic age. Indeed, many Christians in and beyond Latin America accepted this challenge, and still the situation deteriorates. At the same time, liberation theology comes under attack from aspects of the Roman Catholic hierarchy, including the Vatican institutional structure. Over the years, persecution of political and religious figures by the political and religious power structure become commonplace.

Gutiérrez's Job can be seen as a claim on history beyond the political and church structures of the day. The powerful of the world will be judged in the long sweep of history; the apparent defeat of the poor represents a mystical and prophetic journey to God. The acceptance of God's love and delay, at first sight a lessening of the struggle by and for the poor, for Gutiérrez means waging battle in another arena. The power of the poor in history, those exploited and believing masses of poor people, are destined to be disappointed and surprised, as is Gutiér-rez's Job. Regardless of political and church persecution, Gutiérrez finds solace and strength in Job's assertive statement, "I will not restrain my tongue." Perhaps this quote from Job is Gutiérrez's own cry of anguish and defiance. Though chastened, he continues the struggle. The judg-ment of one's commitment is left to God. "Perhaps those who live, and try to express their faith and hope amid unjust suffering will some day have to say humbly with Job, 'I spoke without understanding marvels that are beyond my grasp,' and put aside the harsh language," Gutiérrez writes. "Yet who knows but that the Lord may tell them, to the surprise of some: 'You have spoken correctly about me.'"[45]

The shift in emphasis from the judgment of history to the judgment of God is implicit in Gutiérrez's own journey. Does this shift, coming as it does within an apparent failure in history, represent the failure of God and Jesus, of Christianity, as self-evident responses and solutions to the suffering of the innocent? Has the wager with Marx been lost? Is Christianity impotent, or worse, essentially a structural and symbolic form of oppression rather than a road to liberation? Does failure move beyond institutional Christianity and into the realm of faith in the Christian God? If there is a God, if Christ is among and even suffers with the poor, what kind of God establishes presence simply through suffer-ing, a suffering which seems to have no end? Richard Rubenstein notes that an essential task of the theologian is to reduce the cognitive disso-nance between belief and reality, between the promises of relief, of pres-ence, of liberation and the apparent reality of absence and continued suffering. With Job, Gutiérrez attempts to accomplish this theological task by maintaining a structure of faith that threatens to dissipate in the light of experience. Clearly Gutiérrez's earlier, more systematic expres-sion of liberation theology can no longer be sustained. Could it be that at the end of a systematic theology of liberation, and in the face of dis-appointment, persecution, and suffering, Gutiérrez is reestablishing a Judaic understanding of living in God's presence at the very time when it is being lost in Jewish life precisely because of suffering in the Holo-caust? Gutiérrez's Job represents a paradox of staggering proportions: as the Jewish experience in the Christian West forces Jews to articulate their suffering and the abandonment of God within a Christian theo-logical sensibility, Christians who suffer within and because of the Christian West recover a Judaic sensibility in order to survive their brothers and sisters in the Christian faith.

Job is neither a detour for Gutiérrez nor the end of the story. The radical claims of systematic theology, even in the liberation mode, recede; as Gutiérrez writes on Job, he initiates his larger project focusing on Bartolemé de Las Casas, the sixteenth-century Spanish priest and bishop who initially supported and then vehemently opposed the conquest of the Americas. Gutiérrez's writings on Las Casas represent a major contribution to the history of resistance to the expansion of Europe and European Christianity. In the movement from systematic theology to Job to Las Casas, Gutiérrez comes full circle: the counter-testimony to Christianity that Marx enunciated is affirmed and challenged. Through complicity and resistance, Las Casas finds his own voice and a way of articulating Christianity beyond the blood of conquest. As with James H. Cone and his discussion of Martin Luther King Jr. and Malcolm X, Gutiérrez's final destination is neither systematic theology nor biblical interpretation. Rather a history of resistance captivates both Cone and Gutiérrez and provides the possibility of a theology emerging from that history. Yet it also true—and one is aware of this from the first page of Gutiérrez's writing on Las Casas—that the history of resistance yields less than a theology. What it does yield is a witness in history that involves a richer yet no less problematic tapestry than systematic theology.

As he does with Job, Gutiérrez draws the figure of Las Casas with great detail and imagination. For Gutiérrez, the contribution of Las Casas is hardly limited to the debate regarding colonization and the defense of the native peoples of the Americas. In his defense of the native peoples, Las Casas also contributes decisively to the question of human rights, religious freedom, democracy, and the desire to understand the "other" of Western civilization. What has been lacking in most studies of Las Casas, is emphasis on Las Casas as a man of faith whose theological reflections were important in his day and ours. Gutiérrez views Las Casas as a person who prophetically denounces injustice and, at the same time, proposes concrete solutions. Though he holds strong opinions, Las Casas learns from both people and events, and so his thought continually evolves. For example, Las Casas defends the Native Americans, respects their human dignity, and their right to be different, at the same time believing in the importance of evangelization. This evangelization can only occur, however, with the free consent of the indigenous people. For Gutiérrez, Las Casas forms a historical perspective and political vision that evolves from his faith in Jesus Christ, a Christ "whom he encountered in the afflicted and crucified Indians."[46]

As in the analysis of Job, Gutiérrez is unsparing in his criticism of political and religious oppression. Gutiérrez's description of the spread of Christianity in the Americas, as "evangelization at gunpoint," is scathing in its use of irony. To those who may be scandalized by his historical analysis of war being waged in the service of evangelization, Gutiérrez poses the even more difficult question of whether Christians are so far from this attitude in the present. An example is the contemporary defense of "our continent, of Western Christian civilization through repression, murder, torture, and imprisonment." These measures are often sanctioned by rulers who, like the conquistadors and the *encomenderos*, also call themselves Christian. For Gutiérrez, the modern mentality is different only in inventing more subtle methods of extending its interests and exploiting the poor. Here Gutiérrez uses Las Casas, as he used Job, to speak for himself in the present. Las Casas speaks ironically of "our Spanish saints" who perpetrate crimes against the Indians and, in the same mode, writes of the people of Peru whom Francisco Pizarro and his "holy disciples have extirpated by the law of robbery." Las Casas also analyzes the methodology of evangelization by which the Portuguese work "elegant miracles," that is, "robbing [the Indians], taking them captive, burning them alive and cutting them to pieces." Indeed Job and Las Casas speak more harshly to religious presuppositions and authorities than seems allowable today; by using a biblical and historical figure the accusation is a step removed from Gutiérrez as author. Yet the persecution of Job and Las Casas by religious authorities is clearly a pattern evident in Gutiérrez's own life and ministry. Like Job, Gutiérrez will not remain silent; like Las Casas, Gutiérrez will witness in history.[47]

There is a twist in Gutiérrez's identification with Las Casas. Las Casas is adamantly opposed to the conquest and the evangelization that accompanies it. He argues almost from the beginning for the right of the native peoples to exist in their own integrity and to be protected from political, military, and economic domination by the Europeans. Since for Las Casas the conquest and resistance to it are charged with religious meaning, the perpetrators are guilty of greed, idolatry, murder—in short, sin. Those who defend the Indians are speaking the prophetic word, siding with God, and testifying to the presence of Christ amid suffering. "An early death for the Indians, and sin on the part of those who oppress them," Gutiérrez exclaims. "It is in this context in which Bartolomé receives the call to denounce these conditions, and to proclaim the reign of the God of life in its stead. The liberation of the 'Indian oppressed' looms before his eyes as a colossal exigency. In the Indians, he sees Christ himself, humiliated and scourged." This understanding, so haunting in its symbolic power, leads Las Casas and Gutiérrez as well to affirm resistance to conquest and the possibility of a proper evangelization of the native peoples. Evangelization of the Indies is an important reason, in fact the only reason, for the Spanish to be in Latin America. Gutiérrez complains with Las Casas that the quest for wealth has replaced the proclamation of the gospel. To accept the gospel, the Indians need to be respected and free. As Las Casas writes: "Living, the Indians will have an opportunity to be instructed in the faith and to be saved, instead of dying." The task of the Spanish Christian is to defend the Indians' life and freedom so that the gospel can be freely accepted and so that Indians can be given something other than "death for doctrine." The transformation of the conquest to service and defense of the indigenous, of course, can benefit the Spaniards, too. Instead of living "on the blood of the Indians," as Las Casas phrases it, the Spaniards can move toward a fidelity to the faith they seek to impart. This in turn will help further a real evangelization, proclaimed through deeds of solidarity and persuasion. The key to evangelization comes into view when Gutiérrez writes that "only by loving the Indians as Christ has loved us can we proclaim to them."[48]

Las Casas' journey ends in the defense of the Indians and the call for a proper evangelization. And it is also here that Gutiérrez's journey begins. Latin America inherits the conquest and the evangelization, the Christendom of the conquerors and a fledgling struggle of the poor, many of whom are Christians. Gutiérrez affirms the theology adopted at the meetings of the Latin American Bishops at Medellín, Columbia, in 1968 and Puebla, Mexico, in 1978. It articulates the option for the poor and the call for a new evangelization of Latin America, this time by the poor and the members of the races, cultures, and social classes that have been historically marginalized. The challenge, according to Gutiérrez, is to find "new avenues for the transmission of the gospel message." The plurality of modern Latin America, forged to a large extent in the wake of 1492, is a major element in Gutiérrez's hope for the future; to exclude or denigrate any culture or people is to replicate and therefore extend the consequences of the original conquest. For Gutiérrez it is clear: "Racism is an assault on human dignity and Christian conscience."[49]

Surely there is no question today that racism is an assault on human dignity. But can it be asserted after this history, which Gutiérrez recounts so movingly, that racism is an assault on Christian con-science? In his work on Job and Las Casas, Gutiérrez painstakingly builds an argument for an alternative religious and Christian witness. By probing prophetic protest and witness in detail and with attention to the ambiguities of life and faith—by probing the cry of Job and the transformation of Las Casas—Gutiérrez avoids pious assertion and programmatic declaration. For Gutiérrez, Christian life is a journey through history in which issues arise that challenge assumptions. On the journey the Christian vocation is tested and evolves over time. One can see this in Gutiérrez's own meditation and writings; while main-taining essential sensibilities, the distance from *A Theology of Libera-tion* to *Las Casas* is great. One wonders, then, at the inability to ques-tion evangelization at its core, for it was this initial evangelization that helped destroy Gutiérrez's own people, the native people of Peru. What is it, if not the 500 years of continuing evangelization, that has helped to legitimate and extend this destruction and poverty? Were Gutiérrez's ancestors lacking something essential in their life and cul-ture that somehow the message of the gospel supplies? Was it possible then, and is it possible today, to evangelize without military, econom-ic, cultural, and religious conquest?

Gutiérrez seems to confirm, albeit unintentionally, Malcolm X's view that the European Christian conquers with the gun *and* the Bible, leaving behind a trail of devastation where life and possibility can only be articulated in the conquerors' language and religion. Since a central aspect of Christian history and evangelization has been racist, it is unlikely that a Christianity of the poor and the oppressed will be allowed to flourish—that is, become empowered. Is the entire thrust of evange-lization found in the hope expressed in Paul's letter to the Philippians, that every knee should bend to Jesus Christ, an inherent violence against cultures and peoples? And does this continue today in the ongoing evan-gelization of Africa, Asia, and the former Soviet Union?

A Negotiated Surrender

One can see in the later Gutiérrez the attempt to hold together the world which has conquered and the world of the conquered, as if by accepting a division of this world the Christian faith will dissipate and the suffering of the poor increase. At one level, this decision is strate-gic, for it may be possible to use the symbols of the powerful for the benefit of the poor. Yet it is also true that this strategy may render impotent the demands for empowerment. The universalist symbolism of the Christian message makes it difficult, almost impossible, to maintain a particular subversive understanding of Christianity. Is it possible to hold to Cone's initial sense of authentic Christians being Black in America, or Gutiérrez's sense of Christ being among the dispossessed of Latin America, without being pulled back by the institutional power of the church and the symbolic power of universalism in the Christian ethos?

For Cone and Gutiérrez the quest for unity may be strategic. But it may also involve the difficulty of imagining themselves as Christians while holding to a strict division between those who claim to be Christian, the powerful, and those who are authentic Christians, the powerless. In the long run, however, do Cone and Gutiérrez really believe that the powerful church will do anything but usurp, transform, and even destroy the particularity of the peoples from which they come and for whom they speak? Cone and Gutiérrez may understand at a subconscious level that only Christians flourish in Christian civilization, and that survival is predicated on the appeal to dominant Christians to expand their universe of inclusion. Appealing to division may call down further calamity onto the dispossessed.

A shared Christian language and symbolic universe may seem a ticket of entry into the world of the dominant as a promise of basic security. Historically speaking, it was the basic "inclusion" of Africans and Latin Americans that prefaced their dispossession; despite its language of inclusion, evangelization was, at its most fundamental level, a rite of exclusion. For with Christianization, native peoples were deprived of their world only to enter a world where they did not belong and from which there was no escape. In short, they entered a void. Do Cone and Gutiérrez think that the rite of exclusion, the Christianization of Africans and Latin Americans, will one day become the avenue of inclusion? And finally, what kind of inclusion could this be? Cone seems to sense this in his comment that all people, white and Black, can exclude and exploit the poor. Do these African Americans who exploit—that is those who have been admitted to the system—articulate their success in the same Christian language and symbolism, albeit nuanced and modernized, as those who blessed the slave ships? On this point, of course, Jewish leaders and theologians must be very careful, for Jews have successfully used the same strategy—that is, appealing to the dominant Christian ethos for status, security, and affluence. The evangelization that Jews refused at great cost has been accepted by

Jews today without officially changing religious affiliation. James Baldwin recognized this decades ago when he noticed the Christianization of the Jewish people even as Jews protested their particularity.

But it is not simply the acceptance of a viewpoint—an evangelical sensibility—which helped in the destruction of the world and the people from whom Gutiérrez descends. His own defense of what is left is disciplined in the public realm by those who are heirs to the conquerors. Like Cone's later work, Gutiérrez's fifteenth anniversary edition of the English translation of *A Theology of Liberation* is sobering. Numerous changes are made: an instructive example is that the entire section "Christian Brotherhood and Class Struggle" has been rewritten. As Gutiérrez notes, this section "gave rise to misunderstandings that I want to clear up. I have rewritten the text in the light of new documents of the magisterium and by taking other aspects of the subject into account." The new section is largely taken up with citations and quotes from John Paul II's encyclical *Laborem Exercens*. Though Gutiérrez's essential points are retained, the strategy is now defensive. The authority which has done so much to usurp, reorient, and even destroy liberation theology is used to authenticate the once dynamic and still salient discussion of class in society and church.[50]

Though one might argue the alternatives to the continuing acceptance of the religion of the conqueror, at the same time one can admire the beauty of the language used to defend the defenseless. That this language is disciplined and usurped, that even the courageous bow before the strength of the Christian symbolic and institutional universe, is perhaps simply the fate of the historic journey of defeated peoples. Still the question remains for Jews and oppressed Christians whether the strategic opening to the dominant leads to a liberation worth bequeathing to those who come after, or whether participation in that universe will rescue the terminal belief, only to haunt future generations?

3

In the Shadow of Christian Life

Atrocity and the Concentric Tradition of Reading

On April 7, 1994, Pope John Paul II officially honored the memory of the Jewish victims of the Holocaust at a Vatican ceremony. The ceremony was in the form of a concert and featured the music of Max Bruch and his variations on "Kol Nidre," an 1881 composition for cello and orchestra that evoked the solemnity of Yom Kippur, the Jewish Day of Atonement, as well as Leonard Bernstein's "Kaddish," a musical meditation on the Jewish prayer for the dead. Richard Dreyfus, the Hollywood actor, recited the Kaddish to Bernstein's music; Howard Nevison, the cantor of Temple Emanu-El in New York, intoned in Hebrew the 92nd Psalm, "O Lord, it is good to give thanks," to a composition written by Franz Schubert in 1826 for the dedication of a synagogue in Vienna.

It was the first time in history that the memory of the Jewish victims of the Holocaust had been officially honored by the Vatican. And it was dramatic, for just as "Kol Nidre" was performed, the pope entered the room accompanied by the chief rabbi of Rome, Elio Toaff, and the president of Italy, Oscar Luigi Scalfaro. The equality of both faiths was emphasized by a simple gesture: the pope and the chief rabbi sat on identical gilt and brocade thrones. John Paul II spoke briefly: "The candles lit by some of the survivors seek to demonstrate symbolically that this hall has no narrow limits, but that it contains all the victims: fathers, mothers, sons, brothers, friends. In our memory they are all present. They are with you; they are with us." Rabbi Toaff, who did not speak at the concert, released a statement citing the pope's effort to commemorate the Holocaust as "much appreciated by the Jews" and that the concert "assumes a significance that goes beyond that of a simple artistic event." The event elicited much emotion. As the Kaddish was read the pope was visibly moved; many in the hall wept openly.[1]

The Vatican ceremony took place just months after the "Fundamental Agreement between the Holy See and Israel" was completed— an agreement of mutual recognition and exchange of Vatican and Israeli diplomatic personnel. Among other items, the agreement contained sections on the freedom to worship, protection of shrines and churches, and a condemnation of historic and contemporary anti-Jewishness. The latter is discussed in the text: "The Holy See takes this occasion to reiterate its condemnation of hatred, persecution, and all other manifestations of anti-Semitism directed against the Jewish people and individual Jews anywhere, anytime, and by anyone. In particular, the Holy See deplores attacks on Jews and desecration of Jewish synagogues and cemeteries, acts which offend the memory of the victims of the Holocaust, especially when they occur in the same places which witnessed it." At a press conference before the signing of the agreement, Israeli Deputy Foreign Minister Yossi Beilin noted that behind the agreement was a history "full of hatred, fear, and ignorance" with "very few years of light and many more years of darkness." Beilin posed rhetorically the question whether there was room for reconciliation and answered that it is not for the present generation to determine: "Can we ignore the memories of so many years? No. This would be wrong." Monsignor Claudio Maria Celli spoke of the agreement as historic with fundamental religious and spiritual significance, mentioning the paragraph condemning anti-Jewishness and the Israeli-Palestinian accord signed earlier in the year, but prescinding from a recitation of church history in relation to Jewish people. For Beilin, the moment was hopeful and awkward as a chapter in Jewish suffering seemed to close. For Celli, the moment was pragmatic; a confessional tone and context was avoided.[2]

Just a year earlier in October 1992, the pope traveled to Santo Domingo to open the Fourth General Conference of Latin American

Bishops. Speaking on the 500th anniversary of Columbus' journey to the Americas, he thanked God for the ability to celebrate, together with the bishops and the Christians of Latin America, the "planting of the Church, which has furnished the New World with such abundant fruits of holiness and love during these five centuries." John Paul II continued: "With the coming of the gospel to the Americas, the history of salvation expands, the family of God grows and multiplies .... In the peoples of the Americas, God has chosen for himself a new people whom he had brought into his redemptive plan and made sharers in his Spirit." The pope then thanked God for the "throng of evangelizers" who gave their lives to evangelize peoples who did not yet know the message of Jesus, "some of whom even offered human sacrifices to their Gods." The lives of these missionaries gave witness to the "humanity that results from the encounter with Christ." Quoting Hebrews 11:12, the pope expressed gratitude for those who, by their witness and preaching, opened countless men and women to the "grace of Christ," multiplying Christians like "the stars in the sky and as countless as the sands on the seashore."[3]

Gratitude to the evangelizers who followed Columbus could be appropriately shown in the task of the new evangelization called for by Pope John Paul II. The agenda for the bishops' conference was to trace guidelines for an evangelizing activity that "will place Christ in the heart and on the lips of all Latin Americans" and to make the "truth about Christ and the truth about the human being penetrate even more deeply into all strata of society and transform it." John Paul II's opening of the bishops' conference reiterated aspects of his address in the city of Higuey in the eastern interior of the Dominican Republic. Preaching in Spanish, he spoke in moving language: "Since that far off 1514, the watchful and loving presence of Our Lady of Altagracia has continuously accompanied the beloved children of the whole nation, causing the *immense wealth of Christian life* to flourish in their hearts through the light and grace of her divine Son.... We are celebrating, dear brothers and sister, *the arrival of the message of salvation on this continent*."[4]

Like the agreement signed between Israel and the Vatican, missing from this address was any substantive confession or critical understanding of Christianity's role in the conquest. In the opening address to the bishops, the pope refers to the controversy over 1492 by asserting that the Catholic church has been a "tireless defender of the Indians, a protector of the values present in their cultures, and a promoter of humane treatment in the face of abuses of sometimes unscrupulous colonizers." In a message to indigenous people titled "Forgive All Who Wronged You," John Paul II asserts that the church has always been at the side of the indigenous people through her religious, priests, and bishops and therefore knows the people's suffering: "In this fifth centenary, how could she possibly forget the enormous suffering inflicted on the peoples of this continent during the age of conquest and colonization! In all truth there must be a recognition of the abuses committed due to a lack of love on the part of some individuals who did not see their indigenous brothers and sisters as children of God, their Father." Las Casas is mentioned here as he was at Higuey, along with the intriguing comment made by the pope at the bishops' conference: "The data of history show that a valid, fruitful, and admirable labor of evangelization took place, thereby opening the way to the truth of God and the human being in the Americas—so much so, indeed, that the evangelization itself became a kind of tribunal for holding accountable those responsible for such abuses."[5]

There was indeed a tribunal which discussed, debated, and even eventually accepted the humanity of Native Americans. That is, Native Americans were ultimately deemed fit for the evangelization mission of the church—for the "wealth" of Christian life. Was this tribunal itself a sign of victory that legitimated in more liberal language a process that destroyed the religions and cultures of peoples who are now counseled to forgive? Was the Vatican ceremony honoring the victims of the Holocaust another sign of victory that imposed a decorum on the dead and an obligation of silence on the living? Perhaps the beautiful music, the gilt and brocade thrones, serve as another place of renewal, even rescue, from the questions that now haunt European Christians and the Jewish people. One wonders if Native Americans are welcome to tell their story at the Vatican, to equate if you will, the travails of their Christianization, as a forerunner and as a warning to the Jews of Europe. Or if Palestinians were welcome at the signing of the agreement between the Vatican and Israel, to tell their story and to convene a tribunal that implicates both Christian and Jew in the occupation of Palestine. No doubt it is easier to obligate silence than to do penance while seated on gilt and brocade thrones. It is easier to exclude the victims of power while speaking of their inclusion.

The ceremonies, agreements, and speeches were shadowed, indeed haunted, by the faces of Native Americans, African Americans, Palestinians, Tagalogs, and other struggling people around the world, whose tribunal is history and whose story threatens to disrupt even the most solemn of ceremonies at the highest level of Christian and Jewish life. Perhaps Walter Benjamin's understanding, that there is no document of civilization which is not at the same time a document of barbarism, is important here. Just as such a document is not free of barbarism, Benjamin believed that barbarism also taints the manner in which the document is transmitted from one owner to another. In relation to Auschwitz, 1492, and the Palestinians, perhaps it can be said with Benjamin that there is no assertion of religion and religious life, no tribunal, agreement, or ceremony, no ecumenical dialogue *ex post facto* that is free of its origins—that is, free of its barbarism. When the historical event is over, we are left with speeches and agreements that again silence the victims, even and especially as the victors preach about the immense wealth bequeathed to them.[6]

Gospel of Treblinka/Book of Palestine

It is here that we reencounter that George Steiner's understanding and definition of the Jewish people as participating in a concentric tradition of reading. In Steiner's view, the continual reading of the primary texts of a tradition and the evolution of interpretative texts that comment on the primary texts are crucial in defining the journey of a people. In Judaism, the primary text is the Torah, while the interpretive texts include the Babylonian and Palestinian Talmud. Over the years other texts—Steiner labels these satellite texts—are written as interpretations of the Torah and Talmud and the life of the people which has grown up around them. The continual reading of and commentary on these texts help open a path for the ongoing development of a people. Steiner's vision of the Jews is found within this dialectic of reading and writing, rereading and rewriting of questions and meaning found in the origins of a people and creatively probed over the millennia. The concentric tradition of reading is the constant interplay, elaboration, and development of a people's history through the written and spoken word. No matter how far away in time and geography, the center remains; interpretation revolves around that center even when the language of articulation or the images employed seem distant. The center is the power, that which sends us on the way, but it is also the place to which we return. What appears remote is actually an unacknowledged elaboration of our origins.

The present and future are already latent in the original act of revelation. For Steiner, neither the scattering of the Jews nor the passage of time abrogates the authority or meaning in the primary texts that are affirmed as holy, so long as these are read and surrounded by a series of interpretive and satellite texts. It is these satellite texts that ensure that the past is not relegated to oblivion or a liturgical obscurity. The satellite texts are crucial. They keep alive the holy and interpretive texts, which as time passes become more difficult to identify with in an immediate way. Because these satellite texts maintain a tradition of reading and rereading, the primary texts are also kept alive so that they might in the future "yield existential applications and illuminations of spirit as yet unperceived."[7]

The Jewish people inherit and continue a discussion which has an origin and a destiny. It comprises a series of readings and interpretations that contain themes, arguments, questions, possibilities, and sufferings clustered in a stream of history. Of course, this is true also of the history of Christianity, for that history can also be seen as emanating from readings of a primary text, the New Testament, surrounded by interpretive and secondary satellite texts such as the works of Augustine of Hippo, Thomas Aquinas, and Martin Luther. Hannah Arendt, Richard Rubenstein, Elie Wiesel, and Steiner himself can be seen within the context of a Jewish concentric tradition of reading, as Jürgen Moltmann, James Cone, and Gustavo Gutiérrez can within a Christian concentric tradition of reading. One wonders if the typical separation of Jew and Christian, by virtue of whether one refuses or accepts belief in the messianic mission of Jesus the Christ, is less important than an evolving shared concentric tradition of reading, which begins with a common book and from there develops a diverse and common trajectory.

The difficulty in recognizing this shared tradition has much to do with the history of each community and the interaction between them over time. Here Steiner's understanding of the textual aspect of Jewish and, by extension, Christian life is instructive. Steiner sees the Jewish holy book, indeed the interpretative and satellite texts, as essentially innocent: "Reading, textual exegesis, are an exile from action, from the existential innocence of praxis, even where the text is aiming at practical and political consequence. The reader is one who (day and night) is absent from action." It seems as if the tradition and the reader at different moments transcend, are absent from, or are acted upon by history, but rarely participate in it. At the same time, the tradition is central to the significant history that the commentator inherits and continues. The text almost becomes part of an otherworldly history.[8]

But is this concentric tradition of reading innocent? Are the texts within the tradition innocent? Is the reader absent from action as the texts seem to be absent from history? Steiner is clear on the problematic of modern literature and contemporary history, as we who come after know that a person reading Goethe or Rilke in the evening can work at Auschwitz during the day. The ability to read Goethe and work at Auschwitz creates an almost unimaginable breach in Christian civilization. In fact, it is the actual history, the practice of Auschwitz in the morning after the nightly reading of Goethe, that makes reading of Goethe after Auschwitz so difficult. Steiner does not propose that Goethe leads to Auschwitz, though the reading of Goethe and the practice of Auschwitz suggest a possible connection between the habits of high literacy and the temptations of the inhuman. Steiner asks whether boredom and abstraction within literate civilization prepare it for the release of barbarism. Yet another question seems to be even more relevant and disturbing: Is it possible that within the concentric tradition of reading is a barbarism which erupted into Auschwitz and that barbarism is located within the tradition rather than outside of it?

Certainly those who have interpreted the holy texts have been culpable in the numerous eruptions of barbarism throughout history. One example is the relationship between Nazism and Christianity found in the Institute for the Study and Eradication of Jewish Influence on German Church Life. Founded in 1939, the institute became the central organ for producing Christian anti-Semitic propaganda in support of Nazi government policies and received support from churches, pastors, and theologians throughout Germany. The Nazis wanted a *Judenrein* Germany; the institute's purpose was to produce a *Judenrein* Christianity. Walter Grundmann, a professor of New Testament at Jena and the institute's academic director, articulated the institute's goal as exposing and ending Jewish influence on all aspects of German life, including in the realm of religion and the church. The basis for much of the institute's analysis revolved around the New Testament texts which, at least in the eyes of Grundmann, saw Jesus reviling the Jews, rejecting Judaism, and even suggesting the elimination of both Jews and Judaism. It is Susannah Heschel's view as a historian of the Nazi period that without calling for the murder of Jews, Grundmann made it clear that Christianity originally arose to eliminate Judaism and therefore Christians had a theological mandate to accept and participate in Nazi measures against the Jews. Since Grundmann's work provided a Christian justification for Nazi anti-Semitism, a reader of

Grundmann's work could conclude that the Holocaust did not violate Christian tenets but in fact fulfilled them. As Heschel writes: "If Jesus had come to destroy Judaism, the Nazis were acting as *imitatio Christi*. Nazism may be seen today as an anti-Christian movement, standing in dialectical relation to Christianity, just as medieval Satanism stood toward the Mass of Catholicism, but for certain Christian theologians during the Third Reich, the destruction of the Jews was the ultimate Christian act."[9]

The history of the use of Christian texts to legitimate barbarism clearly precedes the twentieth century. The *Requerimiento*, a document to be read to the leaders of any nation or village the Spanish conquistadors encountered, demanded that all accept the authority of the Spanish crown. Ostensibly a political document, it begins with a theological treatise about God. The document unfolds in a logical manner. God anoints Christ as absolute Lord over the world. Christ then bequeaths this lordship to the pope; the pope in turn gives these lands to the Spanish crown. Native Americans are invited to submit to their new masters, with the proviso that the penalty for refusing to submit will be harsh. As rebellious subjects, those who reject Spanish sovereignty legitimated by the church and by Christ are declared proper objects of a just war. The Spanish are free to wage war against the resistors, confiscate their land, and enslave them. Clearly the function of the document was less to convince the Native Americans—after all, the document was read in Spanish and at such a great distance from the people that they could not even hear, let alone understand it—than it was to convince the conquistadors that what they were doing was legally and religiously justified.[10]

Many Christians prefer to see this *Requerimiento* as a hypocritical document used simply for conquest rather than believed in as authentic and religious. It is important to remember, however, that the Spaniards believed their conquest to be holy, deserving and receiving support from God and Christ. Today it is common knowledge that the conquistadors were greedy and cruel, that they lusted after gold, that they often enslaved and decimated the native inhabitants of the Americas. But a central point—that these conquistadors were Christians who thought themselves on a Christian mission—is often denied. Certainly the adventurers most remembered in history—Christopher Columbus, Hernando Cortéz, and Francisco Pizarro—felt that they had been chosen by God for their mission. Columbus thought that he was being guided by divine providence; Cortez was admired for his religiosity and scrupulous attention to prayer and devotions. The last action of Pizarro, who some historians believe to be the cruelest of the conquistadors, was to draw a cross with his own blood so that he could die with the cross before him.[11]

That Columbus, Cortéz, Pizarro, and Grundmann were sincere Christians, who read themselves, who were read to by others, and who promulgated by the sword and, no doubt, inspirational preaching, the holy texts as they interpreted them, places barbarism within the concentric tradition of reading. For how can those who read these texts today be deaf to the cries of the subjugated or to the fact that these cries emanate from inside the tradition rather than outside of it? Indeed, the question of how one reads Goethe in the evening and works at Auschwitz in the day extends to how one reads the New Testament in the evening and in the morning participates in the decimation of the native peoples.

This is true for the holy texts within the Jewish world as well. A recent use of these texts relates to the Hebron massacre. Just a month after the massacre, more than 10,000 Jews came to the grave of Baruch Goldstein and, as Clyde Haberman, a reporter for the the *New York Times*, observed, many of them bowed deeply to kiss the tombstone and proclaim him a holy man: "Whether young or old, wearing the knitted yarmulkes of modern Orthodox Zionists or the black suits of the Hasidim, they approached the burial mound, surrounded by stones placed in mourning, as though it were a shrine." Another reporter, Wendy Orange, found Hasidim dancing and singing "Goldstein our *moshiach*, our *moshiach*." Many of the crowd of mourners were crying, praising Goldstein: "Our martyr, our saint, our holy man." In sight of Goldstein's grave were graffiti, most of it quoting Psalm 149: "To execute vengeance upon the Gentiles." Next to these was the slogan, "Death to the Arabs." Just days before, a group of 200 rabbis gathered at Goldstein's settlement, Qiryat Arba, and promulgated a religious ruling that soldiers must disobey any order to remove Jews from Hebron or other parts of the territories. Among the rabbis was former Ashkenazic Chief Rabbi of Israel, Abraham Shapira, who ruled that the Torah "forbids evacuation from parts of the Land of Israel. You must refuse it as you would refuse an order to eat pork."[12]

Long before the rise of the religious right in Israel, however, Jews also used holy texts to support acts of barbarism. The sermon of Rabbi Morris Raphall, delivered at the B'nai Jeshurun synagogue in New York City on January 4, 1861, is an example of Jewish religious support for slavery. In the sermon Raphall not only supported slavery with sources from the Hebrew Scriptures, he essentially called for the excommunication of Jewish abolitionists:

> How dare you in the face of the sanction and protection afforded to slave property in the Ten Commandments—how dare you denounce slaveholding as a sin? When you remember that Abraham, Isaac, Jacob, Job—the men with whom the Almighty conversed, with whose names he emphatically connects His own most holy name, and to whom He vouchsafed to give the character of "perfect, upright, fearing God and eschewing evil"—that all these men were slaveholders, does it not strike you that you are guilty of something very little short of blasphemy?

Rabbi Raphall was more than a local rabbi; he was the highest-paid clergyman in America and the first rabbi to deliver the opening prayer at a session of Congress. His sermon was given extensive coverage by the New York press, and a prominent southern rabbi praised Raphall's sermon as the "most forceful arguments in justification of the slavery of the African race." No doubt Christians in favor of slavery welcomed a Jewish confirmation, as did a number of Jews who during the nineteenth century actively traded in slaves, ran slave markets, and owned slaves. Rabbi Isaac M. Wise, another prominent rabbi, criticized those members of the Protestant clergy who opposed slavery:

> Who in the world could act worse, more extravagant and reckless in this crisis than Protestant priests did? . . . The Protestant priests threw the firebrand of abolitionism into the very heart of this country. . . . You know who made Jefferson Davis and the rebellion? The priests did, and their whiners and howlers in the press. The whole host of priests would rather see this country crushed and crippled than discard their fanaticism or give up their political influence.[13]

Surely it can be said that readers of the Jewish texts are able to justify the dispossession of Palestinian land and the slavery of African peoples, just as readers of the Christian texts can justify Auschwitz and 1492. But it is not simply justification after the fact that is problematic; it is the force of theological argument to accompany or even instigate this brutality. If Christians should not be able to read their texts without the shadow of Auschwitz and 1492, then Jewish texts are likewise shadowed by the suffering of Palestinians and African Americans. Still one wonders how these texts and the carriers of these texts come to the justification of atrocity, occupation, and slavery. Those interested in the renewal of Judaism and Christianity cite these justifications as misinterpretations and aberrations. Did not other readers, Jewish and Christian, come to different conclusions, that is oppose 1492, slavery, Auschwitz, and the occupation of Palestine?

Clearly the answer is complex because the responses to these texts have varied. Yet the tendency is to dismiss what characterizes the mainstream of Christianity or Judaism as aberrational while upholding the exceptions as the center of the tradition. Too often the barbarism that Jews and Christians have benefitted from is repressed or elevated as a gift that the victim is seen as lucky to have received. As the Jewish writer and activist Roberta Strauss Feuerlicht reminds us, Jewish memory in relation to African Americans is short and mythologized: "Historically, the relationship between Jew and Black in America has not been one of equality. Jews were traders and masters; Blacks were merchandise and slaves and servants. In America there is no record of a Black who traded in Jews or of a Black who owned Jews; I doubt there are any Black housewives who have a Jewish 'girl' come in one day a week to clean. Where Blacks were available, neither Jews nor any other whites touched bottom." For Jews, the relationship between African American and Jewish history begins in the civil rights movement of the 1960s, while the Jew as beneficiary of slavery and whiteness is rarely mentioned. It is this same suppression of memory and mythology of goodness which allow the pope to declare that 500 years of misery should be understood as the beginning of salvation for the continent of Latin America.[14]

The ability to repress the barbarism and mythologize the gift is connected with the texts themselves and the way certain texts are privileged. Clearly the Hebrew Scriptures and the New Testament are not innocent. Like other texts, they arise within a history of struggle, hope, deceit, generosity, and murder. Yet a prior question is why the history that followed these texts—including, for example, the Holocaust and the treatment of Palestinians—are not themselves seen as texts which are defining and, from the moment of their inception, to be read, interpreted, and meditated upon. Have these texts become part of the tradition of concentric reading? Below are two texts which can be seen in this light, the first a reading from what might be called the gospel of Treblinka, in the form of an interview with the wife of the commandant of Treblinka; the second a reading from what might be called the book of Palestine, reported by Doron Meiri in the Israeli newspaper *Hadashot*, February 24, 1992:

A Reading from the Gospel of Treblinka

And now I began to see the terrible change in him. No one else saw this. And I too had only glimpses; occasional glimpses of another man, somebody with a different, a totally changed face; someone I didn't know; that face that you too saw later, in the prison—red, suffused, swollen, protruding veins, coarse—he who was never coarse or vulgar, who was always loving and kind. I asked him again and again, "Paul, why are you still there? It's a year now, more than a year. All the time you said you'd manage it, you'd wrangle a transfer." "Paul," I'd say, "I'm afraid for you. I am afraid for your soul. You *must* leave. Run away if must be. We will come with you, anywhere."

I could no longer be with him . . . you know . . . near him. It was quite terrible, for both of us. We were staying in the mountains with this friend of my mother's, a priest, Father Mario; she had arranged for us to stay there, for our holiday. And one day I couldn't stand it any longer; I no longer knew where to turn, I *had* to talk to somebody. So I went to see Father Mario. I said, "Father, I must talk to you. I want to talk to you under the seal of the confessional." And I told him about Treblinka. I said, "I know you won't believe it but there is this terrible place in Poland and they are killing people there—they are killing the Jews there. And my Paul," I said, "my Paul is there. He is working there. What shall I do?" I asked him. "Please tell me. Please help us. Please advise us."

You see, I thought—I suppose—the priests had ways; there were convents up in the mountains where one could disappear, hide—I had heard things.

He gave me such a terrible shock. I remember, he brushed his face with his hand and then he said, "We are living through terrible times, my child. Before God and my conscience, if I had been in Paul's place, I would have done the same. I absolve him from all guilt."[15]

A Reading from the Book of Palestine

Blows with wooden sticks, strong kicks and electric shocks, especially on the genitals, are only some of the methods of interrogation used by a police investigation team which is active in the detention centers of Hebron, Ramallah and Jericho. The team, consisting of five policemen who use Arabic nicknames, was established one and half years ago . . . as "a team to interrogate stone-throwers." However, security sources claim, "In a short time the team became a brutal torture unit and through the methods which it had used obtained hundreds of false confessions from Arab detainees." Eight Palestinians from Hebron, aged from 14 to 23, who were detained recently on suspicion of participating in stone-throwing, have given sworn affidavits. . . . According to these affidavits, they were interrogated by torture by five men, who identified themselves as Lutfi, Nur, Zuheir, Samir and Sassi. The detainees testified that they were tortured by the use of electric shocks on their limbs and were also severely beaten on every part of their bodies with wooden sticks, hoses, broken bottles, karate-type blows, and fists. According to them, they were first bound by the police interrogators and put down on the floor, and then "the policemen played soccer with the detainee's body," or else "they played basketball with his head, while beating him and pulling him by the hair." Their eyelashes were burned by cigarettes. The interrogators repeatedly threatened to cut off their penises, put revolvers to their brows and interrogated them in the presence of a growling dog.

The same source adds, "Many people who work here are shocked by these methods. Many heard the shouts of the detainees during the night, and they even wept when the detainees were weeping, but were afraid to talk. . . . Once a soldier named Nissim Levy came to this base. One night he was the officer on duty, or had a similar task. During the night he was simply shocked when he heard the terrible shouts of the detainees. When he discovered why they were shouting, he began to shout too, "What, are we like [Nazi] Germany?"[16]

Perhaps these texts should be read in Jewish and Christian liturgies. Such readings might also lead to a more ecumenical sense of the tradition shared by Jews and Christians. One thinks of the ecumenical possibilities: the Gospel/Book of Slavery, the Gospel/Book of American Capitalism, and the Gospel/Book of Apartheid. Though in each of these events Christian participation has far outweighed Jewish contributions, the possibility of joint ventures increases over time. Though the numbers are not in balance because of demographic realities, Jews are now becoming instrumental in the ongoing nature of 1492.

The holy books are complex in their origin and in their trajectory. In the Hebrew Scriptures, for example, the oppressed flee, prophesy, and invade another land; invasion, expropriation, and slavery are legitimated, discussed, minimized, rejected. The Israelite society escapes poverty yet recreates it, just as it recreates the kingship it fled. The prophets judge poverty and kingship as both inadequate to Israel's calling. At the same time, however, they repress indigenous customs and religiosity, which they label idolatry. The creation of monotheism and the justice-oriented vision of the prophets, while widely celebrated, is similarly more complex than the text or its interpreters have allowed. Indeed, here the struggle over the interpretation of the text is preceded by a

struggle within the text itself. The textual interpretation of the Yahwis-
tic cult of the Israelites battling against the foreign Canaanite Gods of
Baal and Asherah—thus fighting a foreign syncretism which might
compromise the monotheistic cult of Yahweh—can be interpreted differently if one acknowledges that Baal and Asherah were part of Israel's
Canaanite heritage. The emergence of Israelite monolatry thus represents a break with its own Canaanite past and a triumph of the Yahwis-
tic cult as supreme and only God over the earlier, more inclusive worship of Yahweh, El, Asherah, and Baal. One can see this in the study of
the prophets Jeremiah, Ezekiel, and Isaiah, as they adopt a similar perspective: that the emergence of Yahweh as a singular God represents a
struggle within the Israelite nation and religion.[17]

Normative Judaism, which arose in the fourth century of the common era, and whose interpretation of the scriptural text has been
defining over the last 1500 years, is therefore heir to the triumph of
monotheism over popular religiosity, which could include, among
other things and without anxiety, the worship of Yahweh and the sun.
The rabbis, of course, enshrine the victory of their interpretation with
the label "advance," though this is clearly a retrospective assessment.
Can one argue against the Christianization of Latin America—that is,
the triumph of a certain form of monotheistic religion over indigenous
religions—without raising the triumph of monotheism in Judaism as,
among other things, a form of repression and injustice?

There are many struggles within the New Testament canon which,
though unresolved in themselves, are even broader when juxtaposed
to texts that were not admitted in the canon. The canonical Gospels,
too, emerge from certain figures or circles within the early Christian
movement, represent a series of choices, and emphasize certain stories
over others. The New Testament is hardly systematic and the gathering
of all the texts, including those excluded parts, yields a series of contradictory trajectories and future possibilities. The recollections and
reflections which become the Gospels are made in the wake of the early
Christian disappointment with the seeming failure of Jesus; the disappointment is in many cases filtered through a polemic with Jewish
leadership and movements. The disparities and plurality of views in
these texts are harmonized in creedal formulations during the Constantinian empire. Though the New Testament is read as the story of
Jesus, its Constantinian formation is enough to give one pause.[18]

The creedal formulations are solidified by imperial law in the fourth
century, which makes Judaism and various Christian groups pariahs.

The context of the formation of Christianity and the canonization of the New Testament is one of intra-Christian and Christian-Jewish controversy, mediated by empire. Constantine, seeking a unified Christianity as the Roman Empire's new religion, orders the Christian bishops to meet in Nicaea and resolve the theological disagreements between them. Even if one is not already disturbed at Constantine's involvement in church life, the description of the imperial banquet celebrating the Council of Nicaea's conclusion is startling: "Detachments of the body-guard and troops surrounded the entrance of the palace with drawn swords, and through the midst of them the men of God proceeded without fear into the innermost of the Imperial apartments, in which some were the Emperor's companions at table, while others reclined on couches arranged on either side. One might have thought that a picture of Christ's kingdom was thus shadowed forth, and a dream rather than reality." As biblical scholar John Dominic Crossan comments: "A Christian leader now writes a life, not of Jesus, but of Constantine. The meal and the Kingdom still come together but now the participants are the male Bishops alone and they recline, with the Emperor himself, to be served by others. Dream or reality? Dream or nightmare?"[19]

From this point on, empire is integral to Christianity. Rather than aberrational, expansion becomes a main theme of Christian life. At the heart of evangelical life is empire and conquest. These themes are already present in texts that become the New Testament, as normative Christianity is defined within the Constantinian empire and the empires that follow, including the empires formed in 1492. Surely while the New Testament itself cannot be blamed for 1492 and Auschwitz, it has been open to interpretations that legitimated these events. At the same time, the Hebrew Scriptures, which in themselves contain aspects of empire and conquest, are less forceful in worldly affairs by the community which canonized them because the Christian community, having usurped these texts, became powerful and oppressed the Jews. When Jews are empowered, however, as they are in the post-Holocaust world, these texts operate in much the same way as they do in Christianity, as texts to legitimate conquest and oppression. Here we are dealing strictly with the historical record rather than a theoretical construct of the beauty of the Jewish and Christian Scriptures and traditions. Is it possible today to read these texts without the haunting images of destruction and death carried out by the communities whose origins are in these texts? The external destruction is coupled with the internal struggle for hegemony, for the normative, which we now inherit as Judaism and Christianity. One wonders if the external thrust and internal struggle are somehow connected and whether the victims outside the traditions can be somehow bonded together with the victims inside of what becomes the normative traditions of Judaism and Christianity.

The Moral Core of Judaism and Christianity

The texts of Judaism and Christianity emerge from history, are defined within history, and also effect history. That is, the texts come from and are formed within, and help shape human experience. The claims within the texts are also formed and carried by the community in history. In this sense, history can verify or challenge the claims within the texts and the authenticity of their carriers. For every Jewish and Christian testimony there are counter-testimonies—in the text, in the community, in history. As feminist theologian Sharon Welch writes in relation to Christianity: "The atrocities of the Inquisition, the witch-burnings, the Crusades, the justification of imperialism and colonialism, the perpetuation of sexism, racism, anti-Semitism, the silence of most churches in the face of the horrors of war and the Nazi Holocaust should cause even the most committed Christian to question the truth of Christianity's claims." Gordon D. Kaufman, a Mennonite theologian, makes a similar point: "The central Christological symbols that emerged in the primitive Church have been used to authorize these evils and Christian symbolism, therefore, must bear some responsibility for them."[20]

Daniel Maguire responds to Welch and Kaufman not by denying their insights but by seeing the values of Judaism and Christianity as suffering a "rough birthing of ideals." As an ethicist, Maguire proposes to find the moral intelligence that "survives like winter wheat under the scandals of Jewish and Christian history and apply it to the contemporary public conversation." For Maguire, Jewish and Christian values are revolutionary and therefore subvert and reorient personal and societal foundations. These foundations include community, authority, status, the sacred, alienation, and power. His argument is that the original Jewish and Christian teachings accomplished such a revolution. They pioneered transtribal modes of community, sought to build community on the basis of shared ideals and commitments, and explored new forms of egalitarian and cooperative social authority. In doing so, Judaism and Christianity bonded the sacred to the moral and committed communal morality and politics to the abolition of poverty as the path to peace and justice. Further, they marked out gender and ethnic alienation as the prime target for sociomoral reformation.[21]

The prophets are at the heart of this revolution as "connoisseurs of conscience." They believe that history is permeated with divine concern, and that concern prompts their moral passion. The prophets speak out against poverty, relativize royalty, and experience the loneliness of truth-telling. The overall biblical testimony is persuasive for Maguire as well. Over against the Western understanding of justice, which includes avowed impartiality, private definition of property, individualistic definition of rights, and a static and conservative view of public life, the biblical view includes a bias in favor of the poor, a social definition of property, rights defined in terms of social solidarity and need, and an evolutionary and revolutionary view of public life. Still, to argue for this prophetic biblical relevancy in our time is difficult. For God is not the controlling symbol of modern life, and the traditions and theocentric language that have carried these insights are themselves suspect. Therefore to reassert the prophetic and biblical witness in this context is to affirm the commonality of theist and atheist in the moral passion for justice and peace. To be open to and influence both groups, Judaism and Christianity are to be seen as carriers of a "classic" sensibility that emphasizes the values of excellence, universality, and hope. According to Maguire, the Bible does what Aristotle, Immanuel Kant, Mohandas Gandhi, Elizabeth Cady Stanton, Carl Jung, and other pioneers of humanity have done: "Under varying formalities, all were probing the mystery of the human to the fullest extent of their reach, and all enjoyed a special and communicable success."[22]

If the moral core of Judaism and Christianity is compromised by the history of both religions and communities, Maguire's "rough birth" is extensive and ongoing 3000 years later. Can the fruits of this birth, which may be realized in the distant future, justify the pangs that the birth has elicited? Perhaps it is more realistic to see the birthing as tremendously problematic, because the core itself, including the prophets, is problematic. What the prophets helped to repress is no doubt as important as what they announced. The prophets whom Maguire analyzes and the vision that they and he affirm is the version of the priestly, Deuteronomistic vision of exilic Yahwism. There was in fact an alternative vision, a nonpriestly, non-Deuteronomistic, nonprophetic view of what Yahwism was, a view, for example, which allowed for the worship of other Gods along with Yahweh and which encouraged the worship of Yahweh through rituals condemned in the biblical text. Could the core of Judaism and Christianity be itself a form of domination that then extended its control over others, whereas the alternative core, less exclusive and less uniform, could have led somewhere else? Of course, it is possible, even probable, that this alternative core is itself ambivalent. Perhaps holding in tension those cores, rather than the victory of either, might have produced a different history.[23]

Yet Maguire's analysis provides an interesting perspective. The argument for the relevancy of the core of the religious traditions is defensive; it cannot be made from a theological standpoint nor from the supremacy of Judaism and Christianity as religions. Maguire does not argue for his view as dominant but as part of an ongoing public discussion that involves the Bible as a classic text among other classic texts, untouched, or only peripherally shaped, by the history of Judaism and Christianity. The theological inspiration for the texts and their carriers are for Maguire secondary because that inspiration can no longer maintain a self-evident legitimacy. In short, Maguire, as a Catholic Christian, must argue from a humanistic viewpoint. Still the tone is almost evangelical, as if these biblical and prophetic values are salvific for the modern world. As Richard Rubenstein points out, however, it is these same values—"the progressively intensifying night-side of Judeo-Christian civilization" found in, among other places, the land of the Reformation—that also facilitated the emergence of the world of the death camps. Can the moral core of a Judaism and Christianity, with its historical baggage jettisoned, reorient a society formed by the nightside of this self-same core and tradition? Despite his limited claims, Maguire still stands within the context of Christian renewal, attempting to rescue the tradition even as its claims atrophy.

Rosemary Radford Ruether also sees Judaism and Christianity as part of the classical Western tradition, but she provides a more critical perspective on its use in the modern world. For Ruether there is no question that the classical tradition has justified and sacralized domination. As a feminist theologian, she understands that the idea of the male monotheistic God has reinforced domination in many spheres, including that of men over women, humans over animals and the rest of creation. Yet as these classical traditions sacralized patriarchal hierarchy, they also struggled with injustice and sin and sought to create more just and loving relations among people, the earth, and the divine. Ruether is clear that even part of the effort to name and struggle against evil has often reinforced domination and created "victim-blaming" spiritualities and ethics. Still, a totally negative judgment against past biblical and Christian cultures is counseled against. Ruether writes that it would be surprising if there were no "positive insights that could be reclaimed from three thousand years of collective human struggle about the meaning of life and the way to live justly and well." Some of these insights are found in the covenantal and sacramental aspects of Judaism and Christianity, which stress accountability and the beauty of the earth. Ruether's discussion of the Western Christian tradition makes no claim to superiority or religious truth. Rather the tradition is discussed in terms of accountability, since her tradition and culture have shaped and continue to shape much of the world, especially in imperialist colonialism and neo-colonialism. For Ruether, the Western Christian tradition is the "major culture and system of domination that has pressed humans and the earth into the crisis of ecological unsustainability, poverty, and militarism we now experience."[24]

Whereas Maguire argues for the core of the classical tradition with little mention of God, Ruether is interested in redefining our understanding of God. Clearly the male sky God, who defines evil and metes out justice and retribution, is part of the problem of Judaism and Christianity. However, to those who seek a simple substitution of the sky God with the earth god, Ruether is clearly opposed, as she sees the danger of reverse scapegoating and simplistic assumptions about nature as originally paradisiacal. Rather, it is the meeting of these two voices—the voice of power and law speaking on behalf of the weak and the powerless, and the voice that speaks from the heart—which beckons us into communion. The first voice, that of the more traditional God, and the second, that of gaia, the living and sacred earth, are for Ruether our own voices: "Both of these voices, of God and of Gaia, are our own voices. We need to claim them as our own, not in the sense that there is 'nothing' out there, but in the sense that what is 'out there' can only be experienced by us in the strength and frailty of human existence. Through human agency we can intuit the source of life and that which lies behind the whole." For Ruether, the truth of our intuition is tested in our relationships and whether they bear the fruits of compassion or of enmity.[25]

Ruether moves beyond the theism/atheism categories of the God of history discussed by Richard Rubenstein and Elie Wiesel. And while she affirms with Maguire the overreaching, common importance of our humanity, she shifts the discussion of God into the relationship of humans to each other, the earth, and that which is beyond expression. The questions of suffering and God remain, though raised in the context of right relationship to each other. Here the intuitive sense of connectedness and blessing, of the beauty of life and the world, is motivation to overcome systems of domination which define a world of disconnectedness and evil. It is the realization of right relationship as a substratum of the classical tradition that allows Ruether to speak of Judaism and Christianity as part of the solution to the present crisis, rather than as an answer to the haunting question of mass death. Unlike Maguire, there is little evangelical thrust in Ruether's work, as the revolutionary core that Maguire sees as the heritage of Judaism and Christianity is seen by Ruether to be in a dialectical tension with itself. On the one hand, Judaism and Christianity spawn systems of domination; on the other hand, they contain hints of personal, social, and ecological healing.

Does Ruether's understanding of the interconnectedness of life, of striving for right relations with ourselves and the earth, respond to the sufferings of Auschwitz and 1492? Are there answers to the questions posed by those events in Ruether's concept of the voices of God and gaia being our own? If we accept these voices as authentic, does this silence the haunting accusations of Rubenstein and Wiesel? Does this analysis displace the responsibility of God, or was the responsibility for human suffering displaced on God? How does this understanding of God respond to the sufferings of African Americans and Latin Americans in the present? Do they need a patriarchal God—the thundering God of law and justice—to combat the other side of the patriarchal God—the God of conquest and retribution? Or do they all—Rubenstein, Buber, Wiesel, Cone, and Gutiérrez—in their heart of hearts actually agree with Ruether: that there is no sky God which delivers us and, though sin abounds, only we as persons and communities can experience and halt this sin.

One wonders if the healing of self, community, and the earth that Ruether proposes responds to the void, the terrible aloneness of mass destruction and death. In a meditation on the Yom Kippur service, Deborah Lipstadt finds the phrase *Toleh Eretz Al B'limah* (God suspends the earth over a void), part of a poem describing the power of God, raising this question: "In its simple four words it seemed to contain the theological challenge facing every believer in a post-Auschwitz world. How can we continue to believe when we know that not too long ago millions of people were allowed to fall into that void, never to emerge?" Within the context of that void, Lipstadt, herself a commentator on the Holocaust, sees the need to control the things that are in our hands, that is "how we live our lives, how we relate to one another, the good deeds we do, how we practice repentance, prayer, and charity in their broadest manifestations" because these things "help determine how we face that which is out of our control." To be sure, the mystery and void remain; the questions are unanswered. At the same time, Lipstadt believes that we must also turn to God, "reaching out to the one who has suspended us—not for an answer but for a moment of communion, of connection." If it is true that the hiding of God's face is stressed in Holocaust theology, Lipstadt also believes it is possible for us to hide our face from God: "We must let God in even as Job did in the depths of his bewilderment."[26]

With Ruether and Lipstadt the challenge moves from a warrior God of history who is responsible, available, and absent, to a solidarity of commitment and struggle within history, which may suggest another interpretation and approach to God. Both agree that the sources of tradition remain with us and at the same time are limited. These sources are neither self-evident nor self-fulfilling; however, they must be analyzed, sifted through, and approached. The total negation of the traditions is unnecessary and destructive, for they are part of our heritage and who we are. Negation is also paralysis, and that is why the human and divine must be approached again and anew, though sometimes in a halting manner. Neither for Ruether or Lipstadt is this relationship easy or able to cover over destruction and the void. It is less a militant assertion than a humble probing. Yet, especially for Ruether, the tradition itself is simply an opening, a window on an evolving world in which others have often failed but whose struggle might help us glean a future possibility. Perhaps Ruether and Lipstadt see the tradition as an attempt to gather the parts of the texts, the peoples, and the earth, who have been and are being thrust into the void as a way of remembering and asserting human possibility.

Atrocity and the Task of Theology

The German philosopher and social critic Theodore Adorno wrote that after the Holocaust there could be no poetry. George Steiner interprets this statement to mean that after the Holocaust eloquence is suspect, if not impossible. The issue, as both Steiner and Adorno realize, is more than poetry or eloquence, but whether God is available to us and whether we can speak about God. Is theology possible after Auschwitz and 1492, especially since theology was and is involved in both? Surely, there will always be theology, or rather theologies, of conquest, rescue, resistance, core values, mutual relatedness, and earth-healing. Over time, theology has moved from certainty to history, from proclamation to testimony, from salvation to resource. Perhaps when all is said and done we are left with the images of voice and void. Surely, theology, like poetry, has continued after Auschwitz and 1492. In the midst of suffering theology has been strident, elusive, explorative, strong, weak, haunting, and, yes, even at times eloquent.[27]

What perseveres is the search for God and relatedness. Steiner analyzes it this way:

> The density of God's absence, the edge of presence in that absence, is no empty dialectical twist. The phenomenology is elementary; it is like the recession from us of one whom we have loved or sought to love or one of whom we have dwelt in fear. The distancing is, then, charged with the pressures of a nearness out of reach, of a remembrance torn at the edges. It is this absent "thereness," in the death-camps, in the laying waste of a grimed planet, which is articulate in the master-texts of our age.[28]

Steiner is hinting here that the texts that we carry today, unlike the texts of old, can offer only glimpses of a reality beyond ourselves. The texts are not in themselves innocent, nor are they divorced from history. Because of this knowledge the concentric tradition of reading offers diminished possibility, views, tendencies, perhaps some clues. The danger of the post-Holocaust era is twofold: either continuing as if nothing happened or slipping into the void where connection is lost and the context for meaning and value atrophies. Systematic theologies conform to the former, just as a total rejection of theology ensures the latter.

The tendency of theology is to recreate a shattered universe of discourse and to rescue humanity from the void. In this way, the analysis of written memoirs of Holocaust survivors is applicable to theology and its attempt to systematize and therefore overcome the void. In these memoirs, one finds a strategy of style and imagery that seeks to ease the reader into an unfamiliar, almost unimaginable, world. The impulse to portray and refine reality through familiar and comforting literary devices seems irresistible. Lawrence Langer, who has written extensively on this subject, cites a memoir of a woman who describes the SS man who greeted her and her mother on the ramp at Auschwitz in this way: "His pale blue eyes dart from side to side like a metronome." In this description, Langer sees the "literary *transforming* the real in a way that obscures even as it seeks to enlighten." This effect is often true of theology: it tends to transform experience in a way that obscures even as it seeks to enlighten. That is why Pope John Paul II can speak of the immense wealth of Christian life and the message of salvation that has come to Latin America. It is also why Gustavo Gutiérrez's Job can find solidarity in unmerited suffering and hear God's voice as he sits on a dung heap. The words and images transform the reality itself, as immense wealth, even Job on a dung heap, are familiar to us. As we know the story of Job, its retelling lifts us from reality. The story of Job is easier to hear than it is to witness people on the outskirts of Lima or Cairo scavenging from the garbage dumps or literally living in them.[29]

Most oral, as opposed to written, Holocaust testimony portrays confusion, doubt, and moral uncertainty. Still, even in this testimony there is a longing to return to a vocabulary of redemption and salvation. It is a search for moorings in a universe so violated that old designations like tragedy and history lose their force. For Langer, these testimonies embody the issues of atrocity and barbarism, rather than proffer a resolution: "In them, the cherished voices of continuity, adaptation, and renewal speak with the authority of their absence, immersing us in a world whose inhabitants remain adrift even as they clamber ashore." The temptation is all too human and theological as well, for when knowledge leads to unflattering images of human nature, the temptation is to reclaim that nature rather than to confront the meaning of its dissolution.[30]

In the actual experience of conquest and mass death, one finds a world of doubt and disorder that the survivor has difficulty communicating. In fact, where oral testimony moves into written testimony an ordering takes place that often violates the experience itself. That is, language and the telling of story are an ordering and transformation that become intelligible and communicable to others outside the experience. But the ordering is shadowed by the inability to find a language to explain atrocity. "Sandwiched between a vocabulary ('redeeming' and 'salvation') that prods us away from the event toward a consoling future (a vocabulary, one might add, with a distinctly Christian flavor) lies the predicament of a son involuntarily sending his mother to her probable death." For Langer there may be a language *about* Auschwitz, but there has never developed a language *of* Auschwitz. There is no language to articulate a maternity infected by atrocity, for example, at least not a language that leaves the experience untampered with.[31]

Perhaps, then, we are left with theologies about conquest and Holocaust rather than theologies of the experience of both events. We can only testify to events that, in their brutality, undermine language and belief. Is it the task of theology to always come after, to collect, order, and articulate—and therefore transform—that which threatens to overwhelm human sensibility, including our sense of continuity and meaning? This process is clear in the theologians we have explored. In the early work of Cone and Gutiérrez, they wrestle Jesus away from those who claim him and place Jesus with those who are slaves and who are conquered. They seek to transform the experience of suffering into a victory, thereby ordering a situation of disorder and defeat. In their later work, Cone and Gutiérrez are humbled, and they suggest the suffering of their people as insights rather than salvation. Even here, however, an ordering is discernible. Malcolm X and Martin Luther King Jr. both horribly murdered, become martyrs in the struggle of a people; in Cone's work they become part of a tapestry he himself weaves. For Gutiérrez, Job is the ordering for a situation of suffering and disgrace. The shift in Gutiérrez's early work from Jesus to Job as center is instructive. Rather than a militant struggle and salvific presence, which Jesus represents, Job becomes a fellow sufferer who journeys with the people rather than saves them. Still, Job serves as a point of order. Job rescues the anonymous poor from what is—without theology—a meaningless death.

Cone and Gutiérrez as Christians reach in their own life what Rubenstein and Wiesel as Jews reach in theirs—the end of systematic theology. Ruether's work is encyclopedic in its reach and knowledge. It is inspired by a Christian commitment but also exemplifies this terminus when she declares that our relationship to each other and the earth is our destiny. The texts have been infected by atrocity and so has theology. Can we say about theology what Adorno and Steiner understood about poetry and eloquence, that there can be no systematic Jewish and Christian theology after Auschwitz and 1492? Still, if it is true that both Pope John Paul II and Gutiérrez transform the experience of suffering as they theologize, thus elevating chaos into order, they remain in different categories: to speak of the immense wealth of Christian life is to continue 1492 and participate in an ongoing conquest. To posit Job as a victim and survivor of the message of salvation is a covering which is also a form of resistance; it seeks to end 1492 by addressing the arena of salvation from a different perspective.

Yet here is the difficulty. Do Cone and Gutiérrez, while retaining the label Christian and functioning as Christian theologians, actually acquiesce or even help facilitate the conquest of their peoples? Las Casas is important here. Does Gutiérrez's affirmation of evangelization make him an accomplice with the pope's assertion? From a different perspective, a realistic question is whether Cone and Gutiérrez can afford at this moment in history to abandon the language and theology which has opened the void and, at least to some extent, covered it over. Is the ordering which is the conquest also the only means available to mitigate the effects of the conquest? If language and theology are infected with atrocity, it may be that resistance is infected as well.

The very language of conquest becomes inverted into the language of resistance. This is the other side of contracting colonialism, as the Spanish subjugation of Tagalog society demonstrates. If religious conversion was crucial to the consolidation of Spanish power in the Philippines by exercising a profound impact on the patterns of authority and submission in a colonial society, it also provided the Tagalogs with a language for understanding the limits of colonial and class domination. The idiom of religious conversion shaped the terms of native surrender just as it created a way of articulating popular resistance to a colonizing power. Here conversion is conceived dialectically. One's submission to and incorporation of the language and logic of Christianity is also the condition that allows for defining and overcoming of a state of subordination. Use of the oppressor's language and symbolic system is a way of avoiding annihilation and at least allowing the prospect of a negotiated surrender. Soon the original language is weakened to the point where it is unable to carry on the struggle, for there is no future inside of it. What is left is the oppressor's language which, when learned and adopted, can be transformed, if not into victory at least into an alternative history of surrender. As Vincente Rafael notes, this alternative history continues to exist within the Christian era, holding forth the possibility of a future realization of a religious, nationalist, and humanist uprising.[32]

Rafael's analysis is similar to that of Otto Maduro. He sees a refusal of dominant religious language as dangerous to a dominant religious power. That is, the language of religion used to oppress can become a form of resistance that can sometimes threaten that power. Maduro sees every religion as in permanent danger of the rise of the prophets. As a Latin American sociologist of religion, Maduro understands the prophets as religious agents involved in a "strategy of conquest of religious power, and capable of mobilizing significant sections of the church's public against the monopoly of religious power exercised by that church." A prophet makes innovations in the religious field, though not every innovation is prophetic. Maduro distinguishes between adaptive innovations (changes and corrections that tend to preserve the religious order) and subversive innovations (that subvert established religious order and thus promote political and cultural change). The strength of the established religious order is to dismiss what it can, coopt what it cannot dismiss, and transform the prophetic innovation into a renewed yet essentially unchanged system. Language is crucial here because, even as it is part of the hegemonic and the resistor, it establishes a bond that limits the horizon of possible change. A cycle is introduced wherein the prophetic, which seems to break with the system, actually renews it.[33]

This linguistic and sociological analysis raises the question of the task of the theologian, indeed the task of theology. Is the task of the theologian representing the victims of 1492 to use the language of conquest as a language of defense, a defense of the nonpersons who die before their time? In the broadest possible sense, the use of God-language by liberation theologians is a defense of human rights, anchoring that defense in a God now claimed by both the victor and the victim. But that language is shaped by a horizon that the conqueror bequeaths. This is what conversion in the Philippines has led to and what Maduro sees in the rise of the prophets: the renewal of the limited horizon even as some of the elements of that horizon are challenged. A defensive cycle is introduced, in which the challenge to unjust power is articulated in the very same language that unjust power is legitimated within. Is liberation theology destined to simply warn against the inevitable, plead against the continuation of barbarism or, at most, mitigate its most horrendous effects?

Holocaust theologians have avoided the language of the oppressor. Yet one wonders if this avoidance is possible only by the empowerment of the Jewish community and the appeal of Jews to Christians to support that empowerment. It is also true that post-Holocaust Jews have had Christian theologians do their bidding. In a sense, Jews have found their place in the Christian West insofar as in practice—that is in politics, intellectual endeavors, and culture—Jews have become "Christians," and insofar as Christian theologians have fought for Jews within the Christian symbolic and linguistic system. The prophetic critique that Jews offered to Christians has likewise been usurped by dominant Christian theologians as fuel for Christian renewal. Despite the rhetoric, Christian attention to the Holocaust has been centered on the renewal of Christianity, as a way of side-stepping the void that Jewish suffering introduces. The ecumenical deal with Christians allows Jews to dwell in a symbolic void even as Jews integrate into Western society and create a nation that displaces another people in the Middle East. Because Jews help fuel Christian renewal, the eruption of barbarism against Palestinians is left essentially unnoticed. Lipstadt can speak about the void that Jews face without mentioning the void Jews have created. Is it true, as many Jews believe, that the Jewish religious system is free to develop on its own, or is it also enfolded in the Christian symbolic and linguistic universe that Jews have joined? If liberation theology is an appeal to dominant Christian cultures in the language of human rights, then Holocaust theology is a language of integration into the Christian West. For Jews in the West, integration is a similar defense of human rights, especially when seen in the context of the Holocaust. But it is also more; it is the key to Jewish status and identity in a post-Holocaust Christian culture and therefore a place of protection from which security and affluence can be achieved. In a strange twist of fate, the emphasis on Jewish suffering is a key to the success of Jews in America.

It has been said that the task of the artist is never to avert his or her eyes. That is, the artist must always be vigilant and free, seeing what must be seen and integrating that sight into the artist's vision. Perhaps it is the task of the theologian to selectively avert her eyes so as to fight for the people and to continue on in spite of the void. Surely the use of Christian language to defend against the onslaught of Christianity is an aversion of the eyes, as is the discussion of the void in Jewish life while remaining silent on the Palestinian catastrophe. Of course, Jews becoming Christians without officially abandoning Judaism is a massive avoidance as well. After all the definitions and defenses, one wonders if theology is simply a way of asserting power, of surviving that power, thus continuing a cycle of deceit which has no end.

4
God of Life, God of Death

Renewal, Ecumenism, and the Debate without End

Who will heal the victims? For those who have experienced conquest and slaughter, the quest for healing remains. Often religion is seen as the place for that healing. The rise of the prophets, the defense of life, the survival of the people—these provide a minimum of continuity and retain the possibility of a future. Yet beyond these elements is a desire to be healed of the trauma of loss, dislocation, and death. Is the articulation of longing for that healing another task of theology? Like defense and survival, the possibility of healing is contextual. What would it take to heal Latin Americans, African Americans, Jews, and others around the world? Are the Christian and Jewish theologies explored earlier essentially pleas for justice and for healing? That would correspond with a practical criterion for theology offered by Richard Rubenstein. "Does [theology] deepen and help to clarify the individual's manifold insights about himself, his community, his religious and ethical values and his place in the timetable of life in such a way that he can realistically function with minimal conflict between his biological, psychological and cultural needs, his actions toward others, his beliefs, and his ultimate aspirations?" Theologians speak about God to better understand the human condition. If theology does not enhance our capacity for meaning, peace of mind, and love, it is misguided. In this definition the task of theology is separated from the question of God. What is within reach—a sensibility, a language, a culture—is what is available to human beings. The judgment is made without reference to the transcendent or, if the transcendent is invoked, it is done so without challenge.[1]

The paradox here is startling. Perhaps it is only within the language from which barbarism erupted that a healing can begin. In this way, the courting of Christian repentance by the Jewish community, illustrated by the outpouring that greeted the Vatican recognition of Israel in 1993 and the Vatican ceremony honoring the victims of the Holocaust in 1994, can be seen as a desire for security *and* healing. The oppressor opens the void and helps to cover the void; opportunism and a desire for rescue of the dominant joins, at least at times, with a profound reckoning. Or rather, a reckoning can be seen within and beyond the cynicism of regeneration without accountability. The language of the oppressed can be seen in this light as well. Announcing the end of rabbinic Judaism as self-evident because of the assault against the Jews and the inability of the tradition to prevent or minimize the assault, Rubenstein was, in Irving Greenberg's analysis, paradoxically pointing toward the rebirth of Jewish theology after the Holocaust. In responding to Rubenstein, Greenberg writes that only now is a "*believing* remnant entering the mainstream of life. Rubenstein and the new theologians are products of this process. The Auschwitz experience itself has stirred up the subterranean depths of Jewish life and religion, giving life even as it destroyed. The truth is that we are on the brink of a great theological flowering."[2]

Almost twenty-five years later Jonathan Sacks, a Jewish orthodox theologian, confirms what Greenberg prophetically predicted: that Jewish responses to the Holocaust reveal not only the divisions in Jewish thought, but also a new impetus toward unity. This unity revolves around a collective sense of peoplehood and the determination to survive. "Faced with its eclipse, the Jewish people has reaffirmed its covenant with history," Sacks writes in language strikingly similar to that of Emil Fackenheim. "We will never fully understand those dark biblical passages in which God turns His people towards life by the threat of death. Why must Jews endure suffering to remain a people? That, like the Holocaust, remains a mystery no prophet has ever fathomed. Like Jacob after his struggle, the Jewish people limps, still scarred by that encounter. But those who remain have like Jacob taken up the journey again, no longer seeking flight from fate but instead determined to survive as Jews." For Sacks, the state of Israel, diaspora Jewish activism, and a renewal of orthodox Jewish life, all express this fundamental affirmation. Jews have returned to be the people of the covenant, though this means struggling with God and with humanity.[3] Jewish renewal is varied and complex. Sacks, who recently became chief rabbi of the United Kingdom, and his predecessor, Immanuel Jakobovits, exemplify a modern orthodoxy which sees the covenant and Jewish law as binding and superseding the historical experience of Holocaust and Israel. While both events are discussed, the main emphasis is on the religious character of Judaism, which history can influence but not overwhelm. The language of Judaism—found in the Bible and the interpretive texts—remains intact; the texts are challenged by atrocity rather than infected by it.[4]

David Weiss, for example, sees the Holocaust as another in a series of sufferings the Jewish people have experienced. Though perhaps unprecedented in scope and certainly contravening behavior expected in the twentieth century, Jewish history is replete with suffering on a mass scale, Weiss argues, while Jews held firm to the original covenant. Entire Jewish communities have been devastated in the long course of Jewish history; these "earlier holocausts" have affected Jews in the same way as the destruction of the Nazi era. To Weiss it seems theologically absurd to hold that the elimination of Judean, Rhineland, or southeastern European Jewry in previous centuries was any more acceptable or challenging than the most recent disaster. "Is the vision of an infinite God who is Guardian of Israel less shaken by the annihilation of only a million Jews at the hands of the Romans, of only several hundred thousand each by crusaders, cossacks, haidamuks, than by the six million dead in German Europe?" For Weiss, a God who differentiates between one and six million is not the God of Judaism. At the same time, Judaism has survived in the face of this suffering before the Nazis and will after them precisely because Jews did not and will not deny God and the covenant.

Indeed, as with other disasters, the Holocaust demands a "searching, penetrating, reaffirmation of faith and commitment," from the Jewish people. Those who propose a new covenant or write of a new epoch are, in Weiss' view, "closing . . . the book on Judaism." Whatever their sincerity or loyalty, the "prophets of the new covenant call not to revitalization, but to the denial of the God of Israel and annulment of the Jews' *raison d'être* in the world." Clearly, Weiss is referring to Richard Rubenstein but also to Elie Wiesel and Emil Fackenheim. For

Weiss, the covenant is irrevocable and the new theologies will be remembered in Jewish history as tragic aberrations. Though they will not halt the history of the Jewish people, by denying the essential affirmation of Judaism they will add to the attrition of Jews from Judaism and Jewish practice.[5]

Paradoxically, Judith Plaskow, who argues for the renewal of Jewish life through a feminist revolution of inclusion, a revolution that Sacks, Jakobovits, and Weiss would find quite difficult to accept, joins them in the minimalization of Holocaust and Israel. In her writing, Plaskow leaves the Holocaust virtually untouched, while the state of Israel is minimally discussed. For Plaskow, the embrace of Judaism is made difficult by patriarchal language and practice rather than the challenges of mass death and statehood. Her embrace of a Jewish feminist identity grows out of an understanding that "sundering Judaism and feminism would mean sundering my being." In Plaskow's understanding, the merger of Judaism and feminism requires a revolution equal to the transition from Biblical to Rabbinic Judaism almost two thousand years ago. The covenant remains a viable option with and only with the revolutionary inclusion of women.[6]

It is renewal of the covenant and maintenance of the Jewish linguistic and symbolic universe in face of the Holocaust and Israel that is highlighted by these Jewish theologians. They maintain or seek renewal of this universe by essentially avoiding these two formative events as central to Jewish faith and practice. Was God absent in the Holocaust? Is God present in the birth of the state of Israel? Does the classic core of Jewish life remain after the Holocaust and Israel? In fact, these theologians see Holocaust theology itself as endangering the continuity of Jewish life. For if the Holocaust and Israel become *the* texts of Jewish life, what happens as these events recede in time and memory? On the one hand, the Holocaust is seen in continuity with other Jewish suffering, so that Jewish practice before the Holocaust is the same after the event as well. On the other hand, these theologians wonder what practice will guide Jews through other events of suffering in the future. If God is banished, whom will Jews address in their mourning? How will the conversation be continued if the 613 commandments are replaced by the 614th commandment, which emphasizes only survival? And what will happen to Jewish life if Israel achieves a normal life in the future? Will Jews retain an interest in a state that functions on its own and is no longer in an emergency situation? Can Jewish life revolve around a state where a majority of Jews do not reside, one that may evolve a culture difficult for Western Jews to identify with? A permanent mobilization of Jewish life is held to be suspect, as it threatens to empty the core of Judaism. Orthodox belief and practice continue as the center of a people experienced in suffering and survival.

If jettisoning this Judaic framework would sunder corporate and individual Jewish life, the attempt to hold the covenant together often takes on a desperate quality. One can see this in Arthur Waskow's discussion of the Nazi Holocaust and the creation of the atomic bomb as "byproducts of the Divinization of the human race." Waskow, a leading figure in Jewish renewal, writes that even the Holocaust was an "outburst of light. Those who say we cannot blame God for the Holocaust are only partly right: it was the overflow of God, the outbursting of light, the untrammeled, unboundaried outpouring of divinity, that gave us Auschwitz . . . and may yet consume the earth." This leads Waskow to explain the perennial question of why Jews have often experienced suffering within the context of chosenness. "The God who chose us from outside history at Sinai is still choosing us from inside history," Waskow writes. "We are God's canary-people; the people God sends down the mineshaft first, to test out whether the air breathes ecstasy and revelation or is full of carbon monoxide. If we keel over. . . . Now God knows, we all know: the air is heavy with poison." Waskow's attempt to clarify his point only makes his attempt to preserve at all costs the framework of Jewish life more suspect. While he does not say that God sent the Holocaust and murdered the Jews as a warning to the world, Waskow is saying that "God and only God made the Holocaust immensely possible; God also made the Holocaust avoidable; we choose."[7]

Israeli philosopher Adi Ophir moves a step beyond Waskow. If Waskow is trying to contain the deconstructive power of the Holocaust within Jewish life by positing an almost mystical understanding of a God whose power somehow unleashed this tragedy, Ophir speculates that the religious consciousness built around the Holocaust may become the center of a new religion. This religion will have a story of revelation that Ophir imagines to be the following:

> In the year five thousand seven hundred since the creation of the world according to the Jewish calendar, in central Europe, Absolute Evil was revealed. The Absolute—that is, the Divine—is Evil. Every act has a part, to a greater or lesser extent, in this Absolute Evil, every act is an expression of it. But until the emergence of the Absolute Evil no one believed that there was a hidden lawfulness controlling every appear-

ance of evil in our world. Until then, no one had placed his or her trust in the absolute, transcendent, one and only Evil, which is the ground of our lives and deaths, the logic of our finitude and suffering, the rock of our destruction and the promise of our annihilation. Indeed, time has passed before the meaning of this horrible event could be digested and understood completely, but how is it possible that an event of such dimensions of horror could have no meaning? From a secure distance of time the individual acts of extermination have been collected—particular pullings of the trigger, particular and repeated acts of the opening of gas-pipes, lighting of furnaces—and they have woven together to form the infinite face of the Absolute. The proper place of each atrocious act is in the infinity of Evil, those six years can already be seen as a single unique revelation of the Absolute.[8]

In this religion God is seen as a vengeful God from whom four commandments issue, the last of which—Remember the day of the Holocaust to keep it holy, in memory of the destruction of the Jews of Europe—is the most important. To shirk this commandment is the archetype of sin: "Not only the organized drive to forget, but also the innocent forgetting, the result of assimilation or simple lack of interest in the remnants of the Jewish possessions which a person carries with him or herself, is an act of terrible renunciation," says Ophir. "Those who cause forgetting, to say nothing of those who deny, cooperate with the enemy. Those who assimilate complete the Nazis' work. Those who are faithful to themselves and to their people will repeat the tale until the end of time."[9]

The formation of a new religion with the Holocaust as an understandable, objectified, and even worshiped center, is exactly what Holocaust theologians did not foresee in their early years. Nor could they foresee the emergence of a messianic-apocalyptic view of Auschwitz as the birth pangs of the messiah. From the vantage point of the 1990s, Richard Rubenstein writes of this resurgence as a "defense of belief in Israel's election against the potentially disconfirming evidence of the Holocaust." Thereby radical messianists seek to prove that what appears to be disconfirming evidence, that is, the existence of Auschwitz, actually confirms faith in covenant and election through the birth and expansion of the state of Israel. Israel is seen as a battleground for this confirmation, and the destruction of the Al Aksa mosque in Jerusalem as well as the cleansing of Palestinians from Israel and Palestine are seen as cooperating with the divine. Anyone who opposes this enterprise becomes the disconfirming other. The Jewish apocalyptic messianists regard the Holocaust as providential because the Holocaust forced Jews back to the ground of their being, the Greater Land of Israel. As Rubenstein remarks, these apocalyptic-messianists have given every indication that they will pursue an apocalyptic finale to the struggle over the expanded borders of Israel. Baruch Goldstein, in his massacre of Palestinians in Hebron, and Yigail Amir, in his assassination of Yitzhak Rabin, were therefore confirming the presence of God in the history of the Jewish people.[10]

The scenario here seems to repeat almost verbatim the initial transformation of the early followers of Jesus into a Christianity aligned with empire. Was not this, too, the beginning of a new religion, armed with a revealed truth and a revealed evil, and encouraged by a militarized savior? Another similarity is found in the history of Christianity, that even at the moment of humility and reform a new militarism is waiting to burst onto the scene. Perhaps Waskow's "divinization of the human race" and Ophir's "Holocaust religion" are simply attempts to order the ultimate disordering, when the voices of God and the earth which Rosemary Ruether spoke about are destroyed by atrocity. Raging against the void produces yet another void. Like other theologians, Waskow takes on his perceived task, to explain, to make sense of, to provide meaning for, the human journey into darkness. Perhaps this is why Ophir sees his exploration as anti-theological, seeking a way to avoid explaining the Holocaust and the creation, yet again, of a religion of death. Since religion often helps to produce and legitimate death, is it any wonder that at times it promotes the worship of death? Perhaps this is what Theodor Adorno and George Steiner posed in their comments on poetry and eloquence: that after Auschwitz and 1492, Jews and Christians had an obligation to refuse such worship.

Attempts at Christian Renewal

As Pope John Paul II officially honored the memory of the Jewish victims of the Holocaust, Ari Goldman, religion editor for the *New York Times*, reported on three attempts of Christian renewal, each invoking the contemporary aspect of traditional belief. The first involved the Frederick Christian Fellowship of Frederick, Virginia, which offered ten dollars to all newcomers attending Sunday worship. On the Sunday of the giveaway about 300 people attended, nearly double the regular attendance. The following week, without monetary incentive, attendance fell, but remained above normal, with some people returning from the previous week. The pastor, the Reverend Randy Goldenberg, who wears blue jeans at worship and makes use of a rock band in the service, commented that the monetary offer was less to raise membership numbers than it was to reach those who felt church a waste of time or irrelevant: "We believe that the gospel is as valid today as it was 2,000 years ago but has to be communicated in contemporary terms."

The second effort at renewal was the statement by the Church Council of the Evangelical Lutheran Church in America repudiating Martin Luther's anti-Jewish writings, in particular his treatise, "The Jews and Their Lies," written in 1543. It was here that Luther called for Jewish homes and synagogues to be destroyed, for prayer books to be seized, and for rabbis to be forbidden to teach. The statement notes that the church continues to honor Luther's "bold stand for truth, his earthy and sublime words of wisdom and, above all, his witness to God's saving word," even as it repudiates Luther's view of the Jews: "We who bear his name and heritage must with pain acknowledge also Luther's anti-Judaic diatribes and violent recommendations of his later writings against the Jews." In a further comment, the Reverend Daniel Martensen, associate director for the Department of Ecumenical Affairs for the denomination, recognized the ongoing cycle of Christian renewal and violence by noting that one reason for the new statement was the use by Louis Farrakhan, leader of the Nation of Islam, of Luther's writing in denouncing Jews.

The third aspect of renewal noted in Goldman's column was the celebration of Earth Day by the New York-based, interfaith National Religious Partnership for the Environment. As part of the celebration, the partnership sent out packets of material concerning the environment to more than 50,000 churches and synagogues in the United States. With the slogan, "Some say the earth doesn't have a prayer; 50,000 congregations have a chance to prove them wrong," and the scriptural passage, "The earth is the Lord's and the fullness thereof," the packet proposed composting, recycling, and looking for environmental principles in the Bible. The mailing created controversy, when the Reverend Robert Sirico, president of the Acton Institute for the Study of Religions and Liberty in Grand Rapids, Michigan, warned of turning environmentalism into a religion, the earth into a God, and thus displacing orthodox beliefs. "There is no Commandment against littering," Sirico wrote in an op-ed piece in the *Wall Street Journal*, "but there is a very straight-forward one about worshiping false Gods." Paul Gorman, the executive director of the environmental partnership, responded that his group was trying to enhance rather than supplant existing religious beliefs. "The religious community has found in its most traditional and orthodox teachings definitive guidance and a foundation for a response to the environmental crisis." For Gorman, the religious groups who developed the material worship the Creator and not the creation, and he reiterated that they are responding from "deep within their own teachings and traditions." As Goldman writes in reinforcing Gorman's defense of the material: "Roman Catholics, for example, talk about expanding its long standing notion of justice to all life. Jewish groups emphasize the Sabbath as a day of rest for both people and the rest of creation. Mainline Protestants talk of Jesus as the Redeemer of all beings and evangelical Protestants take special pains to disassociate themselves from New Age or pagan worship."[11]

These aspects of religious renewal are defended and attacked on orthodox terrain, as both sides seek popular support for their positions. To offer money for church attendance may seem scandalous to some, yet a closer examination places this offer in continuity with traditional practices. Missionaries offer education, housing, food, and a rise in status and identity in return for church affiliation. The interplay of Luther's "witness" and his anti-Judaism is a question of orthodoxy as well. Is it possible to bifurcate Luther, culling the good from the bad, condemning his anti-Judaism while honoring his "bold stand for truth"? Luther's words concerning the Jews are worth remembering, as it was in the land of the Reformation where the death camps ultimately appeared: "Herewith you can readily see how they understand and obey the fifth commandment of God, namely, that they are thirsty bloodhounds and murderers of all Christendom, with full intent, now for more than fourteen hundred years, and indeed they were often burned to death upon the accusation that they had poisoned water and wells, stolen children, and torn and hacked them apart, in order to cool their temper secretly with Christian blood." Can one read these words and still remain within Luther's fold? The argument that ecological concern is at the heart of the Jewish and Christian traditions is likewise suspect, for is it not these same traditions that "freed" humans from the natural order of things and, in Max Weber's analysis, allowed for a secularization of consciousness and disenchantment of the world?[12]

Just two years earlier the same issue of orthodoxy and renewal led to the resignation from the Roman Catholic priesthood of the Brazilian theologian and Franciscan friar, Leonardo Boff. In his letter to the people of Brazil, Boff made it clear that his decision to leave was one of institutional definition rather than a change of theological direction.

Though over the years Boff received a level of respect for his theological writings, he achieved fame through the church's attempt to redirect his theology and eventually to silence him. In his letter, Boff recalls this censorship in detail. For many years he received warnings and punishment from various church officials. These included temporary removal from his academic chair in theology, a dialogue in Rome that ended in a year of imposed silence, and continuing censorship of his essays and books. In Boff's view, the church sought to imprison his theological intelligence through almost any means. He defines the experience of dealing with the institutional church over the last twenty years as cruel and merciless, since the church "forgets nothing, forgives nothing; it exacts a price for everything." The end was clear: either leave or become bitter. "I feel as though I have come up against a brick wall," Boff writes, "I can no longer go forward. To go back would imply the sacrificing of my personal dignity and the abandoning of the struggle of so many years." The option to leave is the continuation of a journey, opting for the God of life and involving himself in the creating of an Indo-Afro-American Christianity "inculturated in the bodies, skins, dances, suffering, joys, and the languages of our peoples in answer to God's gospel," an answer, Boff hastens to add, which has not been realized in the 500 years of Christian presence in Latin America.[13]

The God of Life

As John Paul II spoke of the "immense wealth" of Christian life just four months after Boff's resignation from the priesthood, and as Gustavo Gutiérrez himself was forced to submit his writings to church leaders for approval, Elsa Tamez, Professor of Biblical Studies at Seminario Biblico Latin America in Costa Rica, wrote an essay that articulated at another level the struggle of these two theologians of liberation.

Tamez makes clear that her words are addressed to white and *mestizo* Christians rather than indigenous people. Indigenous people have their own God and their own language about God; the problem lies with Christians who live out their faith within rigid boundaries and who consequently undervalue other expressions of faith that are not their own. The task of Christians is less to address indigenous people or challenge their God than to accompany indigenous people and learn from them, thereby expanding the horizons of the God Christians worship and the horizons of Christians themselves. It is important for

Christians to acknowledge that the God of life, that is, the creator of the universe and lover of truth and justice, did not arrive in the Americas with the Spaniards and Portuguese. For Tamez, it is both ignorant and arrogant to think that the true faith of the native people came into being with the arrival of Christianity or to suggest that native peoples had previously practiced a primitive faith. It would also be arrogant to suggest that previous generations of indigenous people were condemned because they did not know the God of the Christians. In Tamez's view, "such declarations reveal to us a very limited God, reduced to a small, Western European circle."[14]

Tamez explores the meaning of the God Quetzalcóatl, the God of life in Náhuatl culture. In the Náhuatl language, Quetzalcóatl means "feathered spirit." As the serpent is a symbol of the material realm and the feather a symbol of the heavenly realm, Quetzalcóatl is a synthesis of two forces that move to ascend (the reptile) and descend (the bird). Admiration and love for Quetzalcóatl are based on testimonies that ascribe to him the following: creating the new human person through the fifth sun, bequeathing life and movement through the shedding of his own blood, discovering corn for the sustenance of the people as well as giving humans the wisdom to build homes, inventing the calendar and art. In the story of the fifth creation, Quetzalcóatl struggles against the lord of death so that a new humanity can come into existence. In the struggle, Quetzalcóatl is injured, and so the work of creation involves self-sacrifice; his blood is mixed with humanity in order to give birth to a new creation. Quetzalcóatl also accompanies the people after creation as a way of joining with them in their struggle against oppression. In one story, Quetzalcóatl turns himself into an ant to carry corn from the enemy and give sustenance to other gods who will reinforce the strength of the people to continue their struggle.[15]

Here the story becomes more involved, for Quetzalcóatl, the God of life, is confronted over time by the theocracy and militarism of the Aztec empire, with its sun God, Huitzilopochtli. The extension of the Aztec empire also extends the reach of Huitzilopochtli in his vocation as a warrior and conqueror. In the Aztec official religion, Quetzalcóatl is relegated to a distant heaven of generations past, and the principal morals taught by Quetzalcóatl, that is, interior perfection and mystical union with divinity, are now attributed to Huitzilopochtli. Not surprisingly, the Aztecs claim the tradition of Quetzalcóatl as their own and use it to legitimate their own power. Because the popularity of Quetzalcóatl remains, however, the appropriation of his qualities is important for the Aztecs to be recognized as the culture's heirs. The Aztecs invert the attributes of Quetzalcóatl into one that demands death as a pretext for acquiring life. In doing so, the Aztecs see themselves as the elect who will save humanity from the cataclysm under which the Fifth Sun is suffering. The only way to avoid this catastrophe is by killing human beings and offering them as appeasement to this sun. Those sacrificed are slaves, prisoners of war, children, and women from the Mesoamerican cultures conquered by the Aztec empire. The God of life comes to be the God of death; the God who sacrificed himself in order to give life to humanity comes to be the God who demands human sacrifice in order to live. Worse than the cooptation of Quetzalcóatl by Huitzilopochtli is that Huitzilopochtli comes to be considered and adored as Quetzalcóatl, to the point that even executioner priests called themselves Quetzalcóatl. The God of death appropriates the name and language of the God of life.[16]

Tamez is clear that the God of death, though triumphant, did not replace or eliminate the defeated God of life. In fact, within the empire a struggle ensues, a struggle of peoples and Gods. For example, the Aztec empire practiced human sacrifice, legitimated by Huitzilopochtli. But in the ancient Mexican world, many cultures reject such sacrifice, including those who remain faithful to Quetzalcóaltl. For Tamez, it is important to remember the diversity of responses to empire and its God as many, including some Aztecs themselves, reject Huitzilopochtli. This memory is important for indigenous people who have had their God defined only as a God of empire and human sacrifice, and thus have been seen to be in need of the God of love represented by Christianity. It is important for Christians as well, who see the Christian God as an obvious progression over a "pagan" God of human sacrifice. By understanding the complexity of indigenous religiosity, Tamez believes that Christians are forced to see the complexity of their own religiosity, characterized by a similar struggle between a God of death and a God of life.[17]

The struggle between Gods in Christianity is evident during the arrival of Christianity in the Americas and occurs simultaneously with the exploitation, enslavement, and devaluation of the indigenous people and their Gods. Fray Antonio de Montecinos and Bartolomé de Las Casas, for example, speak for the indigenous people and therefore the God of life. They initiate a campaign in favor of the enslaved and utilize Christian criteria for their defense. The notion of Christian liberty supports these scholastics in their argument against the doctrine of natural servitude. They also read biblical texts in favor of the indigenous people, invoking another God, different from the God proclaimed by the envoys and missionaries, who legitimate theft and massacre. Tamez is forceful when describing the victor in this struggle, the God of death: "Gold, the God of death, replaced the true God of life. It is a God that is imposed by force as the only God. It is a God of the law of orthodoxy, a God that does not know grace but offers salvation in exchange for gold, slavery, tribute, and submission." By the time the Spaniards arrive in the Americas, a reversal of the God of life within Christianity has already taken place; absent is the God of Abraham, who would not sacrifice his son, the God of the Exodus, who set slaves free, and Jesus Christ, who comes to give abundant life. Present is the God who conquers and directs the Spanish to subdue, convert, and plunder.[18]

Tamez surfaces the struggle between the indigenous God and the Christian God and, as importantly, the struggles within both communities over the definition and properties of God. In fact, these latter struggles take precedence because it informs the indigenous and Christian community of their own history and responsibility for that history. The interaction between indigenous and Christian mirrors the activity within each community; and when looked at in this way, the question of inferior-superior Gods and culture is replaced by a humbled, internal searching. The triumph of Huitzilopochtli as legitimator of empire reminds the indigenous of their own complex history, as the triumph of the Christian God of conquest reminds Christians that their God is in no way superior to Quetzalcóatl. Rather than abstract theology, history tests every revelation of God through concrete life. If Quetzalcóatl, or any other God, is a God of life, then God is revealed in that life. If the testing ground is whether God is revealed in the life of human beings who live with a sense of dignity, justice, and communion, then monotheism and Christianity do not in themselves guarantee the revelation of the God of life. For Tamez, it follows that polytheism is to be judged with the same criteria: Does this revelation lead to dignity, justice, and communion or to empire and death? As a Christian, Tamez concludes that "any understanding of the Mesoamerican religion which classifies it as barbaric, idolatrous, or diabolical is completely in error."[19]

Even more controversial is the assertion that the struggle within the indigenous and Christian communities over the God of life and the God of death actually brings the supporters of each God into a practical and theological solidarity. Those who are in solidarity with death support a God of death; those in solidarity with life support a God of life. When Las Casas, in the name of God, condemns the practice of slavery and plunder, Tamez believes that his God is the same God that the native victims accept. "If we say that it is the same God it is because both the missionaries, who are the defenders of the indigenous, and the native inhabitants themselves share a coincidence in their perception of reality." To reinforce this point, Tamez uses as an example Chief Tecpanécatl's analysis of the first years of the invasion, which to Tamez is exactly the same analysis which Las Casas made in defending the indigenous people of the Americas. Said the chief: "How much blood was shed! The blood of our fathers and mothers! And why? They know why: because they wanted to rule alone. Because they were hungry for foreign metals and foreign wealth. And because they wanted to put us under their heel. And because they wanted to mock our women and also our wives and maidens. And because they wanted to become owners of our lands and of everything which was our wealth."[20]

In exploring this coincidence of God, Tamez finds that indigenous people are perceptive in understanding and embracing aspects of the Christian God that oppose conquest. Christian missionaries who embrace the God of life within Christianity have greater difficulty in recognizing the same attributes in the indigenous God. In this sense the missionary defense of the indigenous is ultimately without an acknowledged embrace of the indigenous in their deepest sensibility. The Náhuatl culture takes this further step by accepting the Christian God as part of its own vision of the cosmos. In time there comes into being a continuity between the indigenous and Christian God of life in the figure of the Virgin of Guadalupe. Clodomiro Siller, a Mexican writer, sees this as the "indigenous comprehension of their own living religious tradition in new circumstances of colonization and evangelization." Tamez admires the indigenous people for their capacity to recognize the God of life in a culture and religion that invaded them, and she admonishes Christians who lack the wisdom and humility to recognize the God of life in cultures that profess a non-Western, non-Christian faith. The lack of recognition represents an inability to see that the God of the indigenous is also the Christian God who is "revealed to us in the Scriptures, who has revealed Self in the past and will always reveal Self in the history of every culture, since before the time of Abraham, whenever people cry out for justice or manifest in their lives communion, solidarity, love, liberation, justice, truth, faith, and hope." For Tamez, it is this God who challenges Christians in the present, especially through the indigenous and Black victims of the conquest. By their continuing resistance to the history of conquest, these victims "become the 'good news' for *mestizos* and whites. Through them the Spirit of Christ, as well as the Spirit of Quetzalcóatl, are evangelizing us."[21]

Tamez's assertion that there is no difference between the reigning God of the Aztec empire and the God of the Spanish empire is a bold one. She complements this with a further assertion that the indigenous God of resistance is the same God as the Christian God of resistance. In the battle against empire, that which gives strength and sustenance, that which sustains hope and accompanies the people, is God. While the names for God change due to circumstances, the reality of God remains. What indigenous people do is simply incorporate values and names because they are forced to and because they recognize the other side of the God of empire. Of course, indigenous people also resist the incorporation and renaming of Gods. The ultimate recognition and inclusion does not vitiate the horror of Christian domination. The attempt to escape from and defend against this domination is important to recall and Tamez does so by quoting an indigenous priest who spoke the following in 1524: "You have spoken to us a new word, and we are disturbed by it. . . . Shall we destroy the ancient rule of life? Because in our heart we understand to whom we owe our lives, to whom we owe our birth, to whom we owe our growth, to whom we owe our development. For that reason the Gods are invoked. . . . Our lords, that which you have told us we do not take as the truth even though we confuse you."[22]

The view that the Spirit of Christ and the Spirit of Quetzalcóatl evangelizes both the indigenous and the Christian peoples of Latin America is haunted by atrocity. It is the eruption of Aztec and Spanish barbarism that forces the silencing and recovery of the spirits Tamez invokes. Yet ironically Tamez's openness to indigenous reality as a Christian is also at first appearance supersessionist to her understanding of Judaism. It is Paul's argument against limiting God's revelation to the Jews and their understanding of law and circumcision, that she cites as opening the way to the Christian inclusion of indigenous reality. Paul seeks to free the Jewish religion from exclusiveness by arguing the supremacy of faith over law. Because of this understanding, Paul is freed to be with and for those outside of Christianity as well. According to Tamez, Paul includes within the liberating plan of God people who know neither the Jewish law nor Christian religion: therefore, access to God and God's solidarity with the person and community is secured by the primacy of faith over Jewish law and Christian dogma. For Christians, however, the centrality of Jesus Christ remains, and here Tamez asserts her orthodoxy without compromise: "Our faith is rooted in the belief that we have been justified by faith in Jesus Christ and by faith in the One who raises the dead. The obedience of Jesus Christ, the second Adam, has inaugurated the new humanity for everyone." Still, the task of theology is not to establish belief in the God of Jesus Christ as superior to other beliefs; rather its task is to "testify to the victory of God over death through the weakness of the crucified one."[23]

Tamez's analysis finds a series of contradictions and fascinating possibilities that mirror and move beyond the concentric tradition of reading. For Tamez, as for the pope in his quincentenary address, it is important to recognize God or aspects of God's work before 1492 while condemning the practice of human sacrifice. Tamez specifically raises this issue because the presence of human sacrifice in the Americas before the arrival of Christianity has often been used to prove the superiority of Christianity, as if Christianity in its coming to Latin America did not encourage and legitimate the sacrifice of humans on a scale unknown in the pre-Christian Americas. Still, the God of life explicitly rules out human sacrifice, and thus the Gods of the indigenous people Tamez favors do not call for such sacrifice. The point seems disingenuous, for did not the God of Abraham call for such a sacrifice, and did not Abraham prove his fidelity by offering his son, Isaac, in response to God's call? It is strange for Christians to object to human sacrifice when they profess faith in a savior who, as part of the divine plan of salvation, was himself sacrificed.

The place of Paul in Tamez's theology of Christian inclusivity is also problematic beyond his controversial understanding of Jewish faith. For did Paul really preach the validity of all religions and religiosity as paths to God? Or did he argue within a narrow framework he thought expansive, that is, the inclusion in the Judaic covenant of all peoples with their acceptance of Jesus Christ, a Jew, as Lord? As importantly, it was Paul's argument for the expansion of the Judaic framework through Jesus Christ that moved Judaism from an indigenous people's religion to a religion that claims, in its Christian garb, a universal truth and destiny. What Christians inherit as Christianity is an indigenous Judaic religion expanded into a world religion. In this expansion, Christianity arrives in the Americas already carrying Judaic and other indigenous religions and symbols that Christianity had conquered and absorbed. Christianity in the Americas therefore represents a continuation of a history of expansion, domination, and absorption of other cultures and religions, rather than a new departure in its history. In essence, Tamez's emphasis on the centrality of Jesus Christ is itself an acceptance of the empire's domination of an indigenous Judaic path already receding by the time of Paul.

The shift that Tamez represents and the possibility inherent in her work is in recognizing the validity of Gods outside the Judaic and Christian framework as well as their continuation, often disguised, in Christianity itself. To be evangelized by the spirit of Quetzalcóatl is to introduce a question as to the centrality of Jesus Christ and to raise doubts as to who Christians are in fact worshiping. If the God of life is the same God wherever found, in whatever garb and language, then the worship of the indigenous God of life is the same worship in which Christians participate. That is, Christians come to understand the locality and limitations of their God, as they recognize the importance of the God they were taught to look down upon. The definition of idolatry shifts precipitously: false Gods are found outside Christianity *and* within Christianity, so that the value of being Christian is relativized. A powerful reversal is evident in Tamez's theological assertion that the God Quetzalcóatl is superior to the Spanish Christian God. Those who resist Spanish and Christian domination are superior to those who plant and sustain the cross of gold.

One wonders if it is possible to nourish the God of life only by becoming indigenous in belief, thereby combining elements of the indigenous and Christian and abandoning what is now known as Christianity. This possibility may be what Leonardo Boff means when he speaks of building an Indo-Afro-American Christianity as an answer to God's gospel. Is this answer to God's gospel the end of Christianity as it has existed for more than 1500 years? This, of course, is the pope's fear, that another form of Christianity is evolving in Latin America. This may also be the secret that liberation theologians like Boff and Gutiérrez are either unable or are afraid to articulate. Should liberation theologians be seen as mediators, opening a space for a transformed indigenous religion to evolve by defending the people against the continued domination of orthodox Christianity? Still, it is possible that Tamez, Boff, and Gutiérrez may be more inclusive and responsive to local realities, while at the same time guiding the evolution of Christianity in Latin America in ways they consider orthodox. The danger is that mediators and defenders may also, despite protests to the contrary, be guardians of a tradition in much the same way as the church authorities with whom they are in conflict.

Tamez writes forcefully of an evolving understanding of God and the histories and texts that inform that understanding. She seems to put a fence around Christianity, moving beyond Las Casas and Gutiérrez to suggest a mutual evangelization of indigenous and Christian, which might even end the advance of Christianity. The fence around Christianity is for reasons of history—the domination and oppression of another people—and for reasons of authenticity—Quetzalcóatl is as authentic and life-giving in his context as Jesus Christ is among Christians. Further, she suggests that the diminution of Quetzalcóatl may diminish the resources within the Christian community to oppose the Christian God of conquest; the struggle within the indigenous community for the God of life lends insight into the ongoing struggle for the God of life within the Christian community. A fence around Christianity, though, is more significant than what appears at the outset to be a strict separation between indigenous and Christian, for most Christians in Latin America retain memories of their indigenous cultures and religions. The end of orthodox and liberal evangelical efforts to Christianize the masses might mean the evolution of something quite different than theologians envisioned when liberation theology was first proposed. Could it be that the extension of Tamez's argument leads away from the evangelical impulse—for orthodoxy or for justice—and that a new era of religiosity will see the inclusion of Judaic and Christian ideas in a broader framework of indigenous religiosity around the world? Clearly Tamez extends the idea of the ecumenical dialogue beyond the agreement of Jews and Christians to recognize the authenticity of each other to include indigenous religiosity as well. There is no superiority, only a mutual recognition of the God of life in each other's culture and communities. As important, the other may at the same time be present in each community. The indigenous is within in the Christian and the Christian is within the indigenous.

With this understanding the Christian concentric tradition of reading expands considerably, as the texts of all peoples who have been absorbed into Christianity are now to be reappraised in light of the distinction between the God of life and the God of death. The centrality of the Christian texts are undermined or at least have a new reason for scrutiny. The angle of vision is finding the God of life in Christian culture and joining that with the God of life in other cultures. The texts of the Christian faith that are found wanting become witnesses against the God of life. One wonders if the next step is the inclusion in Christianity of indigenous texts and practices that coincide with the God of life. It could be that the declaration of Christ the savior for Christians may ultimately be decentered as the tradition of concentric reading continues to be challenged by other centers. In this way, the gospel of Treblinka is now joined by the gospel of Quetzalcóatl.

Indigenous Jewish Life

When looked at from this perspective, the Christianization of the indigenous and the indigenization of the Christian is of global relevance. An example is the Zion Christian Church in South Africa, which combines fixtures of African myth—ecstatic utterances, prophecy, initiation and purification rites, taboos, exorcism of demons—with Christian notions of trinity, crucifixion, and resurrection. Another example is the theology of Bishop Emmanuel Milingo, former Archbishop of Lusaka, Zambia, which attempts to introduce Jesus into African reality via the role of ancestors as known in traditional African religious practice. Milingo believes that "marrying Jesus" to the African ancestors represents the possibility of making Christianity indigenous in Africa, as the people will believe and trust in Jesus when they experience Jesus as alive among them, as their ancestors are. This bridging of indigenous African and Christian can also be seen in the work of the African American theologian Josiah Young. Young believes that Jesus Christ enriches symbols already present in the image of God among African people, especially for those Africans in the diaspora: "Each child of the Pan-African experience in Christ reincarnates the love of the old Africans who—unnamed in the history of migrations from the once verdant Sahara; unnamed beneath the waters of the Atlantic and unnamed beneath the hostile soil of the Americas—are sanctified in the Providence that not only pulls us toward tomorrow, but also anchors the Pan-African theologian to God whose divinity is revealed in the redemptive legacies of the ancestors." For Young, the ancestors are alive in Jesus Christ, "rising from the macrodimension of a crucifying sinfulness, speaking through the Spirit of transformation."[24]

The interpretation and transformation of indigenous and foreign symbolic universes, rites of worship, and linguistic patterns seems to be the intuitive means through which a people adapts to changing circumstance. Recognizing the God of life within the God of the conquest is therefore necessary in order to endure, yet also tragic in that this endurance severs a universe once assumed and now forever changed. Yet this recognition also functions as way of surviving the eruption of barbarism and, over time, transforming evil in a process of healing. The healing process is twofold. The dislocation of the indigenous religiosity of the Americas, like the dislocation of indigenous Judaism, struggles to survive the "universal" Christian religion. This mutual dislocation is transformed when the defeated continue to absorb and resist the religious language that ironically, in its new identity, is also partially their own.

The defeated may also use the God of life found in the victor's religion to subvert the victor and to address the God of death in their own indigenous community. Recognizing how the dominant religion functions and the strength of the indigenous over the long haul, especially in times of colonialism and evangelization, the evolving religious sensibility may be a bridge of healing in a community ravaged by conquest. Could it be that here lies a way of addressing the language of atrocity, of raising again the question of God's presence? Surely, the merging and transporting of the defeated and the dominant symbolic universe and language allow resources unavailable to either the defeated or the dominant alone.

At first glance, the indigenous/Christian dialogue is a dialogue distant from Jewish life. It is more complex, however, for the Judaism that Jews are born into is an indigenous religiosity which has traveled and evolved, undergoing internal revolution and external conquest for thousands of years. What is considered normative Judaism is actually a product of this history, though normative Judaism, like normative Christianity, disguises change under the banner of orthodoxy. Rabbinic Judaism, for example, is a product of a diverse past that is presented as a system of study, piety, and prayer centered in the holy texts and the synagogue. Yet it inherited and helped to transform a complex array of forces that included, among other elements, nationalism, diaspora-centered particularity, attraction to Hellenistic thought and discourse, and attempts at syncretistic religious expression. Of course, there was a *before* even to Rabbinic Judaism; the tribes of Yahweh, for example, carried their diverse indigenous cultures and symbols as they interacted with various populations when they were oppressed, and later in the conquest and governance of some of these populations. Rabbinic Judaism is the *before* of Holocaust theology; and, as Rabbinic Judaism relates to the tribes of Yahweh, so Holocaust theology relates primarily to what preceded itself: Rabbinic Judaism. Holocaust theology participates in a perennial aspect of Jewish history, that is, a leading group becomes dominant by legitimizing its interpretations of Jewish life over against its opponents.[25]

Though Jewish scholars tend to understand that other religions have evolved, borrowed, even stolen in their journey, Judaism is often viewed as a simple continuity rather than a complex arena of historical development. Yet there have been several Jewish cultures rather than one, and even the superordinating concepts of Jewish history— God, Torah and Israel's chosenness—have different meanings and functions in each culture. Therefore, it is impossible to sum up the totality of Jewish religious truth and the complexities of Jewish history through the principle of unity or a Jewish essence. What we find instead is optimal expressions of Jewish creativity, that is, some systems have been more creative than others. The cultural diversities in the Jewish world demonstrate that Judaism is not a self-sufficient entity. Jews in Jerusalem, Babylonia, Cordoba, and Cracow articulated their experiences in diverse ways. Jewish cultural historian Efraim Shmueli writes of the denial of this diversity: "If we insist on seeking those trends or expressions which were *common* in all our history, we should not be surprised, or disappointed, when we find that these trends share only very general characteristics."[26]

Shmueli explores Jewish history and finds seven different Judaic cultures. These cultures are divided by time period and formative experiences and are identified as the Biblical, Talmudic, Poetic Philosophic, Mystical, Rabbinic, Emancipation, and National-Israeli cultures. Each culture creates its own language and symbols that distinguish each from that of its predecessors. An example is a generation raised in the Hebrew language of a Biblical culture; they would barely comprehend the meaning of images and symbols used by the Talmudic or Mystic cultures. The thought of a people within a historical culture is limited by the imagery it employs, and only within these limitations can certain concepts be used meaningfully. Therefore in each culture a certain set of experiences has a decisive impact upon its formation and becomes unique to that particular culture. The new experiences are articulated in innovative terminology, new images, and reinvigorated symbols. Instead of unity, Shmueli sees the history of Israel as a dramatic arena of conflicts and accommodations, of "controversies partly settled, often left unresolved, of fundamental contradictions in beliefs, valuations, and opinions," all of which brought about change that eventually forged entire cultures distinct from one another in substance as in style. That Jewish history is conflicted and dialectical means that this history is innovative and full of surprises; diversity is a sign of the wealth and generosity of Jewish life rather than of fragmentation and defeat.[27]

This diversity of Jewish life moves beyond even the expansive categories that Shmueli creates. The discussion of early Israelite history and the indigenous religiosity which was repressed and supplanted in the development of monotheism is complimented by Howard Eilberg-Schwartz's analysis of the "savage" in Judaism. As an anthropologist, Eilberg-Schwartz sees the definition of the Jewish people as a people of the book as both instructive *and* misleading. Israelite religion and ancient Judaism emphasize the body as a concrete embodiment of the people and God. The link between circumcision and fertility in Leviticus is an example of this embodied Judaism as the fruit of a juvenile tree is proscribed like the foreskin of the male organ. A male who is uncircumcised and therefore not part of the covenantal community is, like an immature fruit tree, infertile. Hence the biblical analogy between circumcision and pruning. Eilberg-Schwartz comments that cutting away the foreskin is like pruning a fruit tree because both acts remove unwanted excess and both increase the desired yield. One might say that when Israelites circumcise their male children, they are "pruning the fruit trees of God." The embodied perspective that oriented internal Jewish reality and Jewish discourse about nature, the people, and God, is displaced over time to a more universalist and disembodied perspective of the book. Concrete realities and associations like the link between circumcision and the pruning of fruit trees, are replaced with root metaphors so that circumcision becomes a symbolic entry into the covenant. The movement from associations, such as nature and blood, into more abstract metaphors of the human condition and God, occurs over time and accelerates in the nineteenth century with the development of anthropology and Reform Judaism. Aspects of Judaism that seem primitive within the modern framework are disguised, jettisoned, or transformed.[28]

The marginalization of the body and nature is understood within the political and cultural realities of modern life, as a desire by Jews to see Judaism in relation to the higher religions rather than as a surviving primitive religion. Denying or trivializing the savage in Judaism functions to increase the prestige of Judaism and the Jewish people in a hostile European environment. Because of this, prohibitions against boiling a kid-goat in its mother's milk or eating land animals that do not chew their cud and have cloven hooves, are suppressed or seen as either survivals from primitive religious forms or as degenerated practices from an earlier sophisticated form of religion. Instead, the idea of covenant, God, or the divine-human relationship is emphasized. Interestingly, the denial of the savage in Judaism comes from Christian theologians as well, as Christians justify the idea that Jesus is Messiah through the prophecies of the Hebrew Bible. To see the Hebrew Bible as describing a primitive religion is to threaten the status and authority of Christianity. After all, strict rules governing the sacrifice and eating of animals in Israelite religion were continued in early Christianity through the eating of the body of Christ in the Eucharist.[29]

Will the rediscovery of the savage in Judaism lead to a more mature understanding of the multidimensional heritage of the Jewish people? Will Jews recognize that the people of the book are also a people of the body? At the same time, traces of the savage within Judaism continue; and so the indigenous within Jewish life, though suppressed, remains. Could the liberation of the indigenous within the Jewish people engage the Jewish textual tradition and its questions about God in a new way after the Holocaust, Israel, and Palestine? Can the eruption of barbarism upon Jews and toward another people be understood in a more varied and embodied perspective by those who recognize the savage in Judaism than those who see Jews only as carriers of the texts? Perhaps the wounding of Jewish and Palestinian bodies can be addressed more candidly as a people of the body than as a people of the book. The recovery of the primitive in Judaism may also allow Jews to see other indigenous peoples in a new light. For it may be that the God of life in Judaism is quite similar to the God of life in Mexico, Peru, and South Africa.

Once this internal diversity is recognized, a further step may become necessary. Since recognition of the savage in Judaism forces a confrontation with normative Judaism, another, even more painful, issue must be reexamined. The issue of Jesus and where he belongs in Jewish and Christian theology is perhaps the most complex and anxiety-producing question between the two communities. The controversial nature of the issue is apparent, for this Jewish man has been used against the Jewish people in a wave of violence extraordinary in its effects and scope. Indeed, the textual reading of Jesus through his interpreters, especially Paul, has inflicted psychological and bodily injury on the Jewish people. The carriers of the Christian texts have promulgated wave upon wave of barbarism as they worshiped a Jewish man and ate, physically and symbolically, a Jewish body. It is plausible that an aspect of the difficulty Jews find in addressing God after the Holocaust is related to the easy address that Christians have asserted over the millennia in relation to a Jew who has been systematically stolen, exploited, and misinterpreted as a license for conquest. Could Jewish healing be somehow linked to the embrace of one who represents a path within indigenous Israelite culture and ancient Judaism?

The uniqueness of Jesus is a Christian projection and a key to its universal aspirations; at the same time it involves a jettisoning of Christianity's own indigenous roots. Considering Jesus from the perspective of Jewish history has, in the first instance, little, if anything, to do with the assertion of uniqueness or messianic fulfillment. Rather, it has to do with a path within Judaism chosen by some Jews at the time of Jesus, and chosen again in different parts of Jewish history, including the present. This Jewish path represents an interweaving of religion, geography, class, and power in first-century Palestine. John Dominic Crossan sees the historical Jesus as a Jewish Mediterranean peasant and a Cynic. Jesus' peasant village was close to Sepphoris, a Greco-Roman city, and it is likely that he had knowledge of Cynicism as a philosophical system, even as he worked among the farms and villages of Lower Galilee. His strategy, according to Crossan, was eclectic, combining aspects of his Jewish, Mediterranean, and peasant culture. In essence, the strategy was a way of life, stressing free healing and common eating, a "religious and economic egalitarianism that negated alike and at once the hierarchical and patronal normalcies of Jewish religion and Roman power." Jesus and his followers moved constantly rather than settling down at Nazareth or Capernaum. They refused to be seen as brokers or mediators and announced that neither should exist, either between humanity and divinity or between humanity and itself. As Crossan describes it, this group of wandering Jews combined miracle and parable, healing and eating, to force individuals into "unmediated physical and spiritual contact with God and unmediated physical and spiritual contact with one another." In so doing, Jesus announced the unmediated or brokerless kingdom of God. Crossan confirms what other scholars stress in their work as well: that to understand Jesus, one must understand the context of Jewish life in Palestine as primarily an occupied peasant society in the process of revolt. Jesus was part of a Jewish peasantry that spawned a series of popular movements, originally drove out the Romans, and resisted their reconquest of the country.[30]

Here Jesus, and other Jews as well, found a way of penetrating to the deepest aspect of their contemporary history. Did Jesus and those other Jews experience what Clodomiro Siller wrote of with reference to the Náhuatl peoples' contact with Christianity, that is, "the indigenous comprehension of their own living religious tradition in new circumstances of colonization and evangelization"? Were the stories that grew up around Jesus before the formation of institutional, Constantinian Christianity a recognition of this comprehension, which was ultimately denied by Jewish and Christian leadership? Crossan notes that the historical Jesus must be understood within a Judaism of antiquity and tradition interacting with a Greco-Roman culture of armed power and imperial ambition. Yet by the end of the second century of the common era, Rabbinic Judaism and Catholic Christianity were denying this past by retrojecting their ascendancy onto earlier history. In fact, with the massive and unsuccessful revolt of the Jewish people in Palestine little more than a generation after the crucifixion of Jesus, along with thousands of other Jewish rebels, Judaism and Christianity embarked on a very different trajectory.

The devastation of Palestine, which included destruction of the Temple and the city of Jerusalem, mark a turning point for both Judaism and Christianity. Richard Horsley and John Hanson comment that over against the apocalyptic and revolutionary impulses of their time the Pharisaic sages laid the foundation of what became Rabbinic Judaism. As a result of the Roman suppression of the Jewish revolt, moreover, the Christian movement also shifted its focus from Jerusalem and the Temple as a geographic and symbolic center. Surely the rabbis as well as the priests chose an elite and intellectual encounter rather than a popular, peasant encounter with this Jewish movement of resistance and healing. By the time of the formation of "normative" or classical Judaism and Christianity during the reign of Constantine, both establishments had turned their back on this form of indigenous religiosity. Jews and Christians were defined by their holy books, the interpretative reading of which helped to guide and repress the indigenous diversity and subversive quality of the "lower" form of Judaism embodied by Jesus and other Jews.[31]

The recovery of the Jesus indigenous to ancient Jewish life is a significant part of Jewish history rent by the arrogance of Jewish leadership and Christian power. The peasant quality of Jesus' life again suggests a Jewish link with contemporary peasants who carry Jesus with them today. And it also suggests a path that many Jews have taken in practice, while being totally alienated from modern Jewish religion and from the question of God. The strategy of Jesus and his followers, as well as the peasant movements of his time—the combination of free healing, common eating, and a search for religious and economic egalitarianism—are paths that some Jews continue to choose even after the Holocaust, though most often without religious language. At the same time, a confusion of immense importance comes into being when the religious articulation of the practice of free healing and common eating, the search for justice, and subversion of unjust power, is given over to the very religion that usurps Jewish ideas and violates them on a regular basis. In a strange twist of history, the articulation of a Jewish indigenous path is considered by Christians *and* by Jews as the essence of Christianity. Therefore a path which might speak to the eruption of barbarism in the Holocaust and Palestine is considered by Jews as foreign territory. Because of the constant betrayal of this path by the foreign Christian claimant, almost any articulation of religiosity is seen by many Jews as a cover for deceit and conquest.

The cost of this dilemma is incredible. On the one hand, Jews prize themselves on an open and inquisitive community. On the other hand, entire areas of religious life are closed off to those who seek answers to questions that come from Jewish history. The ironic quality is that the Jewish normative tradition prohibits inquiries into areas of Jewish life that might establish a different angle of vision. If Holocaust theology has come to an end of sorts in that its creative years are over, and if the unanswered questions of the Holocaust era remain, all avenues that promise insight need to be explored. Yet the cycle of mistrust and anger is so great that even resources of the Jewish tradition are denied. The issue is less the messianic claims attached to Jesus than it is the remarkable similarities that many Jews have with certain interpretations of Jesus. Since Jesus was a Jew and since other Jews traveled with Jesus, it would be remarkable if no similarities existed. If Jews give over the definition of Jesus to Christians, it is little wonder that Jews who act on behalf of justice go elsewhere for their spiritual needs. In fact, Jews who become Christians may be attracted to this Jewish path, which they do not find in the Jewish community. But this also may be the reason so many Jews are attracted to Buddhism, Hinduism, and religious cults. Feeling that Holocaust theology provides little spiritual nourishment, and feeling guilty for crossing over into enemy Christian territory, they choose the East instead. The question of a future remains, for those Jews who strive for connection to other Jews and the world, and who seek a spiritual path, the answer is often found outside. Sometimes parts of home are located in another religion, stolen, transformed, and foreign in language and symbol. The existence of Jewish life in the West within the often oppressive shadow of Christianity provides a further complication in that Christianity has helped form and influence a Judaism that sees itself as separate and in exile. This image of separateness is complex and often contradictory. Judaism and Christianity established their normative aspects in contrast and competition with each other in the early centuries of the common era. The interaction of Judaism and Christianity continued in the medieval and Renaissance periods, in disputations, borrowings, and theft. In the post-Holocaust period, collaboration between Jew and Christian is manifest. Although from the Jewish side this latter influence is often unacknowledged, two examples will suffice. Judith Plaskow cites her indebtedness to the Catholic biblical scholar Elizabeth Schüssler Fiorenza, in helping Plaskow develop her approach to the recovery of Jewish women's history. Abraham Joshua Heschel was a close friend and confidant of Reinhold Niebuhr, whom Heschel described as a "pioneer for this generation" and a "beacon of light in a dark world," reminding us "what we are." Niebuhr also influenced Will Herberg, another major Jewish theologian in the post-Holocaust era, to search out his Jewish roots, rather than become a Christian, after his disaffection with Marxism. Of Niebuhr's influence, Herberg wrote: "What I owe to Reinhold Niebuhr in the formation of my general theological outlook, every page of this book bears witness." The revival of Jewish theology in Europe in the 1920s and 1930s was very much the product of a Jewish-Protestant dialogue that included, among others, Franz Rosensweig, Leo Baeck, and Martin Buber. This dialogue continued in America with the participation of Heschel, Herberg, Niebuhr, and Paul Tillich, as well as with the students and followers of Heschel, Joseph Soloveitchik and Emil Fackenheim, who devoted themselves to the study of Christian thought. Jacob Neusner, one of the most innovative Jewish scholars of his generation, continues in that tradition and acknowledges it boldly: "My closest colleagues have been faithful Christians, who exhibit enormous esteem for Judaism. . . . Catholic and Protestant Christianity alike have brought forward, in my life, people whose religious convictions have led them to respect my religion, and to want to know more about it."[32]

Clearly, the Jewish encounter with Christianity is profoundly ambivalent. The articulate critique of an oppressive Christianity is complemented by a mostly silent appreciation of elements of Christianity, or at least of Christian theologians like Niebuhr, Tillich, and Schüssler Fiorenza, who have come into solidarity with the Jewish people, have helped in the development of Jewish theologians, and have often shown more appreciation for Jewish theology than have a majority of Jews. After almost two millennia of living together, it is hard to deny that the Christian symbolic universe and Christian discourse about God are part of Jewish life and consciousness. The Jewish attempt to evaluate and define Christianity, as well as the connection between Jewish and Christian theologians, is—analogous to the import of the Virgin of Guadalupe—the comprehension of the Jewish life in circumstances of colonization and evangelization. At least in the West, one can argue that Christianity is as much a part of Judaism as Judaism is of Christianity. James Baldwin's understanding of Jews taking on the characteristics of Christians moves one step further: Christianity is a permanent part of the Jewish psyche and symbolic universe and never more so than when Jews seek to deny it.

Despite this collaboration, the deepest pain in the Jewish psyche remains the abuse suffered at the hands of Christians. The intimacy of the Christian symbolic universe to Judaism, as originating within and elaborating from Judaic sensibilities, accentuates the pain and makes the healing more difficult. Unfortunately, often a mature dialogue with this part of Jewish culture and experience means crossing over into enemy territory, at least as defined by normative Judaism. Here the fear of assimilation to the Christian ethos is evident and makes more difficult a dialogue with part of Jewish history and Judaic sensibility rejected by both the Jewish and Christian establishments. One wonders if the agreements between Heschel and Niebuhr, Herberg and Niebuhr, Rubenstein and Tillich, and even between Plaskow and Schüssler Fiorenza—to join in an ecumenical front that maintains a division between Judaism and Christianity—contribute to the healing of the Jewish world or rather contributes to a separateness that ultimately prevents that healing.

Great similarities exist between the Jewish encounter with Christianity and the indigenous encounter with Christianity outside of Europe. Having learned the language of Christianity in order to survive its onslaught, Jews have also helped to tame and transform both Jesus and Christianity. Nineteenth- and twentieth-century Jewish commentary on Jesus, for example, affirms the following about Jesus: that he belonged fully and completely to Judaism, affirmed the validity of the Jewish law, had nothing to do with the rise of Christianity, and was a Jewish rabbi who taught Jewish ethics. Though Jacob Neusner parts company with aspects of this analysis of Jesus, especially the assertion that Jesus was simply a rabbi like other rabbis, he, like his nineteenth-century counterparts, chooses a safe and predictable ending to his interpretation of Jewish-Christian relations. Instead of affirming the similarities between Judaism and Christianity, Neusner asserts that they are entirely different and grew up together defining their essence through their differences. Blurring the differences between Judaism and Christianity today, including in the discussion of Jesus, is dangerous because it introduces a subversive element to a now-safe status quo. Neusner boldly and revealingly states the goal of his discussion of Jesus. "If I succeed," he writes, "Christians will find renewal for their faith in Jesus Christ—but also respect Judaism. I mean to explain to Christians why I believe in Judaism, and that ought to help Christians identify the critical convictions that bring them to church every Sunday. Jews will strengthen their commitment to the Torah of Moses—but also respect Christianity. . . . Both Jews and Christians should find in these pages reason to affirm, because each party will locate here the very points on which the difference between Judaism and Christianity rests." This mutual affirmation is good news to the Christian establishment. Neusner's book carries a Catholic *imprimatur* from Joseph Cardinal Ratzinger, archenemy of theologians like Leonardo Boff and Gustavo Gutiérrez.[33]

As historians and theologians, these Jews are pursuing what the Tagalogs and the Náhuatls pursued in a different context: at times adopting part of the foreign powers' symbolic universe, at times disputing it, at times even defending it, in order to fend off a further encroachment and to provide the space for the continuing journey of the people. Like liberation theologians, Jewish commentators help alert dominant Christians to the God of death they worshiped and promulgate and hold out the possibility of a God of life that might be found in common.

Indeed, much of the work done in revising Christian theology is greatly indebted to the Jewish experience of Christianity. At a more foundational level, one can cite Rosemary Radford Ruether's work on the anti-Judaism of the church fathers as a way of demonstrating the need for deconstruction of Christian theology, and Carter Heyward's probing of a theology of mutual relation, which analyzes Elie Wiesel's

work in order to understand the development of a theology of alienation in Christianity. Elizabeth Schüssler Fiorenza's provocative and
sensitive discussion of the Jesus movement as a renewal movement
within Judaism is influenced by her German birth, during the Holocaust. Her reflections consistently connect the issue of feminism and
anti-Semitism, at the same time beginning to address the commonali-
ties between dominant Christians and an empowered post-Holocaust
Judaism. For Schüssler Fiorenza, Christian and Jewish theology after
the Holocaust must refuse a patriarchal God, and it can do so only
when it mourns the loss of women's contributions and rejects their
theological dehumanization. Instead, white Christian and Jewish theology must promote the human dignity of all peoples and struggle
against racism wherever it is found. In short, the memory of the Holocaust must "interrupt" all forms of patriarchal theology if the cries of
the dead are to be heard. Schüssler Fiorenza spells out her commitment to a truly ecumenical movement of women that promotes the
biblical image of God's people common to Judaism and Christianity.
"Any struggle against the structural sin of sexism won for Episcopal,
Jewish, or Mormon women benefits the liberation struggle of all
women and vice versa. Solidarity in the struggle with poor women,
third-world women, lesbian women, welfare mothers, or older and
disabled women spells out our primary spiritual commitment and
accountability."[34]

Yet it is instructive that while the Christian understanding of Jewish suffering has often led to a deconstruction of Christian theology
and an expanded solidarity with others who are suffering, this is less
the case with Jewish theology. Contrast the above with David Blumenthal's probing of the lessons of the Holocaust in relation to child abuse.
Blumenthal labels his theology confessional and begins with his own
background as a male, middle-class, Jewish academic, educated in the
rabbinic tradition, and his commitment to the calling of the theologian
as a "voice for God, for the tradition, for the Jewish people, and for
humanity, with a mission to speak the ought." In the end, however,
Blumenthal affirms an abusing God, one who has denied and abused
his people, but one whom the Jewish people will argue with and
remain faithful to. Blumenthal offers this prayer:

> I come before you as a vessel filled with shame and disgrace lest I have
> been arrogant before You and have denied You or Your Torah. It is
> known and manifest to me that I have sinned before You, that I stand

guilty before Your throne. My unintentional, purposeful, and rebellious sins are many, in private and in public. I regret and I repent of them. I ask forgiveness and forbearance of punishment for them.

Yet I also stand before You, my heart filled with pain and shock at what my eyes have seen and my ears have heard. "How can the Lord have spurned in His rage the daughter of Zion, casting the glory of Israel from heaven to earth and pushing the earthly embodiment of His power from His memory on the day of His rage?" "Indeed, You deserted us and shamed us, and did not go out with our forces. You put us to flight from our enemies, and those who hated us tore us to pieces at will. You handed us over like sheep to be devoured, and cast us among the nations. You sold Your people for nothing, and did not make a profit on their sale price. You made us an object of shame for our neighbors, a thing of scorn and derision for those around us. . . . All this happened to us yet we did not forget You, nor did we betray your covenant. Our hearts did not retreat, nor did our steps deviate from Your way. Though You crushed us into a desolate place and covered us with deep darkness, did we forget the name of our God or spread our hands in prayer to a strange deity? . . . Truly, for Your sake we were killed all day long, we were considered sheep to be butchered."

I do not deny You or Your Torah; You denied us, for we were innocent. You crushed us, yet we were guiltless. You were the Abuser; our sins were not commensurate with your actions. The responsibility is Yours, not ours. You must ask forbearance from us, not we ask forgiveness from You. You must return to us, not we come back to You. [35]

The difference between Schüssler Fiorenza and Blumenthal is striking. For Schüssler Fiorenza, the deconstruction of patriarchal Christianity for Christians and for those who come into contact with Christianity is absolutely essential to stop the continuing eruption of barbarism. Solidarity across religious, ethnic, class, and geographic boundaries in the struggle against patriarchy is essential for each particular struggle. Her protest is against the destruction of life too often legitimated by an abusing God who is a projection and defender of patriarchal interests. By comparison, Blumenthal's vision is proscribed and isolated. Schüssler Fiorenza asserts that those who seek to rediscover Jesus the feminist over against Jewish life and beliefs feed into patriarchal anti-Jewishness and relinquish the "history of those Jewish foresisters who entered into the vision and movement of Jesus." In essence, she refuses to reconstruct Christianity at the expense of historical truth and justice. Blumenthal's confessional theology does not mention the suffering of Palestinians at Jewish hands. His statement that a theologian is in "solidarity with one's fellow human beings before God" is therefore clearly limited. His further definition of doing theology as creating a dialogue from the "intertextuality of the traditions, the collective readings of the traditions, the selves of the theologians, the persons of the hearers, and the presence(s) of the divine," is also limited. Clearly, the Palestinian text is the history of their dispossession, which Jewish theologians must now contemplate and interpret. Perhaps it is the limited concentric tradition of reading that Blumenthal explores that leads him to find healing in an abusing God. In doing so he reaffirms an understanding of a God which, in its patriarchal form, legitimated the attempted annihilation of his own people, as well as the enterprise of 1492 and the end of historic Palestine.[36]

After this long history of oppression and this new posture of militarization, can Jews affirm the abusing God to whom Blumenthal prays? One wonders whether this is the same God who motivated Baruch Goldstein in his mass murder of Palestinians in Hebron or Yigail Amir in his assassination of Prime Minister Rabin. Is this simply the other side of the new Holocaust religion of which Adi Ophir wrote? It is instructive that Elie Wiesel finds Blumenthal's work "engaging and original," as it deals with the "most disturbing theme in Jewish traditional thought: how to reconcile memory with hope, divinity with cruelty, language and truth, absolute exile with ultimate redemption." At the same time, Blumenthal affirms what Richard Rubenstein prophesied years earlier, that the choice of abandoning the traditional Jewish God or accepting the abusive aspects of that God would be settled in favor of the latter. Perhaps in the end, the affirmation of an abusive God might also be a desperate attempt to hold together what has been shattered. It is also a way of protecting one's own innocence. Perhaps Blumenthal fears that the initial shattering of the Holocaust will be compounded by the shattering of oppressing another people. Is affirming an abusing God an attempt to placate a God who also might abuse the Jewish people for displacing the Palestinian people? Accepting this God might function for Jews as it does for Christians, as a place where the culpability for sins is accepted without the need for justice. For if Jews have been abused in the Holocaust as innocent people and freeze that abuse as if it is happening today, then the question of Jewish culpability in the present can be deflected and rendered peripheral.

Breaking the Silence

With David Blumenthal our journey comes full circle. His understanding of the task of the theologian, to defend God, to bring together the pieces of broken awareness and shattered relationship, and to be
a healer of the estrangement between human beings and God, is
betrayed by his own oversight and methodology. The pretense to innocence leads to an insularity that not only shields Jews from accountability but also limits Jewish solidarity with others who are struggling
and suffering. Trying to bind Jewish wounds within a Jewish framework leads to an almost uncritical retrieval of the texts that may one
day serve as a resource, but that no longer nurture the continuing journey of the Jewish people. A cycle ensues in which personal fidelity and
peace take precedence over the corporate reality of life and destiny.
Facing the abusing God is easier than facing a humanity that is being
abused, especially when your own people are no longer innocent.
What appears at first glance to be probing may be a sophisticated way
of averting one's eyes.[37]

The attempt to retrieve God and keep the tradition alive imple-
ments Emil Fackenheim's 614th commandment not to grant Hitler a
posthumous victory. But it also creates an obligation of silence. In his
role as a political commentator, Noam Chomsky raises a critique to
the theology of Blumenthal and Wiesel by calling for full disclosure of
Western and Israeli foreign policy. Without religious language, but
with an insistence that is part of his childhood Talmudic training,
Chomsky expands his own textual understanding of the world by taking a global perspective of struggle and responsibility. For Chomsky
the problem is one of hypocrisy; he sees the prevailing pattern as one
of the indignant outrage over enemy crimes with much "self-congrat-
ulatory appeal to high principle, combined with a remarkable ability
'not to see' in the case of crimes for which we bear responsibility."
Chomsky sees Wiesel as fulfilling this sensibility, since Wiesel has
assured the public that Jewish brutalities against Palestinians are
"regrettable exceptions." In doing so, Wiesel averts his eyes and
attempts to avert the public's eyes from the crime at hand. If Wiesel
tells us of the "dreamlike eyes" of the Israeli soldiers, Chomsky suggests listening to reservists returning from service in the occupied territories in the 1980s. They reported acts of "humiliation and violence"
against Palestinian inhabitants as the norm. Chomsky suggests Wiesel
listen to the story of the "soldiers who caught a ten-year-old boy, and

when he did not respond to their demand that he identify children who had thrown stones, proceeded to mash his head in, leaving him looking like a steak, as soldiers put it, also beating the boy's mother when she tried to protect him, only then discovering that the child was deaf, dumb, and mentally retarded."[38]

What Chomsky analyzes in secular speech is applicable to theological language as well. The task is less retrieval of the tradition than an uncompromising honesty in the present, honesty that neither defends nor extends an all-encompassing vision of destruction or redemption. Rather, the struggle is against illusions, especially the "necessary illusions" promulgated by the state and religion. The term "necessary illusions" comes from Reinhold Niebuhr in his Marxist phase, when he urged the "intelligent" to recognize the "stupidity of the average man" and thus provide this grouping with "emotionally potent oversimplifications" required to create a new society. As Chomsky comments, these basic conceptions underwent little change when Niebuhr became an important theologian for those with responsibilities and power during the Cold War era. Interestingly enough, it is this same Niebuhr whom Heschel and Herberg revered and who helped introduce the Jewish community and Jewish theology to the establishment, which he counseled.[39]

Chomsky calls attention to this alliance of church, synagogue, and state by assembling a textual critique of the obligation of silence and necessary illusions. So, too, with Israel Shahak, who accuses many Jewish public figures—rabbis, scholars, writers, and journalists—of being less than honest. "They lie out of patriotism because they believe it is their duty to lie for what they conceive to be the Jewish interest," Shahak writes. "They are *patriotic liars,* and it is the same patriotism which reduces them to silence when confronted with the discrimination and oppression of the Palestinians." Surely the label "patriotic liar," applies to Christians as well, to the pope, priests and ministers, Christian scholars, journalists, and public figures—to all the guardians of state and religious traditions. Like Chomsky, Shahak assaults the hypocrisy of the learned and the powerful, subverting the notion of necessary illusions.[40]

While Chomsky addresses religious figures like Niebuhr and Wiesel, he does so in reference to their influence on public policy and their inversion of ethical standards. For Chomsky, Niebuhr and Wiesel exemplify the transposition of ethics into a cover for injustice, betraying a willingness to gloss over the struggles of the suffering. Shahak's critique is more consciously internal to the Jewish community and therefore even more relevant to the critique of religion as a device to suppress dissent and truth. In fact, for Shahak it is a war against the religious deception of rabbis and Jewish scholars that must be waged. Religion is not always the opiate of the people, but it can be when theologians cover over injustice and atrocity. Those who front for injustice take on the "character of opium smugglers."[41]

Shahak's critique of Jewish religiosity is unrelenting. He accuses the most notable Jewish philosophers and theologians, including Hannah Arendt and Martin Buber, of presenting the best face of Judaism to the world while neglecting the negative attitudes of Jews toward non-Jews. In fact, while Jewish leadership presents the problem of anti-Semitism as the center of the contemporary discussion with non-Jews, the reverse is now the case. With an empowered Israel, the problem is Jewish attitudes toward non-Jews: What Jews demand of others is now demanded of them. Shahak notes that since the close of World War II the number of non-Jews killed by Jews far exceeds the number of Jews killed by non-Jews. "The extent of the persecution and discrimination against non-Jews inflicted by the Jewish state with the support of organized diaspora Jews is also enormously greater than the suffering inflicted on Jews by regimes hostile to them. Although the struggle against anti-Semitism (and of all other forms of racism) should never cease, the struggle against Jewish chauvinism and exclusivism, which must include a critique of classical Judaism, is now of equal or greater importance."[42]

Sooner or later in this battle for truth and survival comes a time when an attempt must be made to understand one's adversary and, at the same time, to criticize aspects of one's own history. Then interpretations of history leave the military battlefield and become a debate without end. "Only then does a humane historiography, which strives for both accuracy and fairness, become possible," Shahak writes. "And it then turns into one of the most powerful instruments of humanism and self-education."[43]

It is a debate without end, to be sure, but also now in the theological realm as well. For it now includes those elements of Jewish life that had come under the obligation of silence: the indigenous (including the path of Jesus); the Palestinians and those who have been hurt by Israeli foreign policy in South Africa and Central America; the joining of the Jewish community with the Western Christian and capitalist establishment; the critical humanist tradition of solidarity in Jewish life. These diverse, problematic, and hopeful elements, joined with Holocaust theology, are the stuff of the Jewish present waiting to be acknowledged. Clearly, the attempt at retrieval will acknowledge some and jettison other elements, for retrieval, like renewal, has an ulterior motive: to resystematize what once was ordered and to recapture an innocence that is disputed by history. Yet, as is true in the Christian symbolic universe, retrieval and renewal come at a time when that symbolic universe itself is already distant and shattered. Piecing that universe together is often a stop-gap measure to hold on to a meaning, to defend in a language, to support a conquest or resistance, to provide a symbolic expression that legitimates or suffers the eruption of barbarism.

5

God in an Age of Atrocity

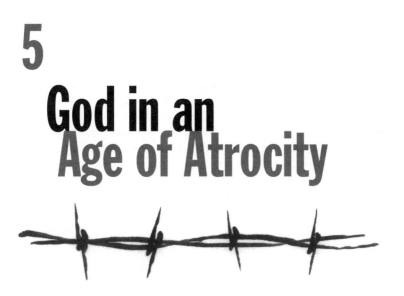

The God of life and the dignity of humanity may be closer to one another than their differing symbolic language suggests. Both convictions contain elements of life and resistance. Both oppose the death of the innocent. Both seek to open a space for further exploration; and though retrieval and renewal are present in some of the perspectives on the God of life and the dignity of humanity, they are secondary in all. Each presents an option that points to a future. One senses a place where theologians and humanists have arrived, however, and a place beyond their arrival from which they cannot announce. They have arrived at a place of depth, which they can articulate but are unable to move beyond. Rosemary Radford Ruether's sensibility is reinforced; the theological voices of God, humanity, and the earth are our voices, voices that carry a sometimes deceptive, sometimes honest, and most often flawed attempt to converse with a reality that is within yet beyond our grasp.

Judaism and Christianity beyond God

The assertion of God's presence, even the God of life, is hardly verifiable. The assertion is better seen within the context of a war promulgated by those who triumphantly announce their own God of conquest and death, though they rarely name it as such. If this war were to end, would we need to name God at all? Would we be able to carry on an evolving conversation on the destiny of life without reference to the

Gods of death and life, to the patriarchal and feminist Gods, or even to the indigenous, Jewish and Christian Gods?

Perhaps, then, we could simply accept these Gods and traditions in the historical, diverse, and enigmatic way that they reside in us. An example of this sensibility is found in Emily Culpepper, who though her own background is Christian, no longer identifies herself as such. When asked whether she drew on her background for sustenance, on her roots, as it were, Culpepper thought the image as one of continuity; from the root springs the tree. Her own spiritual life is more complex, with moments of continuity and radical discontinuity. Instead of roots, the metaphor that Culpepper embraces is one of compost, as her Christianity has decayed and died, "becoming a mix of animate and inanimate, stinking rot and released nutrients." As an organic substance transforming into the ground, compost becomes a matrix into which other elements must be added for future growth. It may be that many of the historic traditions will not survive transformation out of their patriarchal bodies and remain as they have been known. Culpepper asks whether it matters if their "old names are no longer all that is on our lips?"[1]

The word "tradition" comes from the Latin root, meaning to "hand over," and it is here where the difficulty surfaces again. The difficulty, the near impossibility that is the challenge of George Steiner—"In what conceivable language can a Jew speak *to* God after Auschwitz, and in what conceivable language can he speak *about* God?"—remains, though now extended to dominant and oppressed Christians. It is compounded because it is the language of theology that has often carried the evil that makes Steiner's challenge unanswerable. As we have seen, the question of language is even more difficult than Steiner postulates initially because it is not only the problem of reading Goethe in the evening and reporting for work at Auschwitz in the morning; it is the reading of the gospel on Sunday and work at Auschwitz on Monday. In relation to 1492, who can forget the haunting image of the conquistador Pizarro drawing a cross with his own blood as he lay dying, so that he could die gazing upon it? In relation to contemporary Jewish history, who can forget the doctor of medicine and religious Jew who massacred Muslim worshipers in Hebron in order to bring life? Rather than outside, the problem of language and God is inside Judaism and Christianity; it has been and is carried by both religions despite their claims to innocence and redemption.

Justo González, a Methodist minister and church historian,

attempts to resolve the problem by asserting the presence of two different Christs in 1492, Christ the King, who identifies with and legitimates the conquest, and Christ the Servant, who calls Christians to oppose the conquest and identify with the slaves and the indigenous peoples. This is the path chosen by most liberation theologians, and it is from this dichotomy that Gustavo Gutiérrez's Job and Las Casas emerges, as does Elsa Tamez's understanding of the God of life. Yet this theological attempt to reduce the dissonance in believing in such a God is questionable, as atrocity continues unabated.[2]

Joan Casañas, a Spanish theologian who lived in Chile during the Pinochet dictatorship, probes this difficulty. For Casañas, theologians devise grand theories to explain that the God who renounces omnipotence out of love, who becomes weak and exploited with the people, is the same God who will save the people if they seek and adore him. "This approach presupposes that there is a Someone already known now, God the Father Almighty of the Ancient creeds. This someone renounces omnipotence (but has it if desired), wills to cease being powerful (but is powerful), and becomes one of us (precisely because of not being such). Everything follows from a Someone who, by definition taken in advance from the Bible and from church philosophers, is in all things absolutely superior, unique, and separate from collective humankind—the Absolutely Other." Yet from a different perspective Casañas finds revolutionaries to be without a traditional language about God because of the inherent inadequacy of language. When asked to verbalize what they have experienced in their suffering and struggle, they exhibit a great silence, Casañas finds. "They find a void, and undergo a certain vertigo, which seems not unrelated to the experience of many believing activists when they decided to abandon the 'faith'—when they 'lost the faith' as it is said." For Casañas, the search for religious coherence in traditional language may actually mean continuing to conceal and stifle what would otherwise flow spontaneously from revolutionary insight. Casañas is interested in those who, rather than being bound to the language of the bible or of religion, remain in a dialectical relationship with those patterns and that language. This lack of closure allows them to serve as stimulus and a provocation, even a "guide in discovering and bringing to light what lies in the innermost core of the activist experience of struggle for human justice and freedom."[3]

Casañas records moments when the individual within a communal struggle experiences a solidarity and fullness, "an overflowing bril-

liance . . . that they spontaneously, poetically, and more than poetically—with the simplicity of children, but with the force of adults—
divulge the reality that they are experiencing." This experience is
speakable and unspeakable: "The much and more than much; abundance glimpsed from this angle and that; the historical and what goes
beyond it; the unpredictable that may be a reality tomorrow; the
human and what exceeds that which we now grasp as human." In traditional theology this "more" is called God, as if the "more" were given
from outside. Casañas names it "elucidation through abundance." A
question is whether the God that is often invoked in religious traditions began as revelation or in human experience. Was the tradition of
naming God begun because a person or community had such an
"intense experience of the demand for justice that he or she succeeded
in elucidating it in its abundance, calling it God, someone appearing in
the torrent of that abundance?" Casañas seems to be pointing to an
experience found at a certain moment and in a certain context, named,
and followed by individuals and communities who have not had that
experience. Too often that experience has been named as God, lifted
out of context, and then used over against others. The experience is
expropriated from the original moment and group, named as God,
exported, and used as a means of conquest and atrocity.[4]

Similarly, Carter Heyward describes God and justice as the "pattern of the Sacred in our life together." For Heyward, a feminist theologian and Episcopal priest, the shape of God is justice, and she
describes that God as the "movement of the Holy in our common
life." The justice of God accompanies the human journey and is also
part of the future; God is with us now and will come in the future. In
this description, God is beyond the images of jurisprudence and
legalism associated with justice in patriarchal society and resides in
the realm of radical relationality. Radical relationality gives birth to
God, and God becomes, in turn, the matrix of relational power. What
Casañas describes, in a different context, as elucidation through
abundance, Heyward designates the relational power generated in the
human experience as God. Yet, brokenness, despair, and violence
caution us that the naming of the "more" is provisional. Heyward
writes, "The image of God in relation to evil can be envisioned as real
only insofar as we experience the radicality of our relational, collective life together. For none of us on earth—past/present/future, and
not Jesus himself—has the power to overcome despair, brokenness,

and violation. Only together, hands joined and bodies leaning into one another, is there hope for this world and any of us in it."[5]

In Heyward's and Casañas' vision, David Blumenthal's abusing God signifies an acceptance of the broken relation of humans and creation, and projects an appeal of mercy to a God who presides over that brokenness. So, too, with Richard Rubenstein's and Elie Wiesel's lament over the absence of a God of history: it is an appeal to the wrong being in the wrong direction. They are appealing to a reality that emerged at a particular moment in history—for example, the God of Israel in the Exodus event—and fixing that naming for all time. Perhaps this God was simply the God of the Exodus, which was how the former slaves named their elucidation through abundance. From this perspective, Rubenstein and Wiesel are calling on an ancient and decontextualized experience to define their own very particular experience, one which might be defined as a counter-image—elucidation through suffering. Implicit in the analysis of Heyward and Casañas is a critique of the God of life as well, as something out there battling the God of death. For Heyward and Casañas the term "God" is essentially the expression of our collective aspirations and struggle for beauty, love, friendship, creation, and justice. Within the eruption of barbarism, in the midst of atrocity, the God they point to does not yet exist. That is why Casañas sees the human project as the "task of making God exist."

A Fateful Meeting

Until God exists, what do we say to persons, to communities, and to nation-states who practice the politics and religion of atrocity? What words of comfort can be offered to those who experience this violence? Can the language of God which carried atrocity be the language that points toward radical relationality? How do we communicate the sense of abundance without its cooptation into a system that interrupts relationality? By claiming or even arguing with the traditional God, do we delay the coming of God's existence?

It is important to note that Heyward's sense of relationality was influenced by Martin Buber, so deeply criticized by Richard Rubenstein as utopic and naive. It is almost as if the entire discussion of Jewish and Christian theology is haunted by relationality and its efficacy in light of the eruptions of barbarism. Rubenstein's ambivalence toward Buber's theology and his politics, embodied in the confession, "We needed him. Why I do not know," is similar to Gershom Scholem's sensibility regarding Buber. In his memorial essay written shortly after Buber's death, Scholem criticized Buber's conception of Judaism even as he communicated a sense of admiration to the one "who for my generation meant so much in terms of challenge and reflection—even at those times when he became thoroughly opaque, questionable, or unacceptable to us." Steven Schwarzschild, who chaired the symposium on Jewish Values in the Post-Holocaust Future, struck a delicate balance between grateful admiration and philosophical critique when he wrote that Buber—whatever his failures and failings—remains one of the truly great Jews of the century: "Few, if any alternative candidates present themselves with the authority to define our essential Jewish humanness, and this because he struggled heroically with just about all the demons—historical, moral, political, cultural, and religious—that swarm through the night of our century."[6]

The ambivalence toward Buber is understandable, for he continued to raise questions of solidarity and God that contemporary theologians seek to reorient or even bury. On the possibility of solidarity after the Holocaust, Buber spoke forcefully, early, and to a German audience:

> Tokens such as the bestowal of the Hanseatic Goethe Prize and the Peace Prize of the German Book Trade on a surviving Jew. . .are moments in the struggle of the human spirit against the demonry of the subhuman and the antihuman. The survivor who is the object of such honors is taken up into the high duty of solidarity that extends across the fronts: the solidarity of all separate groups in the flaming battle for the rise of a true humanity. This duty is, in the present hour, the highest duty on earth. The Jew chosen as symbol must obey this call of duty even here, indeed, precisely here where the never-to-be-effaced memory of what has happened stands in opposition to it. When I recently expressed my gratitude to the spirit of Goethe, victoriously disseminated throughout the world, and when I now express my gratitude to the spirit of peace, which now as so often before speaks to the world in books of the German tongue, these thanks signify a confession of solidarity with the common battle—common also to Germans and Jews— against the contrahuman, and my reply to a vow taken by fighters, a vow I have heard.[7]

On the subject of God, Buber also remained focused, as if the Holocaust made more urgent his prior discovery. Buber recalls a conversation in which he submitted his ideas of God to an eminent thinker who wondered how Buber could use the name of God so easily, especially after God had been used for so much treachery. Buber responded:

"Yes," I said, "it is the most heavy-laden of all human words. None has become so soiled, so mutilated. Just for this reason I may not abandon it. Generations of men have laid the burden of their anxious lives upon this word and weighed it to the ground; it lies in the dust and bears their whole burden. The races of man with their religious factions have torn the word to pieces; they have killed for it and died for it, and it bears their finger-marks and their blood. . . . We must esteem those who interdict it because they rebel against the injustice and wrong which are so readily referred to 'God' for authorization. But we may not give it up. How understandable it is that some suggest we should remain silent about the 'last things' for a time in order that the misused words may be redeemed! But they are not to be redeemed thus. We cannot cleanse the word 'God' and we cannot make it whole; but, defiled and mutilated as it is, we can raise it from the ground and set it over an hour of great care."[8]

Two decades separated Buber's discussion with the professor and its publication, including the Holocaust and the rise of the Cold War with its concomitant threat of nuclear extinction; yet his understanding of God's availability shifted but remained in place. Buber recognizes the eclipse of God as real and provisional:

Such is the nature of this hour. But what of the next? It is a modern superstition that the character of an age acts as fate for the next. One lets it prescribe what is possible to do and hence what is permitted. One surely cannot swim against the stream, one says. But perhaps one can swim with a new stream whose source is still hidden? In another image, the I-Thou relation has gone into the catacombs—who can say with how much greater power it will step forth! Who can say when the I-It relation will be directed anew to its assisting place and activity!. . . Something is taking place in the depths that as yet needs no name. To-morrow even it may happen that it will be beckoned to from the heights, across the heads of the earthly archons. The eclipse of the light of God is no extinction; even to-morrow that which has stepped in between may give way.[9]

There are many aspects to Buber's challenge to contemporary Jewish theology which are irritating to some and, in the end, difficult to dismiss; hence the ambivalence of almost all major Jewish theologians toward him. For example, Buber, until he was forced to leave Nazi Germany in 1938 and then immediately after the Holocaust, spoke of the need for and the possibility of German-Jewish reconciliation. This was true as well in the realm of Jewish-Christian relations before and after the Holocaust. In the 1930s, Buber concluded that the differences between Judaism and Christianity were balanced by a commonality— a shared book, the Hebrew Bible, and shared expectations, the messianic age. After the Holocaust, Buber held fast to this conclusion. As with his ecumenical focus, Buber held to his binationalist and spiritual Zionism during the Holocaust and after the creation of the state of Israel. Because Buber saw the Jewish return to Palestine as a fulfillment of a spiritual destiny rather than an attempt to normalize the Jewish situation through state power, the return was a spiritual elevation of the Jewish psyche and soul rather than an empowered state that escalated the cost of taking Jewish lives. His vision of communal life, with shared work and a shared spiritual center, occupied Buber in the broader arena as well. After the Holocaust, Buber continued to champion the utopian elements in socialism and posed the decentralist social community characterized by functional autonomy, mutual recognition, and mutual responsibility as the path of regeneration in a world increasingly dominated by bureaucracy, advanced technology, and the state. Naively or prophetically, Buber's positions on God, human beings, and the destiny of the world survived and even grew more urgent with the slaughter of the Jews in Europe.[10]

It is interesting that Buber is often seen as naive and out of touch with reality, a mystical utopic thinker uninvolved with the world. Yet Buber's life was one of profound and extensive engagement. Though for most of his life he was a university professor, Buber worked extensively in areas of Jewish public education as well as in the social and political arena concerning Jewish and Arab rapprochement in Palestine. His lectures and writing had profound consequences for his own life. Buber continued to lecture and organize in Nazi Germany despite pressures from the Nazis, which included banning from public speaking and ultimately the revocation of his citizenship. Buber wrote and organized against the division of Palestine and the coming state of Israel both within Palestine and internationally. His testimony to the Anglo-American Inquiry Committee charged with the task of exploring alternatives to the British mandate in Palestine is well known; here, as in other writings, testimonies, and lectures, Buber argued in public and in a time of great crisis in Europe and Palestine for a binational approach to the Jewish-Arab question. Less well known is his debate with Prime Minister David Ben-Gurion, in which Buber argued for government action on the repatriation of Arab refugees. Buber spoke forcefully to Ben-Gurion about this issue as a "great moral act, which could bring about the moral awakening of the public." The government could take the initiative of calling an international interfaith congress with the cooperation of the Arab countries. Though the outcome of such a congress would be uncertain, Buber felt the main point was to do something concrete and that it be an initiative that arose from the Jewish ethical tradition. Buber addressed this question in light of Jewish history by asking Ben-Gurion, "Were we not refugees in the diaspora?" Buber's last essay before his death proposes a confederative union between the Arab peoples and Israel and a federative union between Jews and Arabs in Israel/Palestine. For Buber, Jews and Arabs should realize a union comparable to that of Switzerland with two partners recognizing the full national autonomy of the other while pursuing cooperative projects and educational opportunities.[11]

It is difficult to argue that Buber was divorced from history. Rather, he entered history from a particular perspective and offered a path that was largely rejected, at least by the more powerful elements of social and political life. In retrospect, his ideas may seem naive if one accepts history as inevitable in its unfolding. If, for example, Adolf Hitler's societal and anti-Jewish program is understood to lead inevitably to the complete Nazification of German society and to the death camps, then Buber was clearly wrong in his argument for the possibility of a ecumenical humanity at the beginning of the Nazi era. The same is true of Buber's crusade for a binational and unified Palestine, if the rise of the state of Israel was not only necessary but in a sense pre-ordained. If the enmity between Jew and Arab is a constituent part of their relationship rather than a politically created struggle in the twentieth century, then Buber was clearly wrong in his hope of a binational state. If the struggle is one over land and development, then different sensibilities and political arrangements can shift the battle into coexistence or even, at some future date, a solidarity in creating a future for both peoples.

Still the argument against inevitability on moral grounds can be important as a witness in history and to future possibility. What Buber argued against was the inevitability of the Nazification of Germany and the militarization of Israel. Perhaps this is the underlying reason for the ambivalence of Rubenstein, Scholem, and Schwarzschild toward him, that the world they inherited was not inevitable and therefore that the world they pass on is not solely determined by the past. The stubbornness of Buber is evident here: he proposed continually, almost relentlessly, that the political, social, and spiritual worlds were intimately tied together and this world was essentially chosen and could be reoriented by individuals and communities. In Buber's view, then, after the Holocaust and 1492, the path away from dislocation and death—the path toward God—remains open.

The key to Buber and the ambivalence he engendered is found in his sense of the openness of history and the religious response to that openness. For Buber, the call of history and spirit is always before the person and the community, awaiting a response. In certain eras the path of response is more difficult to access; in the twentieth century, the totalitarian state, military-industrial-technological complex, dislocation of entire peoples, and mass death are part of this difficulty. Often as not, religion, in its dogmatic and creedal certainty, also conceals the path. Yet the path remains. It is discovered only by the person and the community being present to the possibility of a deeper aspect of life and then by pursuing it through dialogue and common activity.

Buber discovered this sense of presence in his early years as a professor in Germany. One afternoon, as often happened, a young man came to him asking for guidance. Buber, who spent extensive time in prayer, emerged from a morning of religious meditation and listened to the young man query him about the meaning of life. Buber conversed intently with him, yet in learning of the man's death a short while after their meeting, understood that he had missed the essential content of the man's questions. Although Buber had been there in his physical being, because he was dwelling in the beauty of his religious enthusiasm, he was not fully present to the man's concerns. "I learned that he had come to me not casually, but borne by destiny, not for a chat but for a decision," Buber relates. "He had come to me, he had come in this hour. What do you expect when we are in despair and yet go to a man? Surely a presence by means of which we are told that nevertheless there is meaning." From that moment on Buber gave up the idea of the religious experience as being one of exaltation and ecstasy separated from the world and humanity. Rather, the religious became a sense of fullness of claim and responsibility to each other in the everyday events of life. Religion, then, is everything, including all that is lived in the presence and dialogue of life: "As when you pray you do not thereby remove yourself from this life of yours but in your praying refer your thought to it, even though it may be in order to yield it; so too in the unprecedented and surprising, when you are called upon from above, required, chosen, empowered, sent . . . it rests on what has been and beckons to the remainder which has still to be lived. You are not swallowed up in a fullness without obligation, you are willed for the life of communion."[12]

Buber's sense of the everyday, of being present, of understanding even the questions that are not explicitly spoken, of personal and communal response to the moment, are articulated in a somewhat different way by Carter Heyward, when she writes of religiosity as living through the dynamics of alienation toward the realization of our power in right relation. In doing so, we do not move toward a final resolution of life and tensions. "To the contrary, our power draws us into our beginnings— into the heart of creation/creativity, into our relatedness. Here we participate in liberating one another from the isolation, brokenness, and despair wrought by abusive power relations in the great and small places of our lives." Similar is Ruether's understanding of the two forces of gaia and God, which seek communal structures to pursue justice while infusing those structures with heart and compassion.[13]

The presence these theologians speak of is the same presence that atrocity makes so difficult, if not impossible, to affirm. Buber's understanding of the eclipse of the light of God confronts Rubenstein's understanding of God's absence and overcomes it by being present even when that presence seems inadequate. Does this presence and relatedness, heart and compassion, address George Steiner's initial challenge of being unable to stand in God's presence after the Holocaust?

As difficult as the theological questions are and remain, Buber's story about his meeting with the young man is haunting. For after all is analyzed, it is these questions of meaning and purpose in life and our ability to be honest and fully present to them that defines the essence of what it means to be human. Being fully present has less to do with answers to be dispensed than with a readiness to move within and beyond what is already known. Does the meeting itself propose, by its very definition, a place that has already and yet, at the same time, never been explored?

A Deeper Bond of Suffering

George Steiner writes of the loss of assured faith and is troubled in a late and new coloration of his thought which can be perceived as "Christianizing." Indeed, he is finding Christian theology as an "echo chamber indispensable to my uncertainties." This unforeseen modulation troubles him. Steiner also seems to be drawing closer to the sensibilities of the Jewish-Catholic mystic Simone Weil, especially in her "sickening wellspring of Jewish self-refusal." This, he notes, is "somber ground." Could it be that Steiner is close to embracing what he thought terminal because of its legitimation of atrocity? Without a specific answer, Steiner long ago abandoned the possibility that Judaism itself could answer his profoundly Jewish question. Yet it remains that Steiner's struggle to articulate the abyss of the Holocaust has taken him, with many others, beyond Judaism and Christianity as we know it. Does Steiner fear approbation for his journey from his colleague at the symposium of Jewish Values in the Post-Holocaust Future, who might feel him to be in violation of the commandment against granting Hitler a posthumous victory? Perhaps after spending a life defining himself over against normative Judaism but affirming little other than that negative definition, Steiner might embrace a path loathsome to his people and his own personal history. Would this displease his other interlocutor of nearly three decades, Elie Wiesel? But here the question is joined. Does one refuse a victory to Hitler by remaining in a tradition that has ceased to answer the questions the Holocaust raised? Is the willingness to remain in what has lost its viability a victory over Hitler? And what kind of victory would this be? Of course the issue is more complicated, for leaving the Jewish fold and conversion to Christianity is another posthumous victory that the 614th commandment seeks to forestall. After all that the Jews have been through, could the destination be the religion that laid the groundwork for the Nazis? [14]

In his most recent thought, Steiner differentiates between a syllabus—representing cultural, social and pedagogic choices which aim more or less at stable consensus—and a canon—a profoundly personal construct that is private and unvoiced. The canon is the "guarded catalogue" of speech, music, and art that resonates deeply within us and is so familiar as to be part of our "homecomings." For Steiner, the syllabus and canon join the text inside us and have become essential to our interior life. Here Steiner sounds somewhat like the Jewish Buddhist, Rita Gross, who also celebrates "relief from the partial truth of intervention and transcendence; of history and linear time; of going forth, exposure and straight lines," preferring instead metaphors of enclosure, inner spaces, and curved lines. Is this homecoming that Steiner and Gross point to in accord with Buber's sense of "the new stream whose source is still hidden?" Steiner's most recent work is an attempt to answer his own questions as well as to be present to the young who, in his age and wisdom, seek counsel at their moment of decision. But of course in Steiner, as in Buber's story, these are tied together; the search is to be shared with others fully and openly so that a true meeting occurs rather than a paternalistic counseling session. Buber was not responsible for the young man's life in the sense of providing answers that he might cling to. Buber was responsible in that he was called to be fully present.[15]

Perhaps that is why so much religious renewal is superficial. As assertive and defensive, it is neither present to the history of atrocity nor to the metaphors of enclosure and inner spaces. Ultimately, the same is true of singling out the Jewish experience of suffering as unique and incomparable. Doing so misses the deeper bond of suffering and tends to close in on itself, denying a future that moves beyond the past. The hoarding of atrocity—the claim of Auschwitz—is understandable and also impossible over time. Which vision do we pass on to future generations? One is typified in a response to Steiner's plea for considering those being tortured and murdered in the present, where the respondent declared, "I refuse to equate the Sharpesville massacre with Buchenwald, Belsen and Auschwitz." The other is exemplified in Steiner's humble portrait of Marc Bloch comforting a boy as they were both murdered by the Nazis.

Perhaps in the end we are left with disparate images: Abraham Kaplan, the ghetto scribe writing until the end; Francisco Pizarro, the cruelest of the conquistadors, gazing upon the cross as he lay dying; the somber dialogue between Rubenstein, Steiner, and Wiesel; the struggles of Las Casas, Martin Luther King Jr. and Malcolm X; Baruch Goldstein's massacre of Ramadan worshipers in Hebron. And images within images: the cry and acceptance of Job, the voices of God and gaia which are our own, the eclipse of the light of God as well as the God of life, Buber's meeting without being fully present to the young man, the comforting words of the agnostic Marc Bloch. These images do not, as Lawrence Langer warned, transform the real in a way that "obscures even as it seeks to enlighten," nor do they force the aversion of our eyes, as theology often does. They move beyond Irving Greenberg's description of the central religious act after the Holocaust as a "desperate attempt to create, save and heal the image of God wherever it still exists—lest further evidence of meaninglessness finally tilt the scale irreversibly." They also move beyond Greenberg's understanding of "moment faiths" after the Holocaust, "moments when Redeemer and vision of redemption are present, interspersed with times when the flames and smoke of the burning children blot out faith—though it flickers again." Rather, these images exist without an agreed-upon destination, goal, or proper fit—without, as it were, a normative framework of interpretation or institution to legitimate their authenticity.[16]

What did Marc Bloch say to the boy in the last moments before their deaths? What gestures did he use to comfort him? Did he assuage the boy's fear by telling him not to be afraid? Did he speak to him of God, believing it himself at that moment, or perhaps comforting the child regardless of his own unbelief? Did he think life worth living even as he himself prepared to die? And if these were his thoughts, did he dare share them with the innocent boy who would have no time to ponder the deepest of life's mysteries? Perhaps, in a simple way, the boy lent comfort to Bloch, the educated professor, historian, resistor and, most of all, a person who never forgot his humanity. Perhaps the boy's innocence reminded Bloch of his own. Did this innocence counter the men who brought both to their knees and ended their earthly journey? Perhaps Bloch felt at the end, in the eyes of this child, a future still possible after the Nazis, after barbarism, after atrocity. But Bloch the historian also knew that Nazis come in many different forms and dress and carry different labels, even at times the religious designation of Jew and Christian. One wonders if he felt alone in his attempt to comfort the boy, or in a solidarity across the ages with those who struggled to overcome the endless eruptions of barbarism.

In an age of atrocity this is the haunting image left with us; an act of tremendous violence met with a simple and profound tenderness. One feels here, if only for a moment, a presence which has too often been named and, in the rifle shots, a violence which has too often been victorious.

The Possibility of More Truth

No doubt it is difficult for some to imagine that the images of beauty and death, solidarity and solitude, tenderness and violence are, as it were, the final word on atrocity and the language of God. If these images are the defining ones, what can we say about God? If it is the end *and* the beginning of a discussion about God, what is there to say that will lead us beyond violence and death? Can we ever again see God as the place of our safety, our protection, and peace? If God is right relation, if God is indeed our own voice, can the image of senseless murder yield any affirmation beyond a relentless pursuit against injustice and barbarism? At the same time, we are aware that atrocity continues in many places, among them Bosnia and Rwanda. The image of Marc Bloch comforting the boy is joined by ever-new atrocities, like the raping of Bosnian women and the machete-slaying of hundreds of thousands of Rwandans. The search for right relation, the redefinition of God as elucidation through abundance, even the sense of Christianity as compost for a new religious synthesis, these have hardly slowed the new events of atrocity before us.

Here the question of strategy reappears. If atrocity has disciplined the language of God and made it nearly impossible to speak of the God of Judaism and Christianity, and if the search for a new language for God is inadequate to the reality of atrocity (at the same time lacking an institutional base which, while being ambiguous in its message, at least allows for some mobilization of opposition to injustice and barbarism), then perhaps renewal of Judaism and Christianity is the most efficacious possibility for at least mitigating the forces of evil. Still, one wonders if the oppositional stance within Judaism and Christianity forged by this generation can be passed on to the next generation only peripherally touched by these traditions. The tension within one generation—taught the patriarchal God of might and exclusion yet fleeing that God to see God as right relation—experienced a tension unknown to the next generation. In fact the next generation is handed a language of God that may be seen as lacking in strength or even as an imposition on their sensibilities. The danger is apparent. The religious struggle of one generation is often seen to be irrelevant by the next. The diminution of religious language is already occurring; and the secular option as a counter to a false religiosity is, in the next generation, less an option than a given. When secularity becomes the norm and the language of God is no longer wrestled with, then superficiality defines the present and the future. Does a world without the struggle about God understand the image of solidarity and solitude any better than those who always and everywhere know who God is?

Perhaps the defining of God, and the struggle with those who define God differently, is itself part of the problem, a dead end to be avoided. Despite all of the theological questions raised by atrocity, there are those who are simply drawn to a belief in God as a grounding of being and as a hope for a world beyond injustice. This was the experience of Ludwig Wittgenstein when, at the end of his intense philosophical questions, he wrote simply that "life can educate one to a belief in God." As to the definition of God through language, Wittgenstein is dubious: "I should like to say that in this case the words you utter or what you think as you utter them are not what matters, so much as the difference they make at various points in our life." Wittgenstein asks the question as to how one knows what people mean when they say they believe in God. "A theology which insists on the use of *certain particular* words and phrases, and outlaws others, does not make anything clearer. It gesticulates with words, as one might say, because it wants to say something and does not know how to express it." For Wittgenstein it is "practice" which gives words about God their sense.[17]

Since it is the practice of atrocity that makes language about God almost impossible, could a different practice make God-language possible again? For Wittgenstein, the reestablishment of that language seems unimportant; rather the practice points beyond words. The matter of correct language about God is taken seriously but then gone beyond to a "deeper sense" of what is involved. Could that something else be insights, as yet unnamed, that come from a continuing movement toward the depth of our being? Surely the naming in a way that distorts our experience and our movement silences speech. Adrienne Rich, a Jewish poet, writes to this point: "Whoever is unnamed, undepicted in images, whatever is omitted from biography, censored in collections of letters, whoever is misnamed as something else, made difficult-to-come-by, whoever is buried in the memory by the collapse of meaning under an inadequate or lying language—this will become, not merely unspoken, but unspeakable." Misnaming becomes a point of paralysis forced upon us by an empty or violent orthodoxy and, one might say by extension, by a superficial renewal as well. The practice which Wittgenstein writes of—that something else which is the deeper sense—is for Rich an attempt to name the truth which is forbidden: "When someone tells me a piece of truth which has been withheld from me, and which I needed in order to see my life more clearly, it may bring acute pain, but it can also flood me with a cold, sea-sharp wash of relief." Telling this truth is itself a practice that engenders other possibilities: "When a woman tells the truth she is creating the possibility of more truth around her."[18]

What is this truth, and where does it come from? For Rich, truth is naming the unnamed, a turning toward another and a community rather than a turning away. It is what emerges from experience and history and needs to be nurtured and spoken if authenticity is to be approached. It is breaking through a boundary that limits and imprisons the person. It is found in being disloyal to "civilization," that is, to an order that promulgates oppression and atrocity. This truth tends to

get buried in received tradition and the culture that tradition legitimates. Rather, Rich finds these truths often "come by accident or from
strangers."[19]

After the learned discussions about God with the inevitable procla-
mations and dissent, is it possible to end with truths that come only by
accident or strangers? Is this an attempt to escape from the history of
atrocity and from the drive to articulate the anguish of that history,
which was so central to Steiner's understanding of Jewish and Christian life? In its way, the concentric tradition of reading expands *and*
disguises the origins of the traditions themselves. For if we take the stories of the formation of the Israelite community, and even those Jews
who gathered with Jesus, were they not disloyal to civilization as they
knew it? Did they not find and expand their truth by accident and from
strangers? Here, at least in the beginning of these traditions, the telling
of truth created the possibility for more truth. The sad reality is that
these truths, spoken in brokenness and hope, were canonized and
institutionalized, mobilized and militarized, to the point of becoming
a cycle of deceit. Perhaps it is that which comes to us by accident or
through the stranger that permanently subverts truth which has
become loyal to "civilization," including the truth of Judaism and
Christianity. It is a no to the misnaming and unnaming and a yes to
whatever and whoever is "buried . . . under an inadequate or lying language." It subverts and also creates new possibilities because it comes
within a history but without an agenda.

One sees this in Jason Moore's "Dawn," a poem that combines the
horror of Auschwitz with the dawn of Zen meditation.

> On the horizon
> at the end of Auschwitz
> is dawn.
> I feel the dead
> and the living
> within me.
> There is rice
> there is tea
> there is silence.
> At dawn, sitting
> I hear bells
> and the soft cries of passion.
> You are far away
> You are nearer than my breath.[20]

In this poem, images are transposed and arrive without warning. Auschwitz, that most horrible place of death, comes to an end with a dawn of serenity; the dead remain, though now with new life emerging. The words that surround Auschwitz, with their evocation of horror and ideological militancy, become surface to a calm found in the practice of sitting in silence. This Zen practice is a stranger to Judaism and to the horrors of Auschwitz. Auschwitz is no longer the defining point, although it remains in memory as the silence points to a depth which is present to the passion of life. Earlier, Jewish poets, including Moore, evoked the horror of the Holocaust, and even the experience of causing suffering to the Palestinians by reference to the Holocaust, without sensing a future beyond the past. Sitting at dawn is less a plea for a future than a depth open to the accident and the stranger, an openness and a listening faithful to the moment.

There is a cost to this openness and a struggle that is almost hidden in Moore's "Dawn"; or rather Moore has already moved within and beyond the cost after a long struggle. For is not a healing silence, a silence that is the bridge to new life, blasphemy after the Holocaust? And, to many, would not sitting at dawn seem a cheap way out of the terrors of a history and a language scarred by atrocity? Rich portrays the possibility and cost of such a search in her poem "Transcendental Etude":

> But there come times—perhaps this is one of them—
> when we have to take ourselves more seriously or die;
> when we have to pull back from the incantations,
> rhythms we've moved to thoughtlessly,
> and disenthrall ourselves, bestow
> ourselves to silence, or a severer listening, cleansed
> of oratory, formulas, choruses, laments, static
> crowding the wires. We cut the wires,
> find ourselves in free-fall, as if
> our true home were the undimensional
> solitudes, the rift
> in the Great Nebula.
> No one who survives to speak
> new language, has avoided this:
> the cutting-away of an old force that held her
> rooted to an old ground
> the pitch of utter loneliness
> where she herself and all creation
> seem equally dispersed, weightless, her being a cry
> to which no echo comes or can ever come.[21]

For Rich, this breaking with acceptable patterns of thought, this free-fall to utter loneliness, this walking away from the argument and jargon, is also where the drive to connect to oneself and others gains force. Here the "dream of a common language" is born. This is a language struggled for within atrocity and the telling of truth which is costly. Here, also, the search takes on strength. Rich writes of this strength:

We know now we have always been in danger
down in our separateness
and now up here together, but till now
we had not touched our strength.[22]

The strength of which Rich writes moves beyond the superficial reconstruction of a dead language into a construction of a reality that gathers insights and truths from people who are outside or can no longer live within the collapse of meaning. It is a journey toward what Carter Heyward defines as "radically honest cosubjectivity," a process that seeks an understanding of what may be more nearly objectively true. Here testimony is welcomed from the diversity of life as insights that are shared and evolve, deconstructing and constructing a common space with particular sensibilities. Neither the common space nor the particularities are defined in advance, as they are today in Judaism and Christianity. Rather they emerge as more truth is spoken and lived. As this occurs, a trend of philosophy that Andrea Nye surfaces in the thought of Rosa Luxemburg, Simone Weil, and Hannah Arendt, might well apply to theology: "There is no heroic striving for the certain foundations of knowledge, for communion with an all-powerful God, for the ultimate blueprint for a just state, no sigh of resignation at the end that there is no truth. . . ." At the same time, claims of descent that have been marked by, among other things, rivalry, hostility, and schism diminish or even cease. So too the need to claim an identity by refuting the thinkers and theologians of the past and the need to identify with paternal figures and patriarchal religions. Could then the elements of these thinkers, theologians, and traditions be freed to end or resurface insofar as they help increase the possibility of more truth?[23]

For some this method of reconstruction may seem to be one of anarchy, without restraint or boundaries. How, after all, will we determine what is good and evil, right and wrong, acceptable and unacceptable? How will we know what is Jewish and what is Christian, what is religion and what is atheism? What will determine whom we include and exclude, which communities we will gather with, and which ones are to be shunned? Without these boundaries how are we to know the proper form of worship, the correct canon, the approved creedal statements? The corollary fear is anarchy within the cultural, political, and sexual arenas, for if our ability to distinguish ethical and communal boundaries diminishes then perhaps all is permitted, even atrocity itself.

Still, it is within these received boundaries that barbarism erupts, historically and in the present. The conquistadors knew who was Christian and who was not; the Nazis even imposed a legal definition of Jewishness that included faithful Christians with a Jewish past. The rite of inclusion and exclusion, and with it the definition of normal and abnormal, is at the center of atrocity as well. The Nazis knew homosexuals as persons who confused these separations and definitions, as do some churches and synagogues today. They also realized that power often comes from promoting and enforcing these dichotomies in law, culture, and theology. Crossing boundaries in religion, culture, politics, and sexuality constitutes a deep threat to an order that continues to function in a hierarchical and patriarchal way. The received boundaries are themselves confusing, repressing, and dangerous, and at the same time they are continually transgressed. The terrible secret of those who define and enforce received boundaries is the closeted fascination with and pursuit of the pleasures of the legally, morally, and religiously outlawed. In many cases the boundaries are constructed and renewed, albeit in more liberal language, to contain and repress places among us that are otherwise without boundary or clear definition.[24]

Establishment and maintenance of these boundaries are necessary to create a God whose boundaries are known, defined, and without change. One wonders if the transgression of boundaries here on earth prefaces a similar transgression in relation to the boundaries of God in heaven. Perhaps this is why the "other"—Native American, Jew, gay and lesbian, Palestinian—is fought with such vehemence, one might say with a religious ferocity. In their own contexts, each challenges a boundary that will not hold unless enforced well beyond the objective danger posed; each challenges a boundary through an alternate conception of reality that includes the possibility of further exploration and embrace within and among persons. That these boundaries are constantly crossed is, for the purveyors of atrocity, a signal to increase their enforcement.

Yet not only must the more obvious enforcers of received boundaries be held accountable. Often the victims of injustice and atrocity internalize and frame their questions within those same boundaries. It is as if by remaining inside the boundary a shelter can be created, even if the need for shelter comes from that very same place of violence. Heyward writes of her own experience as attempting to keep balance on a very narrow wire that separates acquiescence to, or rejection of, that which oppresses. Keeping balance on the narrow wire is exhausting. Often we remain on the wire because of fear, for to choose is to step into a place that lacks definition or even carries a penalty. "What would happen if I stepped off the wire?" Heyward asks. "What would happen if I stopped trying to balance my love of the church with my love for strong, feisty women who love their sisters, their brothers and themselves? What would happen if I never again worried about whether I was, am, or will be too pushy, too passionate, and too much myself to be a good Christian woman?"[25]

To work through this fear, to somehow move beyond the boundaries that abuse her, Heyward seeks a psychotherapist who experiences the oppressive qualities of the patriarchal and heterosexist world in the same way that she does. However, after some months of therapy, Heyward begins to see psychotherapy, in its professionalization and refusal to join the common journey of healing and freedom, as creating a new boundary with its own rites, symbols, and dogmas. Heyward's flight from the religious world into the world of psychotherapy introduces another boundary which promises freedom but ultimately betrays her. From Heyward's perspective, the betrayal is simply this: Heyward's psychotherapist refuses to see beyond the therapist/client relationship toward a mutually searching and empowering one. In her psychotherapist's ultimate refusal of an evolving friendship, Heyward's world is again shattered: "For what shattered our relationship was not only the disconnections of our lives, but our failure to explore these disconnections together, our failure to prove together our fragmentation into pieces that are political *or* spiritual, professional *or* personal, public *or* private, self *or* other, client *or* therapist." It is in resisting the disconnections, challenging the fragmentation, and making connections, that the possibility of healing emerges and, for Heyward, the final push beyond patriarchal religion and the patriarchal God. The new secular and professional boundary challenges Heyward's evolving perception of God as sacred power in mutual relation, as much as did the old boundary instituted by Christian religion. What appeared to be open to exploration and journey is in fact another closure.[26]

Closure forces Heyward to a recovery of her own childhood and with it a voice she had heard in those years and lost in her adulthood. The initial voice was that of Sophie, Heyward's imaginary playmate, whom she now recognizes as Sophia, ancient figure in Jewish and Christian literature, image of the wisdom of God. By remembering Sophie, a voice which guided her in childhood, Heyward discovers Sophia, a voice which will journey with her as an adult. Five months into therapy Heyward writes of Sophia, whose coming catches her off guard: "She meets us when we least expect to be touched, much less shaken, by the divine. Most of us spend much of our lives running from Sophia, for we have learned to fear the chaos that will be sparked in our lives when she meets us. We are frightened, for as we see ourselves and one another through her eyes, we see the possibility of living more simply and honestly as sisters, brothers, and friends. Gaining our freedom, we pass through our fear."[27]

In Heyward's Sophie/Sophia we hear echoes of Wittgenstein's "life can educate one to God" and Rich's truth which comes by "accident or from strangers." At the same time, it is Heyward's recovery of silence through meditation, a process found in Moore's "Dawn," that allows openness to a future beyond the pain of the past. Recovering Sophie/Sophia represents the possibility of more truth, though one chastened by the boundaries that continually appear. What Heyward learns is that the insights of philosophers and poets, even theologians like herself, are far from easily attained in the actuality of life. A further learning is that the possibility of more truth is less a power to accomplish goals and define reality, or even to provide a certainty for the meaning of life, than it is a wisdom within. When shared with others, this wisdom illumines and expands the human.

Perhaps this wisdom points toward a practice from which a language about God may one day emerge. It is important that this practice does not have God language as its mediator or goal. At least at first glance, this wisdom and practice do little to answer the search of George Steiner, whose anguish is echoed in the many who have struggled with atrocity and the language of God. Within, among, and at the end of Jewish and Christian theologies that seek to respond to the eruption of barbarism and atrocity, and for those whose voices are tragically muted, the attempt to tell the truth and practice it may seem weak, even cowardly. There is no doubt a nostalgia for a strong God, the omnipotent, thundering sky God who can protect and deliver us. Yet we know now that the God who limits the possibility of more truth is the same God who legitimates atrocity. This God makes it more difficult to recognize dawn at the end of Auschwitz and 1492. The very arrival of dawn each morning, however, suggests a path beyond barbarism and atrocity, a path beyond even the language of God. Perhaps this is what Moore hints at when he writes of a dawn where the dead and the living are present to the coming of day, which is life.

Moore ends his poem with the thought-provoking lines, "You are far away / You are nearer than my breath." One wonders who is the "you" that is so far yet so near. Is it the end of Auschwitz or a friend whom Moore is recalling in memory? Is it God? It seems important that Moore invokes rice and tea as symbols of calm and hospitality; they become the bridge from Auschwitz to the unexpected and undefined "you." Perhaps all three—the dead, a friend, God—come together within Moore's meditation. What seems in intellectual discourse to be separate, distant, or even impossible, is brought near and together in silence. Here, the possibility of more truth retreats to an arena where the reconfiguration of past and present can at least be contemplated. Perhaps it is from the place of silence and hospitality that the path beyond barbarism and atrocity might one day become clear and even be welcomed by a world waiting for the end of night.

Is There an End to Atrocity?

As the path beyond barbarism is explored, what will happen to those millions upon millions of people who live on the edge of destruction, those reduced to destitution, and those future victims of atrocity? How will they organize their own defense, and how will those who seek to help in that defense gain moral and political strength to wage the war for human dignity and survival? In the face of this challenge, our guiding insights—elucidation through abundance, the truth that comes to us by accident and from strangers, the place of silence and hospitality—seem humble and individual. How do these understandings become organized to confront injustice and atrocity, or would their organization lead back into the very cycle of militarization from which we are trying to escape?

It is possible that even the abundance that is experienced and the truth that is told are themselves heirs to the very traditions that bequeathed atrocity. The narratives of our lives come from somewhere, and even those who refuse the religious naming of the past do so within the framework of that naming. Elucidation through abundance has different meanings in different cultures; spoken in the West it comes in the categories of Western thought and religion. The increase of truth is similarly bound to the context in which it appears. Casañas finds his understandings among the guerrilla fighters fighting within the cycle of 1492; Rich's possibility of more truth is among women surviving and creating space in a Western patriarchal society. The revolutionary fighters and the women are being "disloyal" to a particular civilization with a particular inheritance.

As heirs and rebels, they take the concentric tradition of reading to a logical terminus. Yet it is difficult to see how their depth can be understood outside these traditions or beyond them. Perhaps the general concepts can be explored in different cultures and across generations to lay the groundwork for a new tradition of reading and activity. The danger, of course, is that this new tradition may critique only what has gone before. An innocence denied the old may come to be embraced in the new; the guardians of tradition are dispatched only to be replaced by new guardians. Heyward found this in her dialogue with Christianity and psychology. A freedom appeared that, at the end of the day, contained the same power and ambivalence in different clothing. But again, is it possible to understand Western psychology outside the framework of Jewish and Christian culture?

If politics is always difficult to imagine without force and coercion, and if the role of religion in mobilizing the political for atrocity *and* against it is equally complex terrain, perhaps the question of commitment is one of direction rather than definition. Here the important act is placing ourselves in the depths of the historical moment rather than concern for the creation of a new tradition. When direction and entry into history are emphasized, the central political and religious option may be seen as the tendency toward community or toward empire. Elsa Tamez approaches this understanding in the religious sphere through her discussion of the God of life and the God of death. Yet the direction toward community or empire is not dependent on God-language, as God may or may not be spoken of. If the direction in a person's life and, ultimately, in a life shared with others, is toward the nurturance rather then the domination of life, then the path toward community is affirmed. The tendency toward empire represents the opposite choice; like the tendency toward community, it can be recognized and shared across cultures and politics. Realization that the desire for community *and* empire is found in religions, politics, and ourselves is humbling and instructive. It forces a continuing appraisal of politics and culture, a discerning of values and the institutions that embody them. Surely critique of empire in history and religion is easier than constructing a history and religion that contain within themselves a knowledge of both tendencies and a boundary that disciplines the empire we seek to confront and transform.

The process of choosing a direction and in that direction making a commitment is complex and fraught with contradictions and possibilities. One thinks of the Filipino artist Renato Ortega whose ballpoint pen meditations began with his drawing of a homeless man asleep on a subway train in New York City. His drawings are diverse in their content and location—from exotic fish to a Japanese bamboo flute—and this diversity mirrors his own journey and that of his people. Born and raised in the Philippines, he and his family now live in the United States. For six years he lived in Japan as a lay associate of an American Catholic missionary order. Raised a Catholic, Ortega practices Zen Buddhism and is a member of San-un-Zendo in Japan. The collection of his drawings bear the title, "Ten Thousand Things That Breathe," and the drawings, like his life, offer a fascinating series of contrasts. To find what "breathes," Ortega travels to the American and Japanese societies that have oppressed his own Filipino people and critically affirms the religions that have shaped those societies. As a descendant of the Tagalog people, his public and intimate language is English; his first drawings were published in the *Catholic Worker*, a newspaper published by a community of people who draw their inspiration from Christianity and live among the poor on the Lower East Side of New York. In exploring America and Japan, he identifies with others within the empires who have also been uprooted. Places of power are found also to contain the oppressed, which is the place from which he comes. The struggle now is to find things that breathe—at home, in the empire, among those who are suffering, and within languages and religions which are foreign and intimate. The breath that he searches for is his own, which can only be found within the context of colonialism and evangelization.[28]

This journey should not be romanticized. Myrna Rosales, a Filipina from the same background as Ortega, travels to the United States and Japan as well, but she also visits the indigenous people in the mountains of her own country. Speaking a sophisticated English and being light-skinned and urban, Rosales feels lost, as if she, a Filipina, is a foreigner in her own culture. The indigenous people challenge her to understand that she comes from the elite, which survives and achieves security within a colonial system, and they counsel her to return to that place with a different understanding of herself and her place in society. Her pain is the separation she feels, as the loss of her own language and culture leaves her without roots. Feelings of guilt are found inside as well, for the indigenous people are victims not only of an external colonialism; there is an internal colonialism that Rosales herself embodies. The cycle of uprooting found in the history of external and internal colonialism is also found within her. Even the common struggle of the Philippines is fractured. The complexity of Rosales' struggle for commitment is made more difficult by the Christian and Buddhist religions she explores. Being Asian in its roots, the practice of Zen draws her. Though she affirms aspects of the practice, she realizes that it, like the Catholicism she grew up with, is foreign to her. Though Rosales sees Christianity as a Western colonial imposition on her people, she returns to it in her journey to Japan. The congregation where she worships is small and Japanese, Protestant rather than Catholic, and located in a land that perpetrated atrocities against her own people. Paradoxically, it is also the land that resisted the Christian missionaries who helped conquer her own people.

One thinks here, too, of the Catholic theologian, John Abraham. Of mixed British, Filipino, and Indian descent, he inherits a faith brought by Western missionaries and now lives among a Muslim majority in Malaysia that sees Christians as foreigners. During political unrest in the 1960s, he is arrested and imprisoned, then upon his release he tries to find his way in Malaysian society. Muslim determination to create a "true" Malay and Islamic society, however, limits the freedom and development of the Christian community. Efforts of Christians to inculturate their religion in a Malaysian and Islamic context are outlawed. Christians are discouraged from using Allah in their references to God; Abraham's desire to learn Arabic as a way of showing solidarity with the Muslims is thwarted, since it is difficult for Christians to study Arabic at the University of Malaysia. To learn the language and religion of Islam, Abraham travels to the West, where he finds his Christian and Muslim teachers traveling regularly to Malaysia to engage in religious dialogues, all the while courting government and Islamic leaders for funding and prestige. In fact, the department in which he studies Islam is dependent on an uncritical relationship with the government, which is increasingly isolating his people. He witnesses and assents to the obligation of silence that his liberal Muslim and Christian teachers in the West adopt in order not to jeopardize a steady stream of government-funded graduate students and professorial grants. The cycle of colonialism goes on around him and also inside him, for where is he to turn as he searches out a commitment that is ecumenically embracing and politically alert? He carries a religion that isolates him in his own country, and he watches as ecumenical Christians who seek a dialogue with the Islamic world bypass his Christian community for the more "important" task of ecumenical dialogue. In fact, theologians, embarrassed by the history of colonialism, often find minority Christian populations an embarrassment better left to fend for themselves. Christian theologians in the West, for example, render Palestinian Christians invisible because they see them as an obstacle to the embrace of the Jewish community. The ecumenical deal with the Jews is extended to other parts of the world as Christians of Malaysia, Pakistan, and Indonesia begin to experience similarities to the Jewish oppression in Europe.

The Future of Martyrdom

If the survivors of Christianity and colonialism have a difficult, sometimes impossible task of personal and social orientation and reconstruction, and if the religions of Judaism and Christianity are of dubious help in these endeavors, the issue of remembering those who did not survive is equally problematic. The victims of atrocity are lost to those who murder them and to those of the victimized community without some vehicle for remembrance. Those who inflict atrocity seek to erase the memory of the dead to erase the memory of their deeds of atrocity. Those who survive seek to remember the dead as a permanent reminder of atrocity and its cost to humanity. Most often the dead are remembered in religious ceremonies, liturgies, and monuments; and in the West these efforts typically have Jewish and Christian elements or sponsorship. Frequently the nation-state becomes involved and what once was a subversive memory against injustice becomes connected with a power that uses the event to demonstrate its innocence and justify its actions. If religion and the state are so compromised, does the sense of abundance and truth, direction and commitment, respond to those in need of comfort and affirmation? Will those in grief demand an identifiable, named, and traditional transcendent power to assuage their grief despite the limitations of such a God? Do people, perhaps even the theologians themselves, need such a God at times of mourning, even if, upon more sober reflection, they find that God wanting?

We need not solve the mystery of what happens to the dead, to recognize the power in remembering the victims of atrocity as embraced by a good and loving God. The mourners' kaddish, spoken over the Jewish dead from time immemorial, never mentions the dead or death itself. It is a prayer for the living, to encourage a memory that brings forth more life. At a moment of sadness and loss, the promise of God's saving presence is proclaimed. The kaddish was said before and after Auschwitz, and inside Auschwitz as well. Is there a need, even a responsibility, to chant the kaddish today because it has accompanied the Jewish people throughout their history? Surely the mourners' kaddish is now impossible to recite without hearing the strains of the new and terrible kaddish that emerges from Auschwitz. If the old prayer promises the deliverance of God, the new one emphasizes the death of that God. The old kaddish exclaims, "May his great name be blessed forever and to all eternity." The new kaddish hurls its accusation, "Never shall I forget the little faces of the children, whose bodies I saw turned into wreaths of smoke beneath a silent blue sky. Never shall I forget those flames which consumed my faith forever."[29]

The contradictions are obvious and too strong to be held together by religion or history. As haunting and important, though, is the question whether, once jettisoned, these prayers can be replaced by images and argument that speak to the agony and hope of the human journey. The author of the new kaddish, Elie Wiesel, added a paragraph to his prayer at the commemoration of the fiftieth anniversary of the liberation of Auschwitz when he implored the mourners to:

> close your eyes and listen to the silent screams that terrify mothers. Listen to the prayers of anguished old men and women. Listen to the tears of children. Remember the nocturnal procession of children, of more and more children, so frightened, so quiet, so beautiful. If we could simply look at one, our heart would break. But it did not break the hearts of the murderers and their accomplices. God, merciful God, do not have mercy on those who had no mercy on Jewish children.

Fifty years after his release from Auschwitz, Wiesel retains the feelings of abandonment, destruction, and death that he prophesied on the thirtieth anniversary of his liberation: "Time does not heal all wounds; there are those that remain painfully open."[30]

What is it that will heal these wounds? The kaddish attempts to heal them by pointing in a direction outside of ourselves, to the coming kingdom and to the power of God. Wiesel is unable to accept this possibility, because he is in a dialogue with a God who can neither prevent atrocity nor heal the victims. He chooses to live with this God and even postulates that it is more difficult to remain in the drama of the believer than to abandon God altogether. But long after Wiesel's decision to remain in the dialogue, his pain lingers. In perhaps his last and most dramatic public moment, he can offer only the solace of eternal punishment for the perpetrators. In a Christian culture that emphasizes a forgiveness without justice and that continues to speak about the "immense wealth" of Christian life as if the gospel of Treblinka has not been written, and in a culture that has honored Wiesel because he has spoken of the Holocaust as a witness to the need for Christian renewal—though he has remained silent on the dark side of contemporary Christianity—Wiesel's words are bold and strangely dissonant. Was the Wiesel speaking at Auschwitz the person of the new kaddish—before his fame, affluence, and concern for status and acceptance overwhelmed him? Was he saying to the civilization and religion that spawned the Nazis, that though they honor him he will never forgive them? Was this his final affirmation that he would not assimilate to Christian categories of forgiveness and therefore would not forgive Christianity itself?

Though Wiesel's defiance is admirable, his life remains unhealed. More than his own situation, he bequeaths to the next generation his "painfully open" wounds. In some ways the situation is worse. The dialogue with the God who cannot prevent atrocity and cannot heal the wounds of atrocity is now complicated by the atrocities that Jews have perpetrated and Wiesel's silence in the face of them. The new kaddish emerges from the Holocaust and expands during the post-Holocaust era; it includes the cries of those Palestinian Arabs whom Sholmo Wolfe dispatched in the mosque after being ordered to clean the blood of the dead from the floor and walls; the hundreds of thousands of Arabs driven from Palestine under the orders of people like Yitzhak Rabin; the forty-nine unarmed and bound Egyptian soldiers executed after their surrender in the 1956 Israeli Egyptian war. It includes Deir Yassin, the Arab village whose inhabitants refused requests to station Arab troops there during the 1948 war but were set upon by and massacred by Jewish soldiers, who, after parading the few survivors through the streets of Jerusalem, executed them.[31]

The leader of the Jewish organization that committed the atrocities at Deir Yassin was Menachem Begin, later to become prime minister of Israel. After the massacre, Begin sent a message to the soldiers: "Accept congratulations on this splendid act of conquest. Tell the soldiers you have made history in Israel." In the employ of the Irgun, a Jewish organization that carried out the massacre, was none other than Elie Wiesel himself. Employed in its French branch, soon Wiesel left the Irgun, never to join it again. One wonders if Wiesel was fleeing the organization that would one day make even his healing more difficult. Perhaps his healing was made more difficult because of his presence at the raw origins of the Jewish state, and perhaps this is why he constructed a narrative after the 1967 war which emphasized the innocence of the Jewish soldiers, the Jewish people, and Jewish history. It is ironic that Yad Vashem, the Holocaust memorial in Jerusalem is just north of Deir Yassin, within eyesight of the village, which is now resettled with a thriving Jewish community. After the massacre, Martin Buber proposed that the resettlement of Deir Yassin be postponed. In a letter to Prime Minister David Ben-Gurion, Buber wrote that the "time will come when it will be possible to conceive of some act in Deir Yassin, an act which will symbolize our people's desire for justice and brotherhood with the Arab people." Was this the time when healing could have begun for the Arabs and for the Jews as well?[32]

Acts of atrocity inflict a pain difficult to heal. Symbolic acts of contrition and confessions embodied in the movement toward justice at least addresses the silence that often accompanies atrocity. Over time it may suggest a path toward healing. A memorial at Deir Yassin, for example, would suggest symbolically that the martyrs of the Palestinian cause, like the martyrs of Jewish history, are not forgotten. It also would symbolize recognition that Jews and Palestinians share a history of struggle and atrocity. Affirming a shared history characterized by so much suffering raises a challenge to move forward in creating a new history beyond atrocity. The martyrs of both peoples are remembered as an act for the future, a future when a healing may take place. The healing is not accomplished in advance or only through a memorial; it is not accomplished through religious language or a pretense to innocence. It cannot be accomplished alone. The healing can be accomplished only by recognizing and acting to build a new community, one of equality and human dignity. Perhaps, on the road to this future, a language of abundance and truth will unexpectedly emerge; the layers of the kaddish will deepen to include a celebration of the path now traveled. Or perhaps if the kaddish is too heavily layered already, a language outside of the tradition will be more suited to the contemporary reality.[33]

The journey into a future beyond atrocity challenges George Steiner's concentric tradition of reading in a new way. The concentric tra dition of reading is textual and historical; it has been found culpable in promoting atrocity and incapable of healing the wounds of atrocity. The layers of culpability and impotence are a problem in themselves, but a further difficulty emerges here. Pointing always back to the origins as *the* center and the holy texts from which Steiner believes the destiny of a people is foretold, interpretations can only refer to, encircle, evolve from, or even burden those origins. It is as if creation occurs only once and destiny is determined in ancient times. It compresses the history of Judaism and Christianity into scriptural canons and treats those canons as if they arrived without a birth, as if there was not a before, a negotiation, a conquest, or even a path from which they emerged.

The Jewish Scriptures are a historical rendering of a path joined by disparate tribes to create a future beyond the oppression they were experiencing; the Christian Scriptures represent the struggle for, a disappointment with, and the hope for another beginning. That these paths were connected to an unfolding vision of a new people and a new society, and that both canons are involved in new injustices, does not dismiss the fact that neither are static or arrive from heaven. The tribes of Yahweh do not refer to themselves for direction and commitment, they are too busy forging a path and a language to narrate their journey. In fact, to set out on their journey, they had to reject the path already destined for them, at least by the religions and societies that held them in bondage and servitude. It was by breaking with the "natural" unfolding of their destiny and by proposing *and* creating another destiny that they became free. It is strange that often we seem trapped in a destiny outlined by these tribes and narrated as a story of liberation by those who refused their destiny as told by others.[34]

By always pointing back to their origins as our destiny are we missing the message they left us? Are we mistaking the narrative of their journey and their God with our own? Is the central message in the details and language of the Exodus or in the fact that these people had the courage to strike out into the wilderness and create life without the safety of a common language, situation, and God? This dilemma is posed also for those who see Jesus at the center of their history. Do they mistake his person as central when the message is of one person among others who demonstrated a courage and tenacity in confronting the culture, religion, and leadership of his time and calling for a deeper reckoning? Can any one say without flinching or without horror that Christian activity in history has been in continuity with Jesus? Can one affirm in fact that the destiny of his followers somehow has or will unfold from his witness in the history of his time? If not, it is difficult to see the possibility of continuing Christianity at all.

In the final analysis, the problem is less in the debatable continuity that Jews and Christians claim with these ancient stories and persons. As Jacob Neusner reminds us, the present generation creates a religion to suit its own time and then retroactively searches for a continuity that is invented and claimed as a natural unfolding. The problem is neither the desire to exclude the history of atrocity, which contradicts the message usually communicated to those who claim this continuity, nor the use of these origins as a way of identifying and finding meaning in the world. Rather the problem is in claiming the centrality of origins as always and everywhere the place to begin in the search for meaning and healing.

Yigal Amir justified his assassination of Yitzhak Rabin within the normative framework of Judaism; and as Amos Elon reports, the university where Amir studied first achieved political notoriety when a professor, Israel Hess, published a treatise entitled *Mitzvah Genocide Batorah*—the commandment of genocide in the Torah. In this writing the Palestinians are pictured as Amalekites, the aboriginal people of Canaan who were decimated by Saul. In defense of this people, God declares a "counter-jihad," and the Amalekites must be annihilated. Hess draws the parallel to the contemporary situation: "The day will come when all of us will be summoned to conclude this holy war to destroy Amalek." David Hartman, an orthodox rabbi who disputes Hess' interpretation of the text, nonetheless concludes about Amir and the texts which he took to heart, "These texts the killer absorbed became his identity. They encouraged hate and destruction. Amir was no aberration. He was wholly *within* the normative tradition that has survived frozen through the ages to our time."[35]

Hartman describes himself as interested in reinterpreting Jewish teaching in a way that is compatible with democratic morality. But is his understanding of Palestinians so different than Hess's, at least as it affects Palestinians in their quest for empowerment? Although Hartman is against killing Palestinians or even oppressing them, he is far from recommending the sharing of Israel/Palestine on an equal basis. Among other things, he rejects an equal sharing of Jerusalem, an essential component for the empowerment and flourishing of Palestinian life. Even in his liberal interpretations, Hartman envisions a strong and moral Israel and a Palestine who exists on the periphery and at the will of Israel. It is difficult to see how his struggle with the "incorrect" orthodox—his use of the same text to dispute their conclusions—can lead to the birthing of a new community. His freedom is more constrained and determined than he would like to admit, and his liberalism is evident only in relation to the promoters of atrocity he seeks to silence. For does he also seek to silence, and from the central texts of the tradition, those Jews and Palestinians who seek to move beyond the limits of Jewish and Palestinian life he outlines?

As late as 1990, for example, Hartman argues for the inclusion of Palestinians, but only to the extent that they recognize the legitimacy and priority of a Jewish state. Even as the Palestinians have lost their land and self-government, Hartman envisions the nightmare of the present situation being healed only when Palestinian voices state with "pristine clarity" that they are willing to give up military power in exchange for political dignity. How political dignity can be achieved when one side dominates the other territorially, economically, and militarily is difficult to understand. At the same time, healing the trauma of the Holocaust is also the responsibility of the Palestinians. As Hartman writes, the Palestinians have to "understand that if they themselves cannot change, Israel cannot heal its own trauma." Palestinian change is recognized by Hartman when they affirm Jewish existence in Israel and the right of Jews to claim a continuity of national identity in the land. In a way, Hartman demands that Palestinians affirm that they were not displaced and that their existence on the land before the modern state of Israel was temporary, awaiting the Jewish return. Hartman is direct on this issue, demanding that Palestinians recognize Jews in the present but also recognize that Jews never left Palestine. Despite their marginality, Palestinians now at least exist for Hartman. In his major work, for which he received the National Jewish Book Award in 1986, Palestinians are not mentioned by name; they are only alluded to in the biblical framework as strangers in the land.[36]

This is exactly the history of dissenting Jews and Christians on so many issues in history. In arguing from the text or in argument with it, the majority of interpreters who find the text central discipline their argument for a different future. The fate of those defined as heretics or prophets is well known, and their fate serves as a warning to the larger community to hold to a certain line or at least to remain silent. How often does the interpretation of the text silence the very wellspring of hope, the desire to speak and to act on behalf of another and justice? The texts and the commentary on the texts establish boundaries dangerous to transgress and so internalized that breaking them is unthinkable. Yet barriers around the boundaries are erected and constantly reiterated; the penalties are constantly brandished and updated. Is this because there exists a desire to see what is on the other side of these boundaries, a constant desire to experience and embrace the "other," to assimilate or expand the world beyond the confines of what has been given and defined as *the* world?

For most people and communities in the contemporary world, the texts and experiences of life are broader than the concentric tradition of reading as defined by Steiner. Of course, he himself is a prime example of the tendency, even proclivity, to read and act outside of his own community. Steiner's view of the world, so shaped by the Holocaust, has also been shaped by his reading of Western literature. Steiner's importance rests outside of his writing on Jewish and Christian themes. Rather, he is known and respected as perhaps the foremost literary critic in Europe and America. At least in terms of time spent thinking through issues and writing to a public, Steiner's texts are primarily non-Jewish in origin, and the many languages that he reads and writes do not include Hebrew. Moreover, he is increasingly drawn to Christianity, as if his destiny might be found there. Steiner's freedom and contribution are found within the broad contours of European life. If he were bound to the Jewish community and limited to the primary and satellite texts of that tradition, could he have contributed as much as he has on the subjects of the Holocaust and Israel? One thinks of his view of Israel to reenforce this point. More than controversial, Steiner on Israel is considered heretical and dangerous. Without a broader tradition of reading and activity, Steiner would be unknown to the world and his distinctive and challenging voice would be different or nonexistent.

Steiner inherits, participates, and expands a European Jewish tradition which is not concentric. Named by Hannah Arendt the hidden tradition, it was held widely by the Jews of Europe before the Holocaust. The hidden tradition was formed at the intersection of Jewish and European life and produced some of the great Jewish intellectuals, literary figures, and artists of the nineteenth and twentieth centuries. The hidden tradition is at home neither in Judaism as it is inherited nor in Europe as it sees itself; between these cultures was a place of insight and provocation in which creativity could be found. Etty Hillesum, a Dutch Jew, who died in Auschwitz and whose diaries were found after the war, exemplified this tradition. During the years

1941–1943 in Amsterdam and in the transit camp Westerbork, Hillesum read widely and her diaries record her reading such diverse authors as Rilke, Dostoevesky, Tolstoy, Jung, Kropotkin, Thomas à Kempis, and Hegel. Her morning meditations included a "few pages of Rilke, a page of the Bible." During bombing raids she listened to Bach and Beethoven. Nowhere does she identify a central text; her sense of the spirit is eclectic. Hillesum is neither Jewish nor Christian in a traditional sense, yet there is a depth in her which is rare. She writes, on the one hand, that in "every ideology hides a little lie" and, on the other hand, "you must also have the courage to say openly that you believe; to say God." Unlike Wiesel's *Night,* in which the entire narrative is an explosive struggle with the Jewish texts and the God portrayed within them, Hillesum's diaries are filled with a deep longing for and acceptance of God. As importantly, Hillesum finds the meaning of the Holocaust in an almost desperate desire to help build a new world after the war is over. Her sufferings and those of the Jewish people are offered as witness to the need for a world where atrocity has no place. In a startling outreach, Hillesum recognizes the agony of German mothers who weep over the fate of their sons, and even searches for the humanity in the German soldiers.[37]

The differences between Hillesum and Wiesel are profound. Hillesum finds a God in the Holocaust who encourages her to be open to love and beauty, and to find the strength to be compassionate even when she is weak and angry. Her God is not an omnipotent God of history, or even responsible for the actions of human beings; rather Hillesum's God is available at the depths of each one of us if we only seek out the internal place where God resides. In August 1941, Hillesum writes of the deep well inside of her in which dwells God. "Sometimes I am there too. But more often stones and grit block the well, and God is buried beneath. Then He must be dug out again. I imagine that there are people who pray with their eyes turned heavenwards. They seek God outside themselves. And there are those who bow their head and bury it in their hands. I think that these seek God inside." Here God is named without reference to any text, though she often uses a variety of texts that do suggest the possibility of God. Unlike Wiesel's, Hillesum's God is a place of refuge and repose, a place of healing, which helps her imagine a better world.[38]

Since Hillesum's God is within rather than outside of her, personal rather than historical, what is on trial in the Holocaust is humanity. As Buber also thought, those who participate in injustice and atrocity are judged and those who seek, even in small ways, to comfort the afflicted are acknowledged as righteous. God is that which she finds inside of her and names God. It is the place of abundance which can be prefigured in literature or philosophy or even the New Testament; it is the place where she can tell the truth and also find it. The possibility of more truth is present here, for as the diaries progress and the situation worsens, that place she calls God becomes more vividly alive, more deeply rooted, easier to call on and kneel before. The diversity of the texts and the interior location allow for centers of strength rather than a sole tradition found wanting, and the personal power of healing that this God elicits expands to a world in need of healing. The final image is one of a solidarity that does not flinch from the realities of her situation and the situation of her people: "I am in Poland every day, on the battlefields, if that's what one can call them. I often see visions of poisonous green smoke; I am with the hungry, with the ill-treated and the dying, every day, but I am also with the jasmine and with that piece of sky beyond my window; there is room for everything in a single life. For belief in God and for a miserable end."[39]

What Hillesum desires above all is a return to the ordinary cadences of life. Heroism is defined within the context of gestures of compassion, small gestures like a smile for the despairing, a cup of water for the thirsty, a seat for the weary. Beauty is found in the tree outside her window, as it appears against the night sky, and in its changes with the seasons. As she is detained in Westerbork and prepares for her travel to Auschwitz, the possibility of love remains. For Hillesum, there is always love; the context of suffering simply deepens the search and expands its reach. Where love once was the physical love of a man, it is now within the place where God resides. This love gives her the power to continue and to reach out to others.

The new world is the restoration of the ordinary, where compassion is practiced, conversation about ideas and life renewed, and love and God are sought. The martyrdom of the Jewish people is for that restoration—to build a world where these elements can take their course, exist in the twists and turns of life, be broken and renewed. The Nazis have mobilized and militarized, distorted and perverted, the ordinary. Hillesum experiences this distortion as the Nazi world creeps in upon her life. After the war, whether she is alive or not, she hopes for a restoration of that life as a witness to the essential goodness of humanity. Neither earthly or eternal punishment is broached as a way to the future, for the Nazis have existed in many places and time periods; martyrdom is a witness against those who pervert the human spirit in its desire to experience the beauty of ordinary life. Who hears this plea, the plea of a compassionate woman, who with her family and people perishes in such a horrible, unspeakable way? Does the concentric tradition of reading and the God that it speaks of, hear her words and accept her testimony? Hillesum's texts are with her to the end, but what do they say to us today? Do Dostoevsky and Rilke, Tolstoy and Freud, and even the Bible outside of the concentric tradition speak to us through her? Do her diaries represent an extension of the Jewish and Christian traditions, a fulfillment, or the end of them? Or does she join with Wiesel and others in an extended commentary on an evolving tradition of atrocity? This tradition is ecumenical in scope and universal in its plea; it is a protest against the disruption of the ordinary and demands a reckoning of humanity and God. Perhaps this tradition is itself a kaddish, a prayer of mourning and hope carried in different languages, texts, and religions, but uniting across these boundaries to create a new place of discernment and challenge. Like the texts of the concentric tradition, they must be read with and among others, as commentary upon, as elaboration of, the violence that is the end of humanity and the hope that is its essence. Wiesel and Hillesum read alternately, together, in light of each other; but also Steiner and Buber, Cone and Gutiérrez, Ruether and Tamez, Rich and Moore; the new kaddish and ten thousand things that breathe—the journey of those who died and those who survive Auschwitz and 1492. For is martyrdom an offering to God or for the continuing journey of humanity? And who has more right to claim this tradition than the living heirs of these witnesses? When freed from the burden of the Jewish and Christian traditions, these authors speak to us in a different and more direct way. Within the concentric tradition their voices become footnotes to a broader agenda; on their own they speak poignantly as witnesses to an age of atrocity.

To claim and define this evolving tradition of atrocity is to feel the dead and the living within, to breathe with the homeless and the silent, to mourn, and in that mourning to seek compassion and justice. Of course, this tradition carries with it the warning that accompanies all traditions, a tendency toward triumphalism and power. For martyrdom can be used to create new martyrs, to continue the cycle of violence for the sake of vengeance. The fear is that the victims of atrocity may be victimized again. Therefore protection is essential and the cost of death must be escalated. The "other" is always to be feared, even as the martyred people join in the same actions that were used against them. The tradition of martyrdom may then encourage a permanent abnormal situation for fear that the ordinary, which was once enjoyed and was suddenly destroyed, is itself a place of vulnerability. The cycle is obvious; those who crave the ordinary and have suffered in its destruction deny to others and themselves its restoration. Those in power are protected from death as a new community of martyrs emerges on the other side of this empowerment. But one wonders what happens to the martyrs of the newly empowered people? Are they compromised, is their witness diminished and perverted, used for political and ideological reasons, when the ordinary of the other is destroyed? Can their memories be restored by recognizing the wrong and beginning to reconcile the claims of the two communities so a new ordinary can be created? Is the restoration of the ordinary the context from which the voice of the martyrs is heard in its fullness and clarity?

We see this in the evolving relationship of Jews and Palestinians. It is almost as if the voices of Hillesum and Wiesel are at stake in this conflict and its resolution, as if the voices of the Holocaust have been heard only in muted or militarized form. Recognition of the brokenness of both peoples, of their mutual losses, grievances, hopes, outrage, martyrs, and even or especially their common humanity, is still in the future. Restoring the ordinary refuses the either/or of Jew or Palestinian, Israel or Palestine. Nor does it look back to the Europe or the Palestine of the 1930s, as if restoration is nightmare or nostalgia. Restoring the ordinary involves the recognition of its loss and its new context; history and the particularities of each people's journey frame the search for a community within and beyond what has been. The ordinary of the past has been supplanted by a violence which has become ordinary; the new ordinary attempts to construct a society where mutual interests and relatedness begin to build relationships of solidarity and hope. This includes autonomous empowerment of Jew and Palestinian and also mutual empowerment. If both have the right to construct a society that escalates the cost of aggression, then the cycle can only end when the fear of atrocity is minimal and shared as a mutual offense. Atrocity against one is seen as an offense against both peoples. Then a new ordinary is created out of the destruction of the past. Sharing Jerusalem is the starting point of this journey, the broken middle of Israel and Palestine, which can become the new middle where the dead and the living, the martyrs and the survivors of both peoples, can be heard, mourned, and celebrated.[40]

As difficult as the formation of the new middle of Israel and Palestine seems to be, the redress and reconciliation demanded after a century of strife, the possibility is visible and achievable. The concentric tradition of both peoples, including the Jewish, Christian, and Islamic traditions, will be voiced and honored, even as they have been primary barriers to the ordinary and significant contributors to atrocity. It is often lamented that in the place where the three monotheistic traditions were created that there is so much violence, as if this is happenstance or a contradiction. Perhaps it is precisely because of the traditions that the area has been historically and is today saturated with atrocity. One day, and in the same way that Christianity and Judaism must deal with their history, Islam will have to deal with its own culpability in the expanding tradition of atrocity. If these three religions are responsible for creating a tradition of martyrs, then perhaps it is in Jerusalem where this tradition can be faced. In their life together, in the middle and the ordinary, which will create patterns of life and texts that reflect that life, Jews, Christians, and Muslims can create a path that recognizes and transforms their own history.

With reference to the Jewish concentric tradition of reading, a new ordinary in Jerusalem might create a 615th commandment, complimenting the 613 of ancient times and the 614th added by Emil Fackenheim after the Holocaust. As the 614th commandment forbids finishing Hitler's work of destruction by instead working for the survival of the Jewish people, so the 615th commandment seeks the restoration of the ordinary in Jerusalem in a context of mutual empowerment and compassion among Jews and Palestinians. If Fackenheim's commandment was a clarion call to mobilization of a community that had just experienced atrocity on a mass scale, the additional commandment is a recognition that a martyred people has also committed atrocity against another people. Fackenheim's commandment represents a permanent mobilization which cannot abide the ordinary and refuses healing as a threat of further atrocity; the 615th commandment is healing found in a commitment to a future beyond atrocity.

As in the 614th commandment we hear the voice of the anguished Elie Wiesel, in the 615th commandment we hear the voice of the hopeful Etty Hillesum. In Wiesel, we hear the anger and the open wound and, too, the atrocities which are to come in the future. In Hillesum, we hear the desire for beauty and future healing. These voices are authentic and humbled; Wiesel's wound remains open, and the world that Hillesum dreamed of is as yet unborn.

Do these voices speak to others, the victims of 1492 and their survivors? How do they rescue their dead from oblivion, raise their martyrs—in numbers, geographical location, and time-span even greater than the Jews? What is the new middle for those of the globe who remain distinctive as tribes and ethnic groups, or exist in segregated or integrated diasporas, or are divided by colonial religions, often within their own countries? What ordinary do they seek, what ordinary can be defined as such when their languages, cultures, and religions were imposed and are now foreign and intimate to their being? Renato Ortega's drawings represent his exile and his at-homeness in a journey that has no homeland. Where do the martyrs of his people find voice and rest? Could exile be the ordinary for him, and is exile in itself a witness to the martyrs who themselves have no way home?

The texts Ortega carries with him are instructive, for they demonstrate again the inadequacy of the concentric tradition. Born a Catholic, Ortega's text is the New Testament, which was brought by the Spanish in the conquest of his own people. In his journey, he encounters Buddhist texts, which accompanied the Japanese in their invasions and conquests in the Philippines and elsewhere in Asia. As he learns about his own history, Vincente Rafael's writing on colonialism and language becomes a text. Through exposure to the Holocaust, Wiesel and Rubenstein become part of his world as well. Do the martyrs of the Holocaust speak to Ortega and join together with the martyrs of his own people?

The struggle with the Jewish text for Jews after the Holocaust because of its inadequacy in the midst of suffering, and the struggle against the external Christian text for its participation in atrocity, seems difficult enough. But when contrasted with Ortega's struggle the difficulty is relativized, for he has as his primary texts those who committed atrocities against his own people. As in liberation theology, he can use those texts to confront the Christianity of the dominant; as Raphael points out, contracting colonialism is a negotiated surrender as the language of submission is also the language of resistance. This religion of colonialism, however, has also become a form of domination in his own country among his own people. The conquest continues, carried by the text that Ortega at once embraces and fights, submits to and revolts against. Even the solidarity with the Jewish martyrs reminds him of his people's conquest and the holy text he inherited as his own. What he finds so horrible, so inexcusable, so reprehensible, what he, like others, would like to bury and flee, is carried by a text and a religion that is an inescapable part of him. Christian liberation movements, which move Ortega, also awaken a profound ambivalence that seems, at times, to offer no way out. The negotiated surrender in colonialism is external *and* internal, as intimate and as ambivalent as the foreign language he speaks as his own.

John Abraham is caught in a further bind with the defining presence of Islamic texts in his country that are also colonial. That they are used to legitimate social and political oppression of the Catholic community, and that he is not allowed to learn or speak the language of the texts themselves, complicates his position and life considerably. The Christian text that is dear to him is also a symbol of the colonialism he fights. And despite resistance to a colonial Christianity, Abraham's Christian identity marks him as part of the colonialist mentality by a militant Islam which refuses the gesture of solidarity found in his desire to learn Arabic. If Abraham embraces the beautiful aspects of the Koran, he embraces a text which carries atrocity to different parts of the world, including against his own people.

Minority Christians—including Palestinian Christians who are caught between Islam and Judaism—are in a position similar to that of post-Holocaust Jews; they are people who come after. They come after, however, and continue to exist within a whirlwind that does not cease. Jews come after and can now think about the consequences of the experience they went through. Others around the world have also survived similar experiences, but they have lodged within them, perhaps permanently, an alien religion and language. Still others are on the brink of another atrocity and live in areas of the world which are within that experience. The relative peace in Rwanda after atrocities there may not last for long, and the Bosnian reality is likely to be unstable for years. Unfortunately, theological reflections on the Holocaust in terms of suffering and God may continue to be relevant far into the next millennium. The age of atrocity, and the difficult question of God in an age of atrocity, may even increase in relevancy in the coming years.

Is there no end to martyrdom? Will the peoples of the world recognize a commonality in atrocity so that it never again becomes the watchword for any people anywhere? Will the ancient traditions take on new life when, one day, they repent of the atrocity they have helped call forth and cease forever to promote or even tolerate atrocity in their name? Will God, the sense of abundance, or even the telling of truth, one day act, speak, confront, cry out for a life that bends toward community rather than empire? Perhaps this will be the time when the dead and living within all of us breathe ten thousand things or more, and when the wanderers on the earth—the heirs of Auschwitz and 1492 who are victims and survivors and subjects of their own history—that is, all who come after, will realize a project of a common humanity and destiny together with the victors.

For too often in history those who are now powerful were once powerless and, if the cycle continues, one day they will again be victims of atrocity. In the cycle of atrocity, the cries unheard today are foretaste of the cries unheard tomorrow. The rescue of the voices of the dead from oblivion is already difficult enough for those of us who come after. Is there a time when it will become impossible to speak, dispute, or even argue with a God whose presence is already so fragile and distant? Will the space from which this question is raised recede until the jasmine and the things that breathe no longer speak of a truth whose telling might increase the possibility of more and more truth? Perhaps, in spite of all, there will always be those who carry the memory of atrocity in their heart and seek to build a world without martyrs.

After our exploration, the task of making God exist remains. It is a task which was bequeathed to us and which we now bequeath to the next generation. Perhaps this generation has helped to clear the way for the next generation, whose task will be to make sure that there are no generations who come after atrocity again.

Epilogue

At the Eschatological End of Humanity

In April 1994, a little more than a month after Baruch Goldstein massacred the Muslim worshipers in Hebron, a wave of massacres decimated the Republic of Rwanda. While Goldstein used a sophisticated machine gun as his weapon, the killing in Rwanda was done mainly by machete. Nonetheless, the slaughter was swift and unrelenting. Out of a population of almost 8 million people, over 500,000 were killed in the first hundred days of the civil war. During that time the dead of Rwanda accumulated at a rate nearly three times the rate of the Jewish dead in the Holocaust. Hutu tribal members were encouraged by political, civic, and even religious leaders to massacre members of the Tutsi tribe. As Philip Gourevitch reports: "Neighbors hacked neighbors to death in their homes, and colleagues hacked colleagues to death in their workplaces. Priests killed their parishioners, and elementary-school teachers killed their students. Many of the largest massacres occurred in churches and stadiums where Tutsis had sought refuge—often at the invitation of local authorities, who then oversaw their execution." One massacre took place in Kibuye, where at least 5,000 Tutsis were herded into a stadium. After their arrival, gunmen in the bleachers shot into the crowded field, forcing victims to stampede back and forth. Some minutes later militiamen went onto the field and finished the massacre with machetes.[1]

African Rights, a London-based human rights group, released a report accusing some Catholic priests of encouraging the killing and the church hierarchy of taking no action to stop the slaughter. This occasioned a letter from John Paul II, who confirmed that members of the church who committed acts of genocide must bear the "consequences of their deeds that they have committed against God and against their future." Still the pope asserted that the church cannot be held responsible for the "misdeeds of its members who acted against evangelical law."[2]

A year later the Bosnian Serb army began storming Srebrencia, a city of refuge created by the United Nations, where more than 40,000 people sought shelter from the war. As the Serbs entered the town, a United Nations officer pleaded with his superiors in Geneva to intervene to prevent a massacre: "Urgent urgent urgent. B.S.A. is entering the town of Srebrencia. Will someone stop immediately and save these people. Thousands of them are gathering around the hospital. Please help." What followed was the summary killing of an estimated 6,000 people. Thousands of Muslims were forced into trucks, brought to killing sights near the Drina river, lined up, and shot. One survivor recalled that as she lay wounded among the dead, a Serbian soldier surveyed the bodies and remarked with satisfaction: "That was a good hunt. There were a lot of rabbits here." Another survivor described the massacre as part mass slaughter, part blood sport.[3]

If the church did not sponsor this massacre, its actions certainly legitimated the policy of "ethnic cleansing" that led to it. For the duration of the war Serbian priests blessed militias on their return from their forays into Muslim territory. The feast of St. Sava, founder of the Serbian church, was celebrated by burning the ancient mosque at Trebinje and killing the town's Muslim population. The mayor of Zvornik, a city with a previously Muslim majority, celebrated its new status as ethnically pure by building and dedicating a church to St. Stephan. Writing of the Christian complicity in the policies of rape, ethnic cleansing, and mass murder, Michael Sells comments that while it would be "wrong to equate the genocide in Bosnia with the Holocaust, it is equally wrong to ignore the moral implications of genocide in Europe, against a non-Christian population, especially on the fiftieth anniversary of the Holocaust."[4]

A week after the pope's letter on the church in Rwanda, Yigal Amir was sentenced to life imprisonment for the murder of Yitzhak Rabin. In his closing statement, Amir declared that he had no remorse for his actions: "Everything I did was for the God of Israel, the Torah of Israel, the people of Israel." Judge Edmond Levy, an orthodox Jew, disputed Amir's religious justification for murdering Rabin and concluded that the attempt to give the murder the "seal of approval of Jewish law is out of place, and constitutes cynical and blatant exploitation of religious law to serve ends that are foreign to Judaism." Yet the seal of approval had already been given many years ago by the state and in Jewish religious discourse. Amir thought that he was simply carrying out the spirit of the law to make invisible or displace Palestinians from the land. If Judge Levy had finally seen where this law leads, namely to the assassination of a prime minister who had helped construct that law, and if with this realization he wanted to transform the law of invisibility and displacement into a law of justice, then his admonition would become a confession. The court would then become a place of reckoning rather than a venue for a reassertion of an innocence which cannot be sustained.[5]

"Those who act against evangelical law," "ends that are foreign to Judaism"—is there no end to the hypocrisy of the religious? To their naiveté? Or willful ignorance? In Bosnia and Rwanda and Israel—but also in the Holocaust and the conquests that went before it—evangelical law and ends within Judaism are followed by the majority. With this understanding the debate shifts ground from the authenticity of those who claim Christianity and Judaism to the question of whether either can be embraced without continuing the legacy of atrocity. John Paul II and Edmund Levy are judges in their own tribunals, but history has its own tribunal which transposes judges into defendants. They are part of what the French intellectual and novelist Albert Camus thought curious and tragic about our century; the transposition of innocence and criminality. "On the day when crime dons the apparel of innocence," Camus wrote, "it is innocence that is called upon to justify itself."[6]

The dialogue Camus had at the Dominican monastery of Latour-Maubourg in 1948 is illustrative of how far things have come and how little they have changed since those terrible days at the end of World War II. As an agnostic, Camus called upon Christians to join with nonbelievers in a joint effort to combat the forces of terror and atrocity. In haunting language Camus envisions a joint solidarity to confront a world where adults and children are maimed and murdered: "We are faced with evil. And, as for me, I feel rather as Augustine did before becoming a Christian when he said: 'I tried to find the source of evil and I got nowhere.' But it is also true that I, and a few others, know what is to be done, if not to reduce evil, at least not to add to it. Perhaps we cannot prevent this world from being a world in which children are tortured. But we can reduce the number of tortured children. And if you don't help us, who else in the world can help us do this?" This solidarity across lines of religious and secular and even between religions, prefigured Vatican II and the contemporary ecumenical dialogue, which sponsors works on behalf of justice and peace. Camus ends his speech with these moving words: "I can only speak of what I know. And what I know—which sometimes creates a deep longing in me—is that if Christians made up their minds to it, millions of voices—millions I say—throughout the world would be added to the appeal of a handful of isolated individuals who, without any sort of affiliation, today intercede almost everywhere and ceaselessly for children and for men."[7]

Yet within this challenge lies the compromise Camus felt almost inevitable. The church might speak to the issues of the day but, at least on the institutional level, would insist on maintaining compromise positions with those in power. The compromise allows condemnation of injustice but limits itself to the "obscure form of the encyclical." Vague generalities couched in religious and moral theories substitute for clear and unequivocal action. Instead, Camus thought the world needed to hear denunciation of injustice backed by forthright and efficacious action, a church witness decidedly missing during the Holocaust.[8]

Camus died before Vatican II and the ecumenical movements so prevalent today. The church has come far since those dark days but would Camus feel, in light of the continuing cycle of atrocity and the response of the church, that his challenge has been met? The obscure form of the encyclical has spread, indeed become a model for the Jewish establishment and, of course, for governments that speak of democracy and human rights. Camus did not foresee this new form of ecumenism, which speaks on behalf of others while acting to rescue the power and prestige of the very churches and institutions challenged by the contradictory relationship of their "encyclicals" and activity in the world. Where today does the church, as its fundamental option and at a sacrifice of its own status, prestige and funding, place itself in danger? If John Paul II believes in nonviolence as the only solution to a world of violence, why then does he celebrate Mass for dictators like Augustin Pinochet in Chile, and why does he admit to communion those who participate in atrocity? Why not bar from the church those who serve in the militaries and militias of the world? And why does the pope recognize, communicate with, and pay papal visits to, governments whose abuse of human rights is legendary? If Judge Levy believes that the justification of murder violates the ends of Judaism, then why not cry out to the Jewish people that the building of a Jewish state has made these ends only too familiar in action even if denied in rhetoric? Why not take the opportunity to declare to the state that Baruch Goldstein and Yigal Amir are not foreign to Judaism but rather have become an integral part of it? For where were these educated and religious men born and trained? Do they speak a language that other Jews are unable to understand? Do they emerge from a religious and political culture distant and isolated from the Jewish people and its history?

One thinks here of John Paul II's condemnation of the Nicaraguan priest and poet, Ernesto Cardenal, who writes so beautifully of a people's revolution and interpretations of the gospels that helped promote the fight for justice. One thinks of the promotion of a Spanish priest, a former Vatican liaison with the Salvadoran army, as archbishop of San Salvador. In a country where more than 75,000 people were killed by the military in the 1980s, and where a previous archbishop, Oscar Romero, was also murdered by that military and is revered by the people as a martyr, the shock was strong. On a papal visit to El Salvador, the pope was able to meet with the president of the country, the founder of whose political party ordered the assassination of Romero, but was unable to visit the graves of the six Jesuits, accused of defending the rights of the poor, who were taken from their residence and executed by Salvadoran army troops. Instead, the pope met with political leaders and celebrated an open-air Mass televised throughout the country. On the eve of the pope's visit the new archbishop spoke of the "series of deviations" promoted by liberation theologians and argued that the church should not be based on classes or limit itself to an economic concept of the poor. Rather, the church should minister to all those "suffering from spiritual poverty," regardless of their social class. "Properly understood, the most orthodox and sound Catholic theology is the true theology of liberation," Archbishop Saenz commented, "Jesus died for our sins, and if we free ourselves from sin, all injustices will disappear."[9]

Perhaps this eschatological view of salvation will one day be realized in a realm beyond the life we know. If in fact salvation has been accomplished and will be realized in the resurrection of the dead, will this mean much if in this life we have come to the eschatological end of humanity? Since Camus' pleas, informed by the Holocaust and the discovery of the Gulags of the Stalinist period, the world has continued on in atrocity. Since Steiner's plea in 1967 about the massacre in Indonesia, atrocity in Vietnam, Cambodia, Guatemala, El Salvador, Bosnia, Rwanda, and other places in the world continues and is in the process of escalation. It seems almost comical to assert crime as the violation of law, evangelical or otherwise, or see the cycle of violence as foreign to Judaism or Christianity. Judge Levy's stern denunciation of Amir is, like the pope's letter to Rwanda, almost beside the point at this time in history. For in historical terms, Amir spoke in the same manner and with the same effect as Sholmo Wolfe did in 1948, when, after the executions of Arabs who had cleaned the bodies and the blood from the mosque, he announced that Tel Aviv was saved and that he would do it again. The pope in Rwanda and El Salvador continues in the line of his predecessors who bless the conquest, argue within it, recognize some who fought it, even adopt some of the language of resistance, yet continue to deal with the powerful as a way to advance the security and prestige of the church.

Yet even if one were not haunted by the complicity of religion and religious leaders in atrocity, the behavior of human beings toward each other is difficult to accept. After Auschwitz to be sure, but now after Bosnia and Rwanda, the question of humanity is as difficult to answer as the question of God. For while God remains a mystery, an assertion in need of debate and questioning, humanity is here, within and before us. No matter its political and religious legitimation, atrocity is carried out by human beings on the bodies of other humans. God may be other, or elucidation, or right relation; humans are us, named and awaiting naming, strong and vulnerable, young and old, male and female. At Auschwitz we reached the end of humanity by ourselves, and with only ourselves, and perhaps this is why the call for God is so insistent, to save us from the vision of what we have become. It could be that the lament over the end of God is really a lament over the end of humanity. If we say that we came face to face with the end of humanity at Auschwitz and therefore realized what it was to come to the end, then how did we allow the cycle to continue in the killing fields of Cambodia, Bosnia, and Rwanda? One wonders if the desire to kill human beings is also somehow the desire to kill humanity, or at least that part of us which aspires to life beyond injustice and atrocity. Does this continuation of atrocity, this pursuit of the eschatological end of humanity, represent a desire to murder the eschatological possibility of God?

This much is certain: the Christian legitimation of atrocity murders the narrative of Christian salvation, just as the Israeli policies of expropriation and torture murder the Jewish covenant. Will both Judaism and Christianity become available to us again once the cycle of atrocity comes to an end? The answer will come when atrocity ends. In our exploration at least, the possibility of Judaism and Christianity being participants in the coming age where atrocity ceases to exist is highly doubtful. Though for some they remain a comfort in this journey at the eschatological end of humanity, for others they are a source of the tragedy itself. Judaism and Christianity are part of the end for millions upon millions of people historically and in the present; despite renewal movements, or even because of them, the future is unlikely to be radically different.

Those who are drawn to God despite religious legitimation of atrocity are shadowed by this knowledge, haunted by a reality already difficult enough to explain without this added burden. Because of this burden, many who are drawn to God are silent, as if they have taken on the secret discipline that Dietrich Bonhoeffer wrote of in his prison cell while awaiting execution for his part in a plot to assassinate Adolf Hitler. Bonhoeffer reasoned that Christianity had little if anything to proclaim after its complicity with Nazism. A time of silence was demanded by that complicity—demanded rather than chosen, a silence imposed by history rather than a decision taken by an embarrassed and repentant Christianity in search of renewal.[10]

And what can Judaism proclaim today? When Jews pronounce the end of humanity in Auschwitz, do they also proclaim it in the prison cells where Hebrew-speaking soldiers torture Palestinian men and women? If God was absent in the death camps, is God present in those nights when the screams echo in the walls of prisons constructed by Jewish hands, speech, and even theology? Perhaps Jews need to adopt a secret discipline similar to the Christian one. Perhaps this common discipline is the final assimilation to Christianity, which comes because Jews too have participated in the eschatological end of humanity.

One thinks of the blood sport in Bosnia and Rwanda and recalls those events of mass death that have come before in history and imagines those that lie ahead. The eschatological end of humanity comes within these events and therefore, like atrocity, recurs and is ever new. At the end of each event is a reckoning with humanity and God: Camus in his dialogue with the Dominicans, Holocaust theologians in dialogue with each other and the world, liberation theologians in dialogue with the powerful in church and society, humanists in dialogue with religion and the state. Each time a record is established, and the need to articulate the end of humanity and to envision a new beginning is realized. Perhaps that is all the human community can do after atrocity and during those brief respites until the slaughter begins again and the dead cry out for a hearing.

In December 1981, soldiers of the Salvadoran army's American-trained Atlactal battalion entered the village of El Mazote and the surrounding hamlets and murdered more than 700 civilians. The slaughter was brutal and swift; more than half the deaths were children. A book written about the massacre has as its index a listing of the dead. At one level, the listing of the names is repetitious, yet one is drawn to it as to a liturgy. Liturgy is typically thought to draw us to life, but this liturgy is a liturgy which draws one to the dead. The few survivors— like the one found naked, her body covered with blood, who could not eat or drink and for weeks talked and cried out to God—chant that liturgy. They chant it for the mother who was found dead hugging her youngest son, who was killed with her, or for the mutilated corpses that littered the streets of El Salvador, sometimes headless or faceless, or with missing hands and legs, sometimes with the genitals found torn and bloody or severed and stuffed into their mouths. Often, cut into the flesh of the victims was a signature of one of the death squads. The torture and the signature assume their place in this liturgy as well. By comparison, the crucified Christ seems almost a relic of a bygone age, a comparatively dignified way to die. Like Job and the testimony of Holocaust survivors, the passion narrative seems a way of averting our eyes to the liturgy of the dead, which has grown so large since the salvation of the world was announced.[11]

Those who practice the secret discipline listen to the liturgy of the dead in an ecumenical spirit and solidarity. For this liturgy crosses geographical and communal boundaries and informs the old liturgies of their compromise and complicity. The tradition building around atrocity challenges and silences the traditions that have contributed to its formation. Is it coincidence that a country made Christian in conquest and slaughter, whose victims cry out to a God who promises salvation yet cannot protect a child found dead in his mother's arms, is named for the Savior that Christianity proclaims?

Years after the massacre, a memorial was placed at El Mazote. Against the backdrop of a field filled with trees and animals, stand statues depicting a family of four. The parents are holding hands with their children as they face a cross that is larger than themselves. The inscription reads: "They did not die, they are with us, with you, and with all humanity."

Notes

Chapter 1

1. Yitzhak Rabin, quoted in *New York Times*, February 26, 1994.

2. Leonard Fein, "Prelude to Murder," *The Jewish Forward*, March 18, 1994; Michael Lerner, "Disarm the West Bank Settlers," *New York Times*, February 26, 1994.

3. Richard Goldstein, "Mourning and Militance," *Village Voice*, March 15, 1994; Todd Gitlin, "Commentary," *New York Observer*, March 14, 1994.

4. Goldstein, "Mourning." Also see Leon Wieseltier, "Bloodlust Memories," *New Republic* 210 (March 21, 1994): 13–15.

5. This event is recounted in Hugh Nissenson's *The Elephant and My Jewish Problem: Selected Stories and Journals, 1957–1987* (New York: Harper and Row, 1988), 95–97.

6. Walter Benjamin, "Theses on the Philosophy of History," in *Illuminations*, ed. Hannah Arendt (New York: Schocken, 1969), 253–64.

7. Hannah Arendt, *Eichmann in Jerusalem: A Report on the Banality of Evil* (New York: Viking, 1964); Elie Wiesel, "A Jew Defends Eichmann," in *Against Silence: The Voice and Vision of Elie Wiesel*, vol. 2, ed. Irving Abrahamson (New York: Holocaust Library, 1985), 171–72.

8. For the exchange of letters between Scholem and Arendt, see "Eichmann in Jerusalem," *Encounter* 22 (January 1964): 51–56; Elie Wiesel, "The Day of Judgment," in *Against Silence*, vol. 2, 176.

9. Hannah Arendt, "To Save the Jewish Homeland: There Is Still Time," in *Hannah Arendt, The Jew as Pariah: Jewish Identity and Politics in the Modern Age*, ed. Ron H. Feldman (New York: Grove Press, 1978), 181–82.

10. Ibid., 187.

11. Viktor Frankl, *Man's Search for Meaning* (New York: Simon and Schuster, 1972), 67, 37.

12. Eric Gutkind, *Choose Life: The Biblical Call to Revolt* (New York: Henry Schuman, 1952), 18.

13. Elie Wiesel, "At the Western Wall," *Hadassah Magazine* (July 1967), 4; Eugene Borowitz, *Renewing the Covenant: A Theology for the Postmodern Jew* (Philadelphia: Jewish Publication Society of America, 1991), 44.

14. My own analysis of Holocaust theology and themes related to it can be found in Marc H. Ellis, *Toward a Jewish Theology of Liberation* (Maryknoll: Orbis, 1987); *Beyond Innocence and Redemption: Confronting the Holocaust and Israeli Power* (San Francisco: HarperCollins, 1990); and *Ending Auschwitz: The*

Future of Jewish and Christian Life (Louisville: Westminster/John Knox Press, 1994). For a survey of Jewish scholars, rabbis, and academics before the twinning of Holocaust and Israel, see *The Condition of Jewish Belief: A Symposium Compiled by the Editors of Commentary Magazine* (New York: Macmillan, 1966).

15. For Michael Berenbaum's perspective on Wiesel, see his *After Tragedy and Triumph: Essays in Modern Jewish Thought and the American Experience* (Cambridge: Cambridge University Press, 1990), 117–25.

16. Elie Wiesel, *A Jew Today* (New York: Random House, 1978), 230–32.

17. For the exchange between Rubenstein and Wiesel see "Richard Rubenstein and Elie Wiesel: An Exchange," in *Holocaust: Religious and Philosophical Implications*, ed. John K. Roth and Michael Berenbaum (New York: Paragon House, 1989), 349–70.

18. On the dramatic story of the development of the Holocaust Museum in Washington, D.C., which includes, among other things, the quarrel between Elie Wiesel and Richard Rubenstein's student, Michael Berenbaum, see Edward Linenthal, *The Boundaries of Memory: The Making of the United States Holocaust Memorial Museum* (New York: Penguin, 1994).

19. Richard Rubenstein, "Journey to Poland," *Judaism* 15 (Fall 1966): 480.

20. Richard Rubenstein, *After Auschwitz: Radical Theology and Contemporary Judaism* (Indianapolis: Bobbs-Merrill, 1966), 128; idem, "Reflections on Power and Jewish Survival," *Jewish Frontier* (May 1980): 17; idem, "Rubenstein and Wiesel," in *Holocaust*, 356.

21. Richard Rubenstein, "Buber and the Holocaust: Some Reconsiderations on the 100th Anniversary of His Birth," *Michigan Quarterly Review* 58 (Summer 1979): 390.

22. Ibid., 396. Rubenstein comments further: "Buber presents us with images of totally unspecified I's and Thou's relating to each other in openness and mutuality, as if mutual acceptance in the real world can ever ignore the claims of class, caste, status and power"(396).

23. Ibid., 401.

24. Ibid., 395.

25. Ibid., 402; "Rubenstein and Wiesel," in *Holocaust*, 369.

26. Elie Wiesel, "Jewish Values in the Post-Holocaust Future," *Judaism* 16(Summer 1967): 281.

27. Martin Buber, "Genuine Conversations and the Possibilities of Peace," *Cross Currents* 5 (Fall 1955): 292–93.

28. Emil Fackenheim, "Jewish Values," *Judaism*, 272. Fackenheim continues: "I think the authentic Jew of today is beginning to hear the 614th Commandment. And he hears it whether, as agnostic, he hears no more, or whether, as believer, he hears the voice of the *metzaveh* (the commander) in the *mitzvah* (the commandment). Moreover, it may well be the case that the authentic Jewish agnostic and the authentic Jewish believer are closer today than at any previous time"(272). Also see idem, *God's Presence in History: Jewish Affirmations and Philosophical Reflections* (New York: New York University Press, 1970).

29. Wiesel, "Jewish Values," *Judaism*, 285; George Steiner, in ibid., 285.

30. George Steiner, *Language and Silence: Essays on Language, Literature and the Inhuman* (New York: Athenaeum, 1970), viii, 159.

31. Ibid., 163–64.

32. Ibid., 39.

33. Steiner, "Jewish Values," *Judaism*, 289.

34. Ibid., 280–81.

35. George Steiner, "Our Homeland, the Text," *Salmagundi* no.6 (Winter-Spring, 1985), 8–9.

36. Ibid., 7, 17.

37. Ibid., 20–21.

38. Ibid., 22–23. Steiner realizes that the return to Zion is also to be found in the holy books and seems to accept the traditional orthodox position of a homecoming to the promised land in the messianic era. However, "the imperiled brutalized condition of the present state of Israel, the failure of Israel to be Zion, prove the spurious, the purely expedient temporality of its re-establishment in 1948. There were, then, armed men about and politicians. The Messiah was nowhere in sight"(23).

39. Ibid., 25.

40. George Steiner, "The Long Life of Metaphor: An Approach to the 'Shoah,'" in *Writing and the Holocaust*, ed. Berel Lang (New York: Holmes and Meier, 1988), 154.

41. Ibid., 156, 157.

42. Ibid., 159, 160. Steiner comments that the Holocaust is the "one and only bond that unites the Orthodox Jew and the atheist, the practicing Jew and the total secularist, the people of Israel and the Diaspora, the Zionist and the anti-Zionist, the extreme conservative Jew (so prominent in the United States today) and the Jewish Trotskyite or Communist" (159–60). It is interesting that Steiner affirms Fackenheim's understanding of the Holocaust as the unifying factor of the Jewish people, though with a caveat. For Fackenheim, Israel is central to this unity as a response to the Holocaust. As we have seen, Steiner sees Israel as one extremely ambivalent response.

43. Ibid., 163, 164. On the question of the uniqueness of the Holocaust, see Stephen Katz, *The Holocaust in Historical Context*, vol. 1 (Oxford: Oxford University Press, 1994).

44. Ibid., 164. Steiner's comments in relation to Jew-hatred are important: "Nothing is more cruel than the blackmail of perfection. We come to hate, to fear most those who demand of us a self-transcendence, a surpassing of our natural and common limits of being"(164).

45.Ibid., 170.

46. Steiner, *Language*, 108; *idem*, "Long Life," 157. For an extended discussion of the perversion of the German language during the Holocaust, see Berel Lang, "Language and Genocide," in *Echoes from the Holocaust: Philosophical Reflections on a Dark Time*, ed. Alan Rosenberg and Gerald Myers (Philadelphia: Temple University Press, 1988), 341–64. Lang refers to, among other things, the Nazis' "elevation of the lie to a principle of discourse"(359).

47. Steiner, "Long Life," 158.

48. Hans Kohn, "Zionism Is Not Judaism," in *A Land of Two Peoples: Martin Buber on Jews and Arabs*, ed. Paul Mendes-Flohr (Oxford: Oxford University Press, 1983), 98–99. For an important wrestling with these issues, see *Dissenter in Zion: From the Writings of Judah Magnes*, ed. Arthur Goren (Cambridge: Harvard University Press, 1982).

49. This poetry is quoted in James Young, *Writing and Rewriting the Holocaust: Narrative Consequences of Interpretation* (Bloomington: Indiana University Press, 1988), 138–39.

50. Ibid., 144–45.

51. Israel Shahak, "Collection: Atrocities as a Method," November 1988, 1.

52. Jason Moore, "Burning Children," *American–Israeli Civil Liberties Coalition* 10 (Summer 1990), 5. Also published in *Palestine Perspectives* no. 48 (July/August 1990), 5.

53. Louis Marton, "Nobel Oblige," *Israel and Palestine Political Report* 140 (February/March 1988), 4.

54. Yitzhak Rabin, *New York Times*, May 5, 1994; Joel Brinkley, "Israel Defense Chief Sees Failure in Quelling Uprising," *New York Times*, December 5, 1989.

55. Rami Heibronn, "Mourning for the Victims of the Massacre at the Hebron Mosque," *JADE*, no. 18 (April 1994), 4.

56. Thomas Friedman, "How about You?" *New York Times*, November 8, 1995.

Chapter 2

1. Daniel Bar-On to Abraham Peck and Gottfried Wagner, March 2, 1994.

2. Richard Rubenstein, "The Holocaust, Holy War and Ethnic Cleansing," public lecture at the conference "Remembering for the Future," Berlin, Germany, March 1994, 3. For Rubenstein's views on Bosnia see his "Silent Partners in Ethnic Cleansing: The UN, The EU, and NATO," *In Depth: A Journal for Values and Public Policy* 3 (Spring 1993): 35–57.

3. Ibid., 7.

4. Ibid., 1.

5. Richard Rubenstein, *The Cunning of History: Mass Death and the American Future* (San Francisco: Harper and Row, 1975), 77.

6. George Steiner, *Language and Silence: Essays on Language, Literature and the Inhuman* (New York: Athenaeum, 1970), 101; Quoted in Michael Sells, "Bosnia: Some Religious Dimensions of Genocide," *Religious News* 9 (May 1994): 5.

7. For an extended discussion of these themes see Rubenstein's autobiography, *Power Struggle: An Autobiographical Confession* (New York: Scribner, 1974).

8. For an interesting discussion of these issues see *Jewish Perspectives on Christianity: Leo Baeck, Martin Buber, Franz Rosenzweig, Will Herberg and Abraham Joshua Heschel*, ed. Fritz Rothschild (New York: Crossroad, 1990).

9. Johann Baptist Metz, *The Emergent Church: The Future of Christianity in a Post-bourgeois World*, trans. Peter Mann (New York: Crossroad, 1981), 18, 19.

10. Ibid., 19.

11. Jürgen Moltmann, "Political Theology and the Ethics of Peace," in *Theology, Politics and Peace*, ed. Theodore Runyon (Maryknoll: Orbis, 1989), 34; Pinchas Lapide and Jürgen Moltmann, *Jewish Monotheism and Christian Trinitarian Doctrine* (Philadelphia: Fortress, 1981), 90.

12. Paul van Buren, *A Christian Theology of the People Israel: A Theology of the Jewish-Christian Reality* (New York: Seabury, 1983), 26.

13. Clark Williamson, *A Guest in the House of Israel: Post-Holocaust Church Theology* (Louisville: Westminster/John Knox Press, 1993), 44; A. Roy Eckardt, *Jews and Christians: The Contemporary Meeting* (Bloomington: Indiana University Press, 1986), 155.

14. Van Buren, *People Israel*, 162.

15. George Steiner, "The Long Life of Metaphor: An Approach to the Shoah," in *Writing and the Holocaust*, ed. Berel Lang (New York: Holmes and Meier, 1988), 163.

16. Edward Said, *The Question of Palestine* (New York: Vintage, 1979); Naim Ateek, "The Emergence of a Palestinian Liberation Theology," in *Faith and the Intifada: Palestinian Christian Voices*, ed. Naim Ateek, Marc H. Ellis, and Rosemary Radford Ruether (Maryknoll: Orbis, 1992), 5, 4.

17. Munir Fasheh, "Reclaiming Our Identity and Redefining Ourselves," in *Faith*, 16.

18. James Baldwin, "Negroes Are Anti-Semitic because They're Anti-White," in *idem, The Price of the Ticket: Collected Nonfiction, 1948–1985* (New York: St. Martins, 1985), 430.

19. Ibid., 428, 427.

20. James Baldwin, "White Racism or World Community?" in ibid., 436–37; Malcolm X is quoted in James H. Cone, *Martin and Malcolm and America: A Dream or a Nightmare* (Maryknoll: Orbis, 1991), 167, 166. Like the discussion of the Holocaust, the Black-Jewish "dialogue" often had more depth then than it does today. For the latest denial of Jewish "whiteness" see Michael Lerner, "Jews Are Not White," *Village Voice* (May 18, 1993).

21. See Noam Chomsky, *Year 501: The Conquest Continues* (Boston: South End Press, 1993).

22. David Stannard, *American Holocaust: Columbus and the Conquest of the New World* (Oxford: Oxford University Press, 1992), 247.

23. Edward Said, *Orientalism* (New York: Vintage, 1978), 74. For a further exploration of some of these themes, see Edward Said, *Culture and Imperialism* (New York: Alfred Knopf, 1993).

24. George E. Tinker, *Missionary Conquest: The Gospel and Native American Cultural Genocide* (Minneapolis: Fortress, 1993), 1–11; Vine Deloria Jr. *God Is Red: A Native View of Religion*, 2nd ed. (Golden, Colo.: North American Press, 1992), 61–77.

25.Vincente Rafael, *Contracting Colonialism: Translation and Christian*

Conversion in Tagalog Society under Early Spanish Rule (Manila: Ateneo De Manila University Press, 1988), x.

26. Ibid., 17.

27. James H. Cone, *A Black Theology of Liberation: Twentieth Anniversary Edition* (Maryknoll: Orbis, 1990), 45, 6, 7. Also see James H. Cone, *Black Theology and Black Power* (New York: Seabury, 1969).

28. Cone, *A Black Theology,* 70, 111, 134. Cone's language is vivid: "To think of the Church in this society is to visualize buildings with crosses and signs designating Sunday morning worship. It is to think of pious white oppressors gathering on Sunday, singing hymns and praying to God, while their preachers talk endlessly about some white cat who died on a cross"(134).

29. Ibid., 78–79, 15, 11, 34.

30. Ibid., 80, 141, 64, 30. Cone develops his understanding of the Bible in relation to liberation themes in James H. Cone, *God of the Oppressed* (New York: Seabury, 1975).

31. Ibid., 26.

32. Ibid., xii, xiv.

33. Ibid., xviii.

34. Cone, *Martin and Malcolm,* 295, 297.

35. For an extended discussion of the history of Christianity and the emergence of liberation theology in Latin America, see Pablo Richard, *Death of Christendom, Birth of the Church,* trans. Phillip Berryman (Maryknoll: Orbis, 1987).

36. Gustavo Gutiérrez, "Toward a Theology of Liberation," in *Liberation Theology: A Documentary History,* ed. and trans. Alfred Hennelly (Maryknoll: Orbis, 1990), 62–77.

37. Ibid., 73, 77.

38. Gustavo Gutiérrez, *A Theology of Liberation: History, Politics and Salvation,* trans. Caridad Inda and John Eagleson (Maryknoll: Orbis, 1973), 277.

39. Ibid., 276, 224. With reference to the concept of universal love Gutiérrez writes: "Universal love comes down from the level of abstractions and becomes concrete and effective by becoming incarnate in the struggle for the liberation of the oppressed"(276).

40. Gustavo Gutiérrez, *The Power of the Poor in History,* trans. Robert Barr (Maryknoll: Orbis, 1983), 39.

41. Ibid., 89, 107.

42. Gustavo Gutiérrez, *On Job: God-Talk and the Suffering of the Innocent,* trans. Matthew O'Connell (Maryknoll: Orbis, 1987), xiv, xvii.

43. Ibid., 102.

44. Ibid., 94, 96.

45. Ibid., 103.

46. Gustavo Gutiérrez, *Las Casas: In Search of the Poor of Jesus Christ,* trans. Robert Barr (Maryknoll: Orbis, 1993), xvi.

47. Ibid., 105, 107.

48. Ibid., 67, 76, 122.

49. Ibid., 458, 450.

50. Gustavo Gutiérrez, *A Theology of Liberation: History, Politics and Salvation,* 15th Anniversary Edition, trans. Caridad Inda and John Eagleson (Maryknoll: Orbis, 1988), 156. See also Gutiérrez's new Introduction xvii–xvi.

Chapter 3

1. John Tagliabue, "Holocaust Lamentations Echo at Vatican," *New York Times,* April 8, 1994.

2. "The Vatican-Israel Agreement," *Christians and Israel* 3(Winter 1993/94): 8–9, 4. Jewish reactions to the agreement were mixed. *Yedioth Ahronoth,* the largest-selling newspaper in Israel, offered this commentary: "The Catholic church is one of the most conservative, oppressive and corrupt organizations in all human history. The reconciliation can be done only if the Catholic church and the one who heads it fall on their knees and ask for forgiveness from the souls of millions of tortured who went to Heaven in black smoke, under the blessing of the Holy See." See "Diplomatic Pact is Signed by Israel and the Vatican," *New York Times,* December 31, 1993.

3. John Paul II, "Letter of Pope John Paul II to the Bishops of Latin America," in *Santo Domingo and Beyond: Documents and Commentaries from the Historic Meeting of the Latin American Bishops Conference,* ed. Alfred Hennelly (Maryknoll: Orbis, 1993), 42–43.

4. *Idem,* "The Almighty Has Done Great Things," *L'Osservatore Romano,* October 21, 1992.

5. *Idem,* "Letter," 43; John Paul II, "Forgive All Who Have Wronged You," *L'Osservatore Romano,* October 21, 1992; ibid., "Letter," 43.

6. Walter Benjamin, *Illuminations: Essays and Reflections,* ed. Hannah Arendt, trans. Harry Zohn (New York: Schocken, 1969), 256.

7. George Steiner, "Our Homeland, the Text," *Salmagundi* 66 (Winter-Spring 1985): 7, 8.

8. Ibid., 5.

9. Susannah Heschel, "Making Nazism a Christian Movement: The Development of a Christian Theology of Anti-Semitism during the Third Reich," in *Reflections on the Thought of Richard Rubenstein: Triage, the Holocaust and Faith,* ed. Betty Rogers Rubenstein and Michael Berenbaum (West Simsbury, Connecticut: Hedgehog Press, 1993), 187. Also see Marshall D. Johnson, "Power Politics and New Testament Scholarship in the Nationalist Socialist Period," *Journal of Ecumenical Studies* 23(Winter 1986): 1–24.

10. For a discussion of this history, see Justo González, "The Christ of Colonialism," *Church and Society* 82(January/February, 1992): 22. On the *Requerimiento,* see Gustavo Gutiérrez, *Las Casas: In Search of the Poor of Jesus Christ,* trans. Robert Barr (Maryknoll, N.Y.: Orbis, 1993), 109–21.

11. Ibid., 19–20.

12. Clyde Haberman, "Hundreds of Jews Gather to Honor Hebron Killer," *New York Times,* April 1, 1994; Wendy Orange, "In the Wake of the Hebron Massacre," *Tikkun* 9 (May/June 1994): 33–34; Clyde Haberman, "Rabbis Are

Urging Israeli Soldiers to Defy Any Orders to Move Settlers," *New York Times*, April 19, 1994. Also see Michael Lerner, "Settler Violence and the Rape of Judaism," *Tikkun* 9 (May/June 1994): 27–28, 97.

13. Quoted in Roberta Strauss Feuerlicht, *The Fate of the Jews: A People Torn between Israeli Power and Jewish Ethics* (New York: Time Books, 1983), 74–75, 76.

14. Ibid., 186–87. Feuerlicht here is analyzing themes from a Jewish perspective that James Baldwin articulated in 1967 from an African American perspective and that exploded again in the early 1990s with publication of the Nation of Islam's *The Secret Relationship between Blacks and Jews* (Chicago: Nation of Islam, 1991).

15. Gitta Sereny, *Into That Darkness: An Examination of Conscience* (New York: Vintage, 1983), 235.

16. Doron Meiri, "A Torture Unit," *Hadashot*, February 24, 1992.

17. Mark Smith, *The Early History of God: Yahweh and the Other Deities in Ancient Israel* (San Francisco: HarperCollins, 1990), xxiii; Susan Ackerman, *Under Every Green Tree: Popular Religion in Sixth–Century Judah* (Atlanta: Scholars Press, 1992), 213–17.

18. See Robert M. Coote and Mary P. Coote, *Power, Politics, and the Making of the Bible: An Introduction* (Minneapolis: Fortress Press, 1990).

19. John Dominic Crossan, "The Historical Jesus in Early Christianity," in *Jesus and Faith: A Conversation on the Work of John Dominic Crossan*, ed. Jeffrey Carlson and Robert Ludwig (Maryknoll: Orbis, 1994), 20–21, 21.

20. Sharon D. Welch, *Communities of Resistance and Solidarity: A Feminist Theology of Liberation* (Maryknoll: Orbis, 1985), 4; Gordon D. Kaufman, *Theology for a Nuclear Age* (Manchester: Manchester University Press, 1985), 50.

21. Daniel C. Maguire, *The Moral Core of Judaism and Christianity: Reclaiming the Revolution* (Minneapolis: Fortress Press, 1993), 1, 21, 48.

22. Ibid., 131, 63.

23. Ackerman, *Green Tree*, 216.

24. Rosemary Radford Ruether, *Gaia and God: An Ecofeminist Theology of Earth Healing* (San Francisco: HarperSanFrancisco, 1992), 10.

25. Ibid., 254–55.

26. Deborah Lipstadt, "Facing the Void," in *Different Voices: Women and the Holocaust*, ed. Carol Rittner and John K. Roth (New York: Paragon House, 1993), 351, 353, 354.

27. George Steiner, "The Long Life of Metaphor: An Approach to the Shoah," in *Writing and the Holocaust*, ed. Berel Lang (London: Holmes and Meier, 1988), 156.

28. *Idem, Real Presences* (Chicago: University of Chicago Press, 1989), 200.

29. Lawrence Langer, *Holocaust Testimonies: The Ruins of Memory* (New Haven: Yale University Press, 1991), 19.

30. Ibid., 37, 80.

31. Ibid., 2. Langer continues: "Tributes are cheering; memorials are sad. Language often seems to be the fulcrum tilting us away from one and toward the other"(2).

32. Vincente Rafael, *Contracting Colonialism: Translation and Christian Conversion in Tagalog Society under Early Spanish Rule* (Manila: Ateneo de Manila University Press, 1988), 7, 8.

33. Otto Maduro, *Religion and Social Conflicts*, trans. Robert Barr (Maryknoll: Orbis, 1982), 106.

Chapter 4

1. Richard Rubenstein, "Homeland and Holocaust: Issues in the Jewish Religious Situation," in *The Religious Situation: 1968*, ed. Donald Cutler (Boston: Beacon Press, 1968), 61. Rubenstein concludes that mainstream Jewish theology does not meet the test of good theology.

2. Irving Greenberg, "Commentary," in ibid., 100–101. For other responses to Rubenstein's essay see "Commentaries," in ibid., 64–90.

3. Jonathan Sacks, *Crisis and Covenant: Jewish Thought after the Holocaust* (Manchester: Manchester University Press, 1992), 50.

4. Jackobovits is an interesting religious and political figure who is probably the last major Jewish establishment figure who is non-Zionist. See Immanuel Jakobovits, *If Only My People: Zionism in My Life* (Washington, D.C.: B'nai B'rith Books, 1986).

5. David Weiss, "The Holocaust and the Covenant," in *Holocaust: Religious and Philosophical Implications*, ed. John Roth and Michael Berenbaum (New York: Paragon, 1989), 72–73.

6. Judith Plaskow, *Standing again at Sinai: Judaism from a Feminist Perspective* (San Francisco: HarperSanFrancisco, 1990), xiii.

7. Arthur Waskow, "Between the Fires," *Tikkun* 2 (1987), 85, 86. Waskow continues: "I do not believe that Auschwitz was inevitable—but the Divine Insurge made it very hard to avoid. I do not believe that the looming Planetary Auschwitz is inevitable, but rather that the Divine Insurge is making it very hard to avoid"(86).

8. Adi Ophir, "On Sanctifying the Holocaust: An Anti-Theological Treatise," ibid., 61, 62.

9. Ibid., 62.

10. Richard Rubenstein, "The Holocaust, Holy War and Ethnic Cleansing," a public lecture at the conference "Remembering for the Future," Berlin, Germany, March 1994, 2–3. Also see Rubenstein's "In Response to Professor Ophir," *Tikkun* 2 (1987): 66–67. For a detailed study of this phenomenon see Ehud Sprinzak, *The Ascendance of Israel's Radical Right* (Oxford: Oxford University Press, 1991).

11. Ari Goldman, "Religion Notes," *New York Times*, April 23, 1994.

12. For an interesting and nuanced study of Luther see Heiko Oberman, *Luther: Man between God and the Devil*, trans. Eileen Walliser-Schwarzblart (New York: Doubleday, 1992).

13. Leonardo Boff, *The Path of Hope: Fragments from a Theologian's Journey* (Maryknoll: Orbis, 1993), 125, 126.

14. Elsa Tamez, "Reliving Our Histories: Racial and Cultural Revelations of God," in *New Visions for the Americas: Religious Engagement and Social Trans-*

formation, ed. David Batstone (Minneapolis: Fortress Press, 1993), 34.

15. Ibid., 37, 39.

16. Ibid., 40, 42.

17. Ibid., 48.

18. Ibid., 50, 44.

19. Ibid., 47, 53.

20. Ibid., 54.

21. Ibid., 56.

22. Ibid., 52. For a view of the resistance to foreign gods, especially by women, see Irene Marsha Silverblatt, *Moon, Sun, and Witches: Gender Ideologies and Colonial Peru* (Princeton: Princeton University Press, 1987).

23. Ibid., 35, 36. For Tamez's lengthy discussion of Paul, see her book *The Amnesty of Grace: Justification by Faith in a Latin American Perspective* (Nashville: Abingdon Press, 1993).

24. Bill Keller, "A Surprising Silent Majority in South Africa," *New York Times Magazine,* April 17, 1994; Emmanuel Milingo, *The World in Between: Christian Healing and the Struggle for Spiritual Survival* (Maryknoll: Orbis, 1984); Josiah Ulysses Young, *A Pan-African Theology: Providence and the Legacies of the Ancestors* (Trenton, New Jersey: Africa World Press, 1992), 162.

25. Efraim Shmueli, *A Reinterpretation of Jewish History and Thought,* trans. Gila Shmueli (Cambridge: Cambridge University Press, 1990), 4. For a discussion of early Israelite history see Norman Gottwald, *The Tribes of Yahweh: A Sociology of the Religion of Liberated Israel, 1250–1050 B.C.E.* (Maryknoll: Orbis, 1979).

26. Ibid., 2, 3.

27. Ibid., 11. Shmueli calls for a more balanced approach to Jewish history: "As every great piece of literature seeks to provide insight into the complex fabric of contesting forces, so Jewish historical writing must now discover the orchestration of the disparate notes which constitute Jewish culture in its dialectical continuity"(9).

28. Howard Eilberg-Schwartz, *The Savage in Judaism: An Anthropology of Israelite Religion and Ancient Judaism* (Bloomington: Indiana University Press, 1990), 152.

29. Ibid., 24, 3, 140.

30. John Dominic Crossan, *Jesus: An Historical Portrait* (San Francisco: HarperSanFrancisco, 1993), 109. Also see Richard Horsley and John Hanson, *Bandits, Prophets and Messiahs: Popular Movements at the Time of Jesus* (New York: Harper and Row, 1985).

31. Horsley, *Bandits,* xi, xii.

32. Plaskow, *Sinai,* 243; Abraham Joshua Heschel, "A Hebrew Evaluation of Reinhold Niebuhr," in *Reinhold Niebuhr: His Religious, Social and Political Thought,* ed. Charles Kegley and Robert Bretall (New York: Macmillan, 1956), 391; Will Herberg, *Judaism and Modern Man: An Interpretation of Jewish Religion* (New York: Farrar, Straus and Young, 1951), x; Robert Goldy, *The Emergence of Jewish Theology in America* (Bloomington: Indiana University Press, 1990), 54; Jacob Neusner, *A Rabbi Talks with Jesus: An Intermillennial, Inter-*

faith Exchange (New York: Doubleday, 1993), 150.

33. Neusner, *Rabbi*, xii. For a study of Jewish interpretations of Jesus, see Donald Hagner, *The Jewish Reclamation of Jesus: An Analysis and Critique of Modern Jewish Study of Jesus* (Grand Rapids, Michigan: Zondervan, 1984). Also see George Berlin, *Defending the Faith: Nineteenth-Century American Jewish Writings on Christianity and Jesus* (Albany: State University of New York Press, 1989).

34. Rosemary Radford Ruether, *Faith and Fratricide: The Theological Roots of Anti-Semitism* (New York: Seabury, 1974); Isabel Carter Heyward, *The Redemption of God: A Theology of Mutual Relation* (Lanham, Maryland: University Press of America, 1992); Elizabeth Schüssler Fiorenza, *In Memory of Her: A Feminist Theological Reconstruction of Christian Origins* (New York: Crossroad, 1983), 349; Elizabeth Schüssler Fiorenza and David Tracy, eds., *The Holocaust as Interruption* (Edinburgh: T & T Clark, 1984), 86.

35. David Blumenthal, *Facing the Abusing God: A Theology of Protest* (Louisville: Westminster/John Knox Press, 1993), 41, 299.

36. Ibid., 4.

37. Ibid., 3, 4.

38. Noam Chomsky, *Necessary Illusions: Thought Control in Democratic Societies* (Boston: South End Press, 1989), 206, 207–208.

39. Ibid., 17.

40. Israel Shahak, "The Jewish Religion and its Attitude to Non-Jews," *Khamsin* no. 8 (1981): 41, 40.

41. Ibid., 34.

42. Israel Shahak, *Jewish History, Jewish Religion: The Weight of Three Thousand Years* (London: Pluto Press, 1994), 103.

43. Ibid., 104.

Chapter 5

1. Emily Culpepper, "The Spiritual, Political Journey of a Feminist Freethinker," in *After Patriarchy: Feminist Transformations of the World Religions*, ed. Paula Cooey, William Eakin, and Jay McDaniel (Maryknoll: Orbis, 1993), 162, 163.

2. Justo González, "The Christ of Colonialism," *Church and Society* 82(January/February 1992), 5–34.

3. Joan Casañas, "The Task of Making God Exist," in *The Idols of Death and the God of Life: A Theology*, ed. Pablo Richard, trans. Barbara Campbell and Bonnie Shepard (Maryknoll: Orbis, 1983), 141, 135, 138.

4. Ibid., 139, 143.

5. Carter Heyward, *Touching Our Strength: The Erotic as Power and the Love of God* (San Francisco: Harper and Row, 1989), 24.

6. Steven Schwarzschild, *The Pursuit of the Ideal: Jewish Writings of Steven Schwarzschild*, ed. Menachem Kellner (Albany: State University of New York, 1990), 207.

7. Martin Buber, *The Way of Response*, ed. Nahum Glatzer (New York: Schocken, 1966), 197.

8. Martin Buber, *Eclipse of God: Studies in the Relation between Religion and Philosophy* (New York: Harper and Row, 1952), 7–8.

9. Ibid., 129.

10. For Buber's understanding of the relation between Judaism and Christianity see Fritz A. Rothschild, ed., *Jewish Perspectives on Christianity: Leo Baeck, Martin Buber, Franz Rosenzweig, Will Herberg and Abraham Heschel* (New York: Crossroad, 1990), 111–58. For Buber's writings on the Jewish return to Palestine, see Martin Buber, *A Land of Two Peoples: Martin Buber on Jews and Arabs*, ed. Paul Mendes-Flohr (Oxford: Oxford University Press, 1983).

11. Buber, *Land*, 244, 305. Buber writes in relation to Switzerland: "The basis on which a federative union can be established is, by necessity, so that for each of the two partners the full national autonomy is preserved: neither one should be allowed to injure in any point the national existence of the other" (305).

12. Buber, *Response*, 18.

13. Heyward, *Touching*, 92.

14. Nathan Scott and Ronald Sharp, eds., *Reading George Steiner* (Baltimore: Johns Hopkins University Press, 1994), 280–81. Steiner writes, "No deeps of light—I find no other expression—thrown into the long midnight of our century surpass those given us by such Jewish visionaries as Kafka, Mandelstam, and Celan. But the legacy of iconoclasm, of juridicial rationalism in Judaism inhibits an idiom that endeavors to come nearer the transcendent possibility, the otherness of informing unreason in the arts" (281). For a further discussion of these themes, see his "Two Suppers," *Salmagundi* 108 (Fall 1995): 33–61.

15. George Steiner, *Real Presences* (Chicago: University of Chicago Press, 1989), 185; Rita Gross, "Steps toward Feminine Imagery of Deity in Jewish Theology," in *On Being a Jewish Feminist: A Reader*, ed. Susannah Heschel (New York: Schocken, 1983), 246.

16. Irving Greenberg, "Cloud of Smoke, Pillar of Fire: Judaism, Christianity and Modernity after the Holocaust," in *Auschwitz: Beginning of a New Era?* ed. Eva Fleischner (New York: KTAV, 1977), 42, 27.

17. Ludwig Wittgenstein, *Culture and Value*, ed. G. H. von Wright (Oxford: Blackwell, 1980), 86, 85.

18. Ibid., 85; Adrienne Rich, *On Lies, Secrets, and Silence: Selected Prose, 1966–1978* (New York: Norton, 1979), 199, 193, 191.

19. Rich, *On Lies*, 193.

20. Jason Moore, unpublished.

21. Adrienne Rich, *The Dream of a Common Language: Poems 1974–1977* (New York: Norton, 1978), 74–75.

22. Ibid., "Phantasia for Elvira Shatayev," 6.

23. Carter Heyward, *When Boundaries Betray Us: Beyond Illusions of What Is Ethical in Therapy and Life* (San Francisco: HarperSanFrancisco, 1993), 134; Andrea Nye, *Philosophia: The Thought of Rosa Luxemburg, Simone Weil and Hannah Arendt* (London: Routledge, 1994), 226, 227.

24. For an interesting discussion of these issues in light of the celebration of the twenty-fifth celebration of the Stonewall Rebellion, see Richard Goldstein, "The Coming Crisis of Gay Rights," *Village Voice,* June 28, 1994, 25–29.

25. Heyward, *Boundaries,* 17.

26. Ibid., 14.

27. Ibid., 18–19.

28. Renato Ortega, *Ten Thousand Things That Breathe* (Kyoto, Japan: Korinsha Press, 1996).

29. Elie Wiesel, *Night* (New York: Bantam, 1982), 32.

30. Quoted in the *New York Times,* January 28, 1995; Elie Wiesel, *A Jew Today* (New York: Vintage, 1978), 222. For an interesting discussion of Elie Wiesel and the subject of healing, see Ora Avni, "Beyond Psychoanalysis: Elie Wiesel's *Night* in Historical Perspective," in Lawrence Kritzman, ed., *Auschwitz and After: Race, Culture, and "the Jewish Question" in France* (London: Routledge, 1995), 203–18.

31. For the text of Rabin's confession of his orders to expel the Arabs from Lod and Ramle, see David Shipler, *Arab and Jew: Wounded Spirits in a Promised Land* (New York: Times Books, 1986), 33–34. For the story of Deir Yassin, see Conor Cruise O'Brien, *The Seige: The Saga of Israel and Zionism* (New York: Simon and Schuster, 1986), 281–82; Benny Morris, *The Birth of the Palestinian Refugee Problem, 1947–1949* (Cambridge: Cambridge University Press, 1987), 113–15; Michael Palumbo, *The Palestinian Catastrophe: The 1948 Expulsion of a People from their Homeland* (London: Quartet Books, 1987), 47–59. Though each of these historians differs on certain details, they affirm the main outlines of the massacre. For the execution of the Egyptian prisoners, see Serge Schmemann, "After a General Tells of Killing P.O.W.s in 1956, Israelis Argue over Ethics of War," *New York Times,* August 21, 1995.

32. Buber's letter is found in Tom Segev, *1949: The First Israelis* (New York: Free Press, 1986), 88–89.

33. A group headed by Daniel McGowan is trying to establish such a memorial. Its working title is "Deir Yassin Remembered."

34. A fascinating account of the tribal revolts that came to form the Jewish people, see Norman Gottwald, *The Tribes of Yahweh: A Sociology of the Religion of the Liberated Israel, 1250–1050 B.C.E.* (Maryknoll: Orbis, 1979).

35. Hess and Hartman are quoted in Amos Elon, "Israel's Demons," *New York Review of Books,* December 21, 1995, 42.

36. David Hartman, *Conflicting Visions: Spiritual Possibilities of Modern Israel* (New York: Schocken, 1990), 241; *idem, A Living Covenant: The Innovative Spirit in Traditional Judaism* (New York: Free Press, 1985), 291. Hartman states that the rabbinic tradition teaches us to say "grace over an incomplete meal" (299). For Hartman that incomplete meal is an intra-Jewish argument over the place of the covenant in a Jewish state. That the meal is now infected by atrocity precisely because of this ability to say grace without including the Palestinians is not addressed.

37. Etty Hillesum, *An Interrupted Life: The Diaries of Etty Hillesum, 1941–1943,* ed. J. G. Gaarlandt (New York: Pocket Books, 1985), 126, 98, 85.

For a commentary on the suffering that moved Hillesum, see Timothy Ryback, "Stalingrad: Letters from the Dead," *New Yorker*, February 1, 1993, 58–71.

38. Ibid., 44.

39. Ibid., 159.

40. This understanding of the broken middle is taken from the late Jewish philosopher Gillian Rose. For a full-length discussion of the meaning of the term in her philosophic discourse, see Rose, *The Broken Middle: Out of Our Ancient Society* (Oxford: Blackwell, 1992).

Epilogue

1. Philip Gourevitch, "After the Genocide," *New Yorker*, December 18, 1995, 80.

2. "Pope Says Church Is Not to Blame in Rwanda," *New York Times*, March 21, 1996.

3. Stephen Engelberg, Tim Weiner, Raymond Bonner, and Jane Berlez, "Srebrenica: The Days of Slaughter," *New York Times*, October 29, 1995.

4. Michael Sells, "Bosnia: Some Religious Dimensions of Genocide," *Religious Studies News* 9 (May 1994), 4,5.

5. Joel Greenberg, "Rabin's Killer Is Given a Life Sentence in Israel," *New York Times*, March 28, 1996.

6. Albert Camus, *The Rebel: An Essay on Man in Revolt* (New York: Knopf, 1956), 4. Camus addresses the political aspect of what we have been discussing with regard to the language of God: "But slave camps under the flag of freedom, massacres justified by philanthropy or by a taste for the superhuman, in one sense cripple judgment"(4).

7. Albert Camus, *Resistance, Rebellion, and Death* (New York: Modern Library, 1963), 55, 56.

8. Ibid., 56. Like Steiner, Camus recognizes the compromise between rhetoric and activity as the terminal condition of Christianity. That is why Camus can write that if this compromise continues "Christians will live and Christianity will die" (56).

9. Larry Rohter, "A Church Asunder Awaits the Pope in Salvador," *New York Times*, February 4, 1996. As for the choice of a televised open-air Mass instead of a visit to the Jesuit graves, one priest complained that the pope was "mounting a spectacle, as if it were the Rolling Stones or Michael Jackson who were coming."

10. Dietrich Bonhoeffer, *Letters and Papers from Prison* (New York: Macmillan, 1972), 80–82.

11. Mark Danner, *The Massacre at El Mozote: A Parable of the Cold War* (New York: Vintage, 1994), 89, 25–26.

Index